*Respectfully dedicated*
*to the memory of*
*Dr. King and the*
*fulfillment of his*
*dream*

# PRAISE FOR THE LEADERSHIP BOOKS FROM DONALD T. PHILLIPS

## MARTIN LUTHER KING, JR., ON LEADERSHIP

"Lessons on making decisions, inspiring creativity, and instigating change."
—*Seattle Times & Post-Intelligencer*

"A different look at King, and a refreshing guide into not only how he learned from his failures, but what he learned from each victory....A welcome gift."
—*Indiana Herald*

"Provides insight into King's ability to rally much of the country around him . . . from which any leader could learn."
—*St. Petersburg Times*

## LINCOLN ON LEADERSHIP

"Remarkable . . . a lively and entertaining study that delivers uncommon good sense."
—*USA Today*

"If Lincoln's example were taken to heart, life undoubtedly would improve up and down the corporate line."
—*New York Times*

"This expert, detailed record of Lincoln's leadership qualities not only illuminates the past, it might also help light the way to the future."
—Mario M. Cuomo, former governor of New York

## THE FOUNDING FATHERS ON LEADERSHIP

"Examines the leadership principles the founding fathers employed to build a nation and demonstrates how these same management practices can be applied to today's business situations."
—Orange County Register (CA)

"Every member of Congress should have a copy of this book and study it carefully."
—Mary Matalin

# MARTIN LUTHER KING, JR. ON LEADERSHIP™

## INSPIRATION & WISDOM FOR
## · CHALLENGING TIMES ·

## DONALD T. PHILLIPS

**WARNER BOOKS**

A Time Warner Company

ON LEADERSHIP is a trademark of Donald T. Phillips

Warner Books, Inc., 1271 Avenue of the Americas,
New York, NY 10020
Visit our Web site at www.twbookmark.com

 A Time Warner Company

Printed in the United States of America
First Trade Printing: January 2000
10  9  8  7  6  5  4  3  2

**The Library of Congress has cataloged the hardcover edition as follows:**

Phillips, Donald T. (Donald Thomas).
   Martin Luther King, Jr., on leadership : inspiration and wisdom for challenging times / Donald T. Phillips.
      p.   c.m.
   Includes index.
   ISBN 0-446-52367-4
   1. King, Martin Luther, Jr., 1929–1968—Views on leadership. 2. Leadership. 3. Afro-Americans—Biography. 4. Civil rights workers—United States—Biography. 5. Baptists—United States—Clergy—Biography. 6. Afro-Americans—Civil rights—History—20th century.   I. Title.
   E185.97.K5P46   1999
   323'.092—dc21                                    98-3795
ISBN 0-446-67546-6 (pbk.)                             CIP

*Book design by Giorgetta Bell McRee*
*Cover design by Mario Pulice*
*Cover illustration by Mark Weakly*

# Contents

**PART III.** Winning with People

**PART IV.** Ensuring the Future

"These are revolutionary times; all over the globe men are revolting against old systems of exploitation and oppression. The shirtless and barefoot people of the world are rising up as never before. The people that walked in darkness have seen a great light. . . . We must move past indecision to action. . . . If we do not act, we shall surely be dragged down the long, dark, and shameful corridors of time reserved for those who possess power without compassion, might without morality, and strength without sight."

MARTIN LUTHER KING, JR.,
APRIL 4, 1967

# Introduction

It has been said that there were three revolutions in American history—spaced approximately one century apart: *The American Revolution (1776–1783)* was a violent war fought to achieve independence from Great Britain. It ended with the establishment of the United States of America as a free nation governed by democracy. *The Civil War (1861–1865),* an extraordinarily brutal armed conflict, was waged primarily over America's enslavement of human beings of African descent. The final result was formal eradication of the institution of slavery. The third revolution was the *American Civil Rights Movement (1954–1968),* a mostly nonviolent period of transformation (but no less a revolution) conducted to change human behavior relating to the doctrine of racial prejudice known as "separate but equal." The concluding result was the elimination of most federal- and state-sanctioned segregation and discrimination practices. Taken collectively, these three major transformational events were something of a march toward achievement of the American dream.

Realizing that slavery was incompatible with the ideal that "all men are created equal," Thomas Jefferson, in his original

1

draft of the Declaration of Independence, provided for the elimination of the institution. However, representatives of America's southern colonies refused to approve the Declaration unless Jefferson's slavery clause was removed. In order to found the nation, therefore, action on the slavery issue was left to future generations.

That monumental decision indicated the founding fathers clearly understood that any massive social change cannot occur all at once. Therefore, in order to realize America's idealistic dream, change would have to happen through a series of steps over a significant period of time. First, a new system of government had to be created—which the founding fathers accomplished. Next, the formal abolishment of the institution of slavery had to occur. Abraham Lincoln took care of that step. And third, unjust laws and behaviors had to be revoked and changed—those that flowed from hundreds of years of ingrained attitudes developed in an economic culture based, in large part, on the monstrous practice of slavery. Dr. Martin Luther King, Jr., who assumed leadership for this daunting task, may have had the toughest job of all. For the realities of human nature ensure that the waging of a violent war, with weapons of individual and mass destruction, will not change the hearts, minds, and feelings of a vast majority of people, especially if they have previously wielded power over the minority.

To clearly understand the series of fateful events in the 1950s and 1960s, it's necessary to place the American civil rights movement in the context of 350 years of African-American history. Only then can the leadership of Martin Luther King, Jr., be fully appreciated.

In August of the year 1619, twelve months before the *Mayflower* reached Plymouth Rock with the Pilgrims, twenty-three people arrived aboard a ship in Jamestown, Virginia. These first African immigrants to America were free men and women. In the common practice of indentured servitude, they sold their services to planters for a certain number of years. Poor Europeans had participated in this system for decades as a means of traveling to and settling in the New World. After their terms of indenture (usually three to seven years) were completed, they were free to move on and live their lives as they chose.

For the next two generations (forty years), Africans and their American-born descendants were free people. They formed their own settlements, worked and acquired property, and mixed into American society. They also voted and held public office.

Gradually, however, powerful social and economic forces, propelled by a worldwide demand for crops grown in America, created a widespread movement toward slavery. Africans, who comprised a small minority of the overall population, were chosen as the group to be enslaved largely because of the color of their skin. Being black, they were not easily able to blend in with the majority of European-Americans. By the 1660s, the American colonies had begun passing laws that made Africans and African-Americans slaves for life. And the highly profitable European slave trade finally reached the shores of America.

From 1700 to the signing of the Declaration of Independence in 1776, the African population of America increased tenfold—from 50,000 to 500,000. Nearly all newly arrived slaves in America were kidnapped from the west coast of Africa or sold by neighboring tribes and then transported across the Atlantic Ocean against their will. They were manacled and chained together, taken aboard cargo ships, and packed like animals into small spaces below deck for the two-month trip to the New World. Malnourishment, disease, and suicide led to death rates as high as 25 percent. Upon arrival, those who survived were sold into slavery at auctions in slave markets, or as retail goods in taverns and warehouses. Many were also purchased in advance or sold on consignment.

During those years, slavery became an ingrained part of the

American economy and culture. A culture of racism and separatism perpetuated itself—one that labeled African-born or African-American people as inferior, unintelligent, barbarous, and simpleminded. Slaves could be sold indiscriminately, families broken apart, and women raped by their masters. Many new laws were passed to strengthen slaveholders' rights. For example, disobedient slaves could be punished with severe physical brutality that included whippings, castration, and branding. Runaway slaves could be killed for resisting arrest.

Despite the tough laws and terrible punishments, slaves were not totally submissive. Periodically, individual acts of resistance or actual slave revolts took place. In 1729 and 1739, slaves rose up and killed their masters in several northern and southern states—which led to further strengthening of statutes and enforcement of laws against disobedience. All the slaves who participated in the revolts were hanged or set on fire, or both.

Several African-Americans also attempted to fight against slavery in the courts. They raised funds, hired lawyers, and filed suits. On rare occasions, chiefly in the North, they won small concessions. Most often, though, the British-based judiciary system slammed the door on their requests.

With time, the slaves embraced American Christianity and blended it with their own African culture. They gathered in remote woods at night because they were not allowed to meet openly. At these meetings, they prayed, commiserated with one another, and sang spiritual hymns and songs—many of which they composed themselves. The Christian religion gave them hope and sustenance. And the music lifted their spirits and became a vital part of slave culture.

The period surrounding the American Revolution began to see some change and progress. The Declaration of Independence provided a grand idea in such simple and general language that African-Americans mired in slavery could not be excluded. "We hold these truths to be self-evident," wrote Thomas Jefferson: "that all men are created equal; that they are endowed by their Creator with certain inalienable rights; that among these are life, liberty, and the pursuit of happiness." The Declaration also stated that "when governments are destructive of these ends as evidenced by bad faith, it is the duty of citizens to alter or abolish these governments." The Declaration gave new impetus to African-Americans to get involved. It gave them hope that, should the new nation achieve its independence from Great Britain, they, too, might eventually win their freedom.

And so, during the American Revolution, thousands of African-Americans from all the thirteen original colonies fought alongside European-American patriots. Crispus Attucks, a forty-seven-year-old escaped slave, was the first person killed by English troops in the Boston Massacre of March 5, 1770. A slave named Abel Benson helped wake the town of Needham, Massachusetts, by blowing his trumpet the same night as Paul Revere's famous ride. There were black Minutemen at Lexington and Concord. They were there with George Washington when he crossed the Delaware and took Trenton. And they fought at the battles of Breed's Hill, Monmouth Courthouse, Saratoga, Brandywine, Yorktown, and nearly all other major engagements. Many African-Americans who did not actually fight in combat helped in other ways. Some were spies and scouts. Others helped build roads or produced and transported supplies.

After the war, many states awarded freedom to those slaves who fought on the American side. Actually, both during and after the Revolution, a trend toward emancipation passed through the northern states, where the economy was not as dependent on slave labor. In 1777, for instance, the Vermont legislature became the first to abolish slavery. Pennsylvania and New York enacted legislation to gradually eliminate the institution. And, with time, the northern states began taking steps toward abolition. By 1790, all had prohibited the importation of slaves—and Massachusetts had not a single slave left in the entire state. About the same time, the new United

States Congress passed the Northwest Ordinance, which prohibited slavery in territories east of the Mississippi and north of the Ohio River. As a consequence, Illinois, Indiana, Ohio, Michigan, and Wisconsin were eventually admitted to the Union as free states.

In the southern region of the United States, however, it was an altogether different story. Most slaves who had participated in the rebellion on the side of America simply returned to their masters and remained in slavery. The institution not only remained strong in the South, but grew considerably as business expanded rapidly. Kentucky and Tennessee were admitted as slave states. Demand for cotton boomed, as did the demand for tobacco, rice, sugar, and other southern staples. It was an economy in which the institution of slavery became ingrained as a method to insure high profits through noncompensated labor.

By 1820 slavery was no longer a national establishment. It was a southern enterprise. Of the 1.5 million slaves in the United States, 99 percent resided in southern states and territories. The conditions in which they lived were abominable— working from sunrise to sunset, living in small, crowded, and dilapidated shacks, with meager rations for sustenance. It was a crime to teach a slave to read or write. They were not permitted to possess Bibles. And they were admonished to think of themselves as inferior and helpless; to obey their masters without question. Slavery was a lifelong condition for millions of African-Americans with no hope that they, or even their children, would one day be free. The culture created by the southern majority was an increasingly downward spiral of oppression.

In the North, conditions were better because slavery was being phased out—but not much better. Racial bias, prejudice, and segregation still remained in practice and in the minds of many European-Americans. Rapid growth in the number of free former slaves seemed only to increase racist views in the North. As such, African-Americans were confined to the lowest tier of society with low-paying jobs and all the accompanying social negatives. They were segregated and prohibited from participating in most societal functions controlled by the majority. The Fugitive Slave Act, passed in 1793, allowed agents to seize any African-American they thought might be a slave. This law led to the widespread abuse of capturing free people in the North and then transporting them to the South to be sold into slavery. Those taken had no rights to appeal—no trial by jury, no witnesses allowed to speak nor individual testimony on their own behalf. And the new United States Constitution had a provision that slaves could be counted as only three fifths of a human being for the purposes of calculating taxes and government representation.

In response, free African-Americans began to organize themselves into social groups and create a society and culture of their own design. As a matter of fact, post–Revolutionary War America brought a wave of African-American institution-building that lasted approximately forty years.

One month before the Constitutional Convention opened in 1787, the Free African Society was founded in Philadelphia. That event set off a chain reaction where fraternal lodges, schools, mutual aid and improvement societies, and various cultural organizations were also established. Colonization organizations for those who wished to return to Africa (though most did not wish to do so) were created. Also founded were wide-ranging correspondence networks (providing for the sharing of information and ideas) that served to link African-Americans geographically for the first time. And, perhaps most significantly because they touched people on a local and daily basis, various independent African-American churches came into existence. The church served as a center for social life and politics and parish preachers quickly became acknowledged leaders of the community.

In the North, workers organized demonstrations against segregation and discrimination policies. In the South, resistance to slavery produced individual instances of theft, destruction of property, trampling of crops, poor work performance, work slowdowns, and sit-downs. Many violent revolts also took place. There was one planned in Charleston in 1822 that would have involved nine thousand slaves had not informers alerted authorities. And in 1831, there was the now-famous revolt led by a slave named Nat Turner, who embarked on a rampage of killing and murder throughout Southampton County, Virginia. As before, such violence and disobedience resulted in more restrictive laws and harsher punishments in an attempt to quell resistance. Violators were whipped, burned at the stake, and hanged. Tougher laws were passed and enforced. The state of Maryland actually set up a law that promoted colonization of free blacks in Africa and authorized them to be deported if they did not leave voluntarily.

But still, the world seemed to be on a path toward the eventual elimination of involuntary servitude. Between 1810 and 1825, the fight for independence in the Spanish-held portion of the Americas eventually led to the total liberation of slaves in the resulting newly independent nations. On March 3, 1820, Congress passed the Missouri Compromise, which admitted Maine to the Union as a free state, Missouri as a slave state, and banned slavery in the northern half of territories acquired in the Louisiana Purchase. In 1833, Great Britain abolished slavery. Fifteen years later, France followed suit. And in the United States of America, a fast-growing radical abolitionist movement emerged in the northern part of the nation.

Abolitionists like William Lloyd Garrison (a former indentured servant) founded the American Anti-Slavery Society and the American and Foreign Anti-Slavery Society. In addition, political organizations (such as the Liberty Party and the Free Soil Party) were formed to run abolitionist candidates for nationwide office.

Frederick Douglass, an escaped slave turned passionate abolitionist, also rose from the masses and, for more than half a century, led the fight for emancipation and equal rights under the law. He traveled the country and the world, preaching his abolitionist views and raising awareness of slavery's inhumanity to man. In fact, he was so well received in Europe that many people urged him to stay because he was better treated there than in his own country. In reply, Douglass said in 1847 to a group of London supporters:

> I choose to go home; to return to America. I will go back, for the sake of my brethren. I go to suffer with them; to toil with them; to endure insult with them; to undergo outrage with them; to lift up my voice in their behalf; to speak and write in their vindication; and struggle in their ranks for that emancipation which shall yet be achieved by the power of truth and of principle for that oppressed people.

Back in the United States, Douglass and other black abolitionists created mass movements of protest on a nationwide basis. They held regional and local meetings, sang freedom songs, and marched in demonstrations. For the most part, they protested without violence in attempting to call attention to the inhumanity of slavery.

African-Americans also held a series of national conventions where strategy was debated, decisions made, and nationwide action agreed upon. Education and dissemination of information became a top priority. *Freedom's Journal,* the nation's first African-American newspaper, was founded. Many articles and pamphlets concerning events and conditions in black society were published. Several escaped slaves published autobiographies detailing the horror of their experiences. And the first detailed works chronicling the history of African-Americans appeared.

Formal education also became of paramount concern. The first African-American gained admittance to and subsequently graduated from Middlebury College in Vermont in 1823.

Others followed suit at such northern universities as Amherst, Bowdoin, Oberlin, and Rutland. And of special significance was the founding of the first all–African-American colleges in the 1840s and 1850s in Pennsylvania, Ohio, and Washington, D.C.

African-Americans also renewed their fight within the court systems. A group of Boston abolitionists, for example, raised enough money to hire famed attorney Charles Sumner to plead a case regarding the unconstitutionality of segregated schools. So many demonstrations, sit-downs, and protests were held in the process that the Massachusetts state legislature, in 1849, finally outlawed school segregation. In addition, free African-Americans, like Sojourner Truth and Harriet Tubman, helped slaves escape to the North through an elaborate and shrewdly constructed "Underground Railroad."

Despite all the small victories and the hope created by the abolitionist movement, the vast majority of American citizens refused to accept slaves and former slaves as equals in society. As a consequence, the practice of segregation in the United States was greatly expanded. Hundreds of riots were instigated by European-Americans in opposition to the crusade for abolition and equal rights. And Jim Crow laws (named after a racial stereotype from a song-and-dance routine) became more common between 1830 and 1860. Segregation was formalized in nearly all public institutions in the North, including theaters, libraries, museums, schools, and modes of transportation, to name a few.

In the early and mid-nineteenth century, the issue and status of slavery in the United States grew to primary and paramount importance in the quest for political power and determination of new territories being added to the Union. The Compromise of 1850, for instance, involved several bills adopted by Congress that abolished slavery in Washington, D.C.; admitted California as a free state; organized the New Mexico and Utah territories without restrictions on slavery;

and enacted a new Fugitive Slave Law that strengthened the previous one of 1793. The Kansas-Nebraska Act of 1854 opened those new territories to settlement by slaveholders—which led immediately to violence and bloodshed between abolitionists and pro-slavery activists.

But tensions between North and South grew to a fevered pitch when, in 1857, the Supreme Court issued its decision in *Dred Scott v. Sandford*. The Court essentially ruled that African-Americans, because they were "so far inferior, they had no rights which the white man was bound to respect," were not considered citizens of the United States—and therefore had no rights under the Constitution.

When Abraham Lincoln, a compromise candidate, was elected president of the United States in 1860 without even being on the ballot in most southern states, the South had had enough. Before Lincoln was sworn in, seven states seceded from the United States to form the Confederate States of America. Jefferson Davis was inaugurated in Montgomery, Alabama, as first president of the Confederacy. And within six months of Lincoln's inauguration, a total of eleven states had left the Union. When Confederate troops fired on the Union-held Fort Sumter in Charleston, South Carolina—a four-year war, the bloodiest in American history, began.

In short order, President Lincoln issued a call for volunteers, and thousands of free African-Americans in the North filled the recruiting stations. Later, in another effort to raise troops, Lincoln became the first president to institute the draft. But many European-American citizens in the North were enraged at the prospect of having to fight a war to free slaves. Lincoln's call for troops resulted in some of the worst race riots in American history. On July 12, 1863, for example, New York's draft rioters turned on any African-American they could find. Blacks were hunted down in the streets and shot or hanged. Women and children were thrown out of windows. New York's Colored Orphan Asylum was burned to the ground, as were businesses and private residences. And thousands of free citizens fled the city for their lives. The riots were a telling indication of just how deeply racism went in America's culture and consciousness.

On January 1, 1863, Abraham Lincoln formally issued the Emancipation Proclamation, which declared that all slaves in the rebellious states (three million in number) were "thenceforward, and forever free." The emancipation did not include nearly a million slaves in border states that had not seceded—nor southern states under federal occupation. When word of Lincoln's freedom doctrine reached southern slaves that summer, spontaneous mass celebrations took place all across the South. Spiritual chants of *Free at last! Free at last! Thank God Almighty, we are free at last!* rang through the plantation countryside. After the festivities wound down, slaves began leaving their masters in droves and heading northward. By the end of the war, more than 500,000 had fled the Confederacy.

Many enlisted in the service of the Union army, which was by then actively recruiting African-Americans. As a matter of fact, 75 percent of the 200,000 black troops who fought in the United States army during the Civil War were from slave states. Although African-Americans served in segregated units, they participated in more than four hundred engagements and fought valiantly for their own freedom and for the preservation of democracy. Twenty percent were killed and thousands more wounded. At least twenty African-Americans were awarded the Congressional Medal of Honor. Those who did not serve in uniform worked in civilian jobs to help the war effort. They built bridges, roads, entrenchments, and fortifications. They took care of livestock, worked on the railroads, and served as spies and scouts. Many historians credit the influx of African-American manpower in the last few years of the war as having helped the Union defeat the Confederacy. But less than a week after Gen. Robert E. Lee surrendered to Gen. Ulysses S. Grant at Appomattox Court House in Virginia (effectively ending the Civil War), Abraham Lincoln was shot dead by a southerner, John Wilkes Booth, in what he claimed was "revenge for the South."

Despite Lincoln's death, a series of monumental steps occurred over the next decade: in December 1865, the Thirteenth Amendment to the Constitution was ratified—thus formally ending the institution of slavery in the United States of America; in 1868 ratification of the Fourteenth Amendment affirmed citizenship for people naturalized or born in the United States; in 1870, the Fifteenth Amendment guaranteed the right to vote for all citizens by prohibiting federal and state governments from denying an individual's right to vote "on account of race, color, or previous condition of servitude"; and passage of the Civil Rights Bill of 1875 ordered equal treatment in public facilities regardless of race, color, or "any previous condition of servitude."

In addition, many new African-American colleges were founded, including Atlanta University, Virginia Union College, Fisk University, Howard University, Morgan College, and Morehouse College. The Homestead Act of 1866 opened up public lands, allowing many former slaves to acquire land in Florida. And across the nation, African-American organizations and churches raised funds for the education and welfare of millions of recently freed slaves. Former slaves and their children could now attend newly created interracial public school systems in the South.

New leaders also began to arise from the masses to assume leadership roles. African-Americans joined the United States House of Representatives, the Senate, and other positions of authority in the federal government. They earned roles in nearly all areas of local and state government as mayors, judges, representatives, superintendents of education, postmasters, policemen. They voted, held jobs, and acquired property. And in many areas of the country, including the South, blacks and whites were served in the same rooms at restaurants. Moreover, it was former slaves who rebuilt the infrastructure of the South. Roads, bridges, railway tracks, government buildings, levees, and dams, to name a few, were constructed by African-Americans.

Such progress in the societal position of former slaves was due to the process (and the period) known as Reconstruction. But less than a decade after the war, northern support for such radical reconstruction of the old system began to wane. An economic depression in the late 1870s focused private-sector thoughts on areas other than those associated with former slaves. In turn, the federal government became less inclined to interfere in the affairs of the southern states.

But African-Americans had simply gained too much freedom too fast for the vast majority of white southerners to swallow. That feeling (coupled with pressure easing up a bit on the South), caused something of a backlash racist movement by the white majority to put African-Americans "back in their place." For instance, a sharecropping system was introduced where former slaves worked the land for owners, who, in turn, provided supplies, food, and clothing. Profits were supposed to be split, but the landowners usually fixed the books so sharecroppers were perpetually in a state of poverty. Many states also passed oppressive "Black Codes" that sought to legally restrain the progress of former slaves. Special licenses were required to perform farming and other menial work. And the right to use physical violence on "servants" under the age of eighteen was made legal.

Paramilitary vigilante organizations, such as the Ku Klux Klan, were organized across the South. As a result, thousands of former slaves were murdered by racist government and law enforcement officials. Violence was so prevalent, it is estimated that in the last two decades of the nineteenth century more than ten thousand African-Americans were lynched in the United States of America.

Because the black vote began to affect the outcome of key elections in the South, state governments started to implement successful steps to keep African-Americans from voting. Poll tax laws were passed and voters had to show proof they had paid their taxes before being allowed to vote. Literacy tests were implemented as a precondition for voting. Polls were closed, or located in hard-to-reach, unpleasant places. These laws, of course, negatively affected former slaves because they lived in dire poverty. And there were, of course, the continued threats and violence against those who attempted to exercise their constitutional right to vote.

From 1875 to the turn of the century, the societal status of African-Americans in the South gradually declined to a new low point of rigidly oppressive racism and separatism. Intimidation, threats, and physical violence became a way of life for former slaves trying to mix into society and earn a living. African-Americans were continually portrayed as ignorant, simpleminded, and corrupt in a racial stereotype that would remain in the minds of the majority for more than a century.

Despite the slow undoing of their personal rights, African-Americans fought back where they could. They responded by staging protests, filing lawsuits, and forming new organizations to combat racism. Not only was there a move toward creation of organized labor unions (such as the Colored Waiters Association of New York), a pioneer protest organization was formed called the National Afro-American League (later renamed the Afro-American Council). It quickly placed local branches in dozens of cities around the nation. In addition, there had been a gradual increase in the number of African-American–owned businesses—from 2,000 at the end of the Civil War to approximately 25,000 by 1900.

Just before the turn of the century, in 1896, the United States Supreme Court issued a monumental decision that would control the destiny of African-Americans for more than fifty years. In *Plessy v. Ferguson,* the Court legalized laws requiring "separate but equal" accommodations for African-Americans. Before that case, only a few states had passed Jim Crow laws for separate facilities. Afterward, all the southern states began enacting widespread, tough, and enforceable laws that kept African-Americans on a completely separate basis from everybody else.

Formally segregated were schools, libraries, hospitals, parks, churches, orphanages, cemeteries, and all forms of public transportation. Public schools became rigidly segregated with poor black schools receiving little funding compared to white schools. Some southern states did not even offer a high school education to African-American children. Into the 1930s there were no state-funded schools offering blacks a four-year college degree in the South. The administration of President Woodrow Wilson officially segregated government employees in Washington. The armed forces were segregated and some branches, including the Marine Corps, did not allow African-Americans in their ranks at all. Nearly every southern city and town had "separate but equal" statutes on their books by 1940. And there were signs everywhere marked "white" and "colored"—for bathrooms, water fountains, telephone booths, and so forth. There was also hard punishment for violators of the "separate but equal" doctrine. Blacks, for example, would be arrested, convicted, and sentenced to serve on chain gangs where they worked from sunrise to sunset, were chained together, and then put behind bars at night.

In an effort to flee the oppression, search for jobs, and find a better way of life, African-Americans in the South responded with the largest mass migration in American history. In the first two decades of the twentieth century, more than 1.7 million people moved to the big cities of the North. And between 1930 and 1960, another four million left the South. As a result, isolated, poor black neighborhoods began to form in nearly every major city in the United States—including Chicago, Cleveland, Detroit, Newark, New York, and Philadelphia, to name a few. Formation of these "ghettos" led, in turn, to overcrowding and higher costs of living than in white neighborhoods. And, as conditions worsened, many people gave up all hope—abandoning efforts to find jobs, loitering on street corners, drifting into crime.

At the same time, white citizens reacted negatively to the mass infusion of African-Americans into their cities and towns. There were bombings of black residences in Chicago, beatings in New York, and murders in Detroit. Consequently, in what has become known as the Red Summer of 1919, African-Americans exploded in race riots in more than twenty cities across the nation. For two weeks, cities such as Charleston, Chicago, Knoxville, Omaha, New York, and Norfolk became quite literally "war zones" where gunfire was exchanged and blood flowed in the streets. In response to these riots, the Ku Klux Klan renewed itself and local chapters spread across the rest of the country. The result was more lynchings in South Carolina and mass murders of blacks in nearly every southern state.

Increasingly, the African-American community in the United States turned more inward—taking action on their own behalf when none was forthcoming from the government or the overwhelming white majority. New leaders emerged at the turn of the century who chose radically new paths to progress. Booker T. Washington, a former Virginia slave, urged African-Americans to concentrate on education and economic advancement and then "lifting others up as we climb." He further advocated learning specific vocations and then set up a system of schools to teach uneducated blacks various trades. As a result, by 1920, there were more than 75,000 African-American–owned businesses scattered throughout the United States.

On the other hand, W. E. B. Du Bois, the first African-American to receive a doctor of philosophy degree, demanded immediate integration into the white majority. He urged organization, teamwork, and consolidation. As a direct result of Du Bois's leadership, the Niagara Movement of 1905 formed and dedicated itself to securing African-Americans "every single right that belongs to a freeborn American, political, civil, and social."

Du Bois was also one of the founding members of the National Association for the Advancement of Colored People. Created in May 1910, the NAACP quickly set up local chapters in all major northern and southern cities. The organization's mission was "to promote equality of rights and eradicate caste or race prejudice among the citizens of the United States" and "to advance the interest of colored Americans." Also in 1910, the National Urban League was created to focus specifically on the economic problems of African-Americans living in major metropolitan areas. And between 1917 and 1925, A. Philip Randolph, the son of a Methodist minister from Florida, helped form several black labor organizations—including the Brotherhood of Sleeping Car Porters.

But when the stock market crashed in 1929, setting off the Great Depression, African-Americans were hit the hardest. They were the first to get laid off and the last to receive jobs when things started to turn around. Unemployment among blacks soared to over 50 percent in some cities—and more than 25 percent nationwide.

The plight of African-Americans on both economic and social levels was alleviated significantly when Franklin D. Roosevelt became president. FDR's New Deal provided work projects and relief checks for people in dire straits—regardless of the color of their skin. When the Daughters of the American Revolution refused to allow entertainer Marian Anderson to sing at Constitution Hall, Eleanor Roosevelt and other leaders of the administration arranged for her to perform at the Lincoln Memorial. Such progressive, action-oriented endeavors on the part of the government caused African-Americans to shift political allegiance from the Republican "party of Lincoln" to the Democratic party of FDR.

Usually, however, President Roosevelt did not act without the firm prodding of civil rights leaders. In 1941, for example, A. Philip Randolph formed a "March on Washington" committee and laid plans for a hundred thousand people to descend on the capital in a protest against unfair practices in business and discrimination in the armed forces. In response to a demand from Randolph (and assurances to stop the march before it began), Roosevelt issued an executive order that banned discrimination in war industries and apprenticeship programs. That executive action, in turn, led to the establishment of the Fair Employment Practices Committee.

With the onset of World War II, African-Americans not only made significant gains in securing jobs, they lined up en masse to join the armed services and risk their lives to fight for America's freedom. More than 1.1 million African-Americans served in the armed forces during World War II. Mostly, they fought in segregated units but, for the first time, they were accepted in all branches of the armed services. Moreover, African-Americans, as they had done during the American Revolution, the Civil War, and World War I, fought valiantly and earned numerous medals for valor.

And yet, when black veterans returned from Europe and Asia after the war, they were thrown back into a system of second-class citizenship in the "separate but equal" South and the ghetto-ridden North. During the war, in protests directly related to these conditions and the treatment of African-American soldiers, race riots broke out in Detroit, Harlem, and Los Angeles. Also, the Congress of Racial Equality (CORE) was founded to formally stage protests. One of CORE's first efforts, for example, was to organize a sit-in in a Chicago restaurant to demonstrate against discriminatory practices.

After World War II, black civil rights groups began to form alliances with white organizations to combat segregation and racial discrimination. The American Jewish Congress, the Anti-Defamation League, the National Catholic Welfare Conference, the American Civil Liberties Union, and the AFL-CIO joined forces with African-Americans on a national scale. Significant progress began to occur on the federal level.

Under pressure from these organizations, as well as the NAACP and A. Philip Randolph, President Harry Truman created a national Civil Rights Committee and issued an executive directive integrating the armed forces.

Gradually, through a series of court orders, and with increasing activism by CORE and the NAACP, public facilities in the North began to open up to blacks. Individual gains in private enterprise were also made—as when Branch Rickey, general manager of the Brooklyn Dodgers, elevated Jackie Robinson to the major leagues, effectively integrating professional baseball.

The South, however, remained rigid and resistant—which only served to motivate more action from civil rights groups. The NAACP led protests, fought with presidents and government bureaucrats for African-American rights, and led a massive battle in the federal courts of the United States. The most significant of these was the momentous case argued by NAACP attorney Thurgood Marshall that tested the legality of segregated schools in the United States. In that opinion, handed down on May 17, 1954, the Supreme Court of the United States issued a unanimous decision in the case of *Brown v. Board of Education:* "We conclude," wrote Chief Justice Earl Warren, "that in the field of public education, the doctrine of 'separate but equal' has no place."

The next year, the High Court ordered nationwide public school desegregation to proceed "with all deliberate speed." President Dwight Eisenhower, however, believed that the Court's decision was ill advised and maintained a hands-off attitude toward the ruling. Partly as a result of the president's inaction, by 1956 nearly every southern state had enacted legislation that declared the *Brown* ruling null and void. In addition, 101 southern congressmen signed what was labeled the "Southern Manifesto," which declared their rigid resistance to public school integration. In Tennessee, Kentucky, and Arkansas, National Guard units had to escort African-American children to school through angry mobs of white citizens. All across the South, White Citizens Councils formed to resist school integration, as they said, "by every lawful means." And once again, the Ku Klux Klan fought back with characteristic violence—including lynchings, bombings, kidnappings, and murders.

With the *Brown* decision, however, a corner had been turned in the long struggle of African-Americans to secure their rights as free people. Clearly, a new period of change had begun. And, as with other periods of great historical transformation, a new leader was emerging *from* the masses to *lead* the masses.

He was a child of the South who embodied and personified the hopes and dreams of African-Americans everywhere. He had experienced firsthand "separate but equal" discrimination practices. He had attended segregated public schools, drank water from "colored only" fountains, been directed to the back of buses, and been excluded from "white only" public places. He had grown up in the segregated streets of Atlanta, Georgia.

Martin Luther King, Jr., was born in 1929—nine months before New York's stock market crash precipitated the Great Depression. He was a teenager during the World War II riots, in college when Harry Truman integrated the armed forces, and just into his first job when the Supreme Court handed down *Brown v. Board of Education*. His mother, a descendant of slaves, was the daughter of a minister. She was a quiet woman with integrity and dignity. His father, a sharecropper's son, had a short temper and fought back against virtually any form of discrimination—especially when it affected him directly.

In later years, Martin recalled riding with his father as a policeman approached their car. "All right, boy," said the policeman to the elder King, "pull over and let me see your license." "I'm no boy," replied Mr. King indignantly. "This is a boy," he said, pointing to his son. "I'm a man, and until you call me one, I will not listen to you." Martin also remembered his father once saying to him: "I don't care how long I have to live with this system, I will never accept it."

The attitude and behavior displayed by his parents, along with personal events experienced in the segregated South, clearly influenced and molded Martin's own feelings and beliefs. As he grew, he, like his father, became outraged by injustice and refused to accept it. When only a junior in high school, for instance, he and his teacher, Sarah Bradley, traveled from Atlanta to Macon by bus so that Martin could participate in a speech contest. On the trip back to Atlanta, after a group of white people boarded the bus at an intermediate stop, Martin and Ms. Bradley were ordered to give up their seats so the new passengers could sit down. "When we didn't move right away," recalled Martin, "the driver started cursing us out and calling us black sons of bitches." His teacher, however, informed her student that they must, indeed, obey the law. So Martin and Ms. Bradley stood in the aisle for an hour and a half as the bus traveled back to Atlanta. "It was the angriest I have ever been in my life," he said. Ironically, the subject of Martin Luther King's speech delivered earlier that day was: "The Negro and the Constitution."

Another time, when he was traveling alone on a train from Connecticut to Atlanta, Martin was escorted to a back table in the dining car where a curtain was pulled so that white patrons would not have to look at him. "I felt just as if a curtain had come down across my whole life," he recalled. "The insult I will never forget."

It was from many experiences like these that, as a young man, Martin developed a hatred for white people, for the oppressive society he was forced to live in, and for injustice of any kind. "As I grew older and older," he said, "this feeling continued to grow. . . . I did not conquer it until I entered college and came in contact with white students through working in interracial organizations."

It was from these beginnings, with these deep-seated feelings, that young Martin Luther King, Jr., rose up from the masses to lead the third revolution in American history. Although inexperienced, unpolished, and impulsive, he learned rapidly and turned out to be not only a great leader, but a *true* leader—one whom most people followed easily, willingly, and passionately.

Well, that begs a fundamental question: Just what exactly is true leadership? And how does it differ from, say, management or dictatorship?

In his landmark book *Leadership,* James MacGregor Burns offered a simple and clear definition which, with slight modification, is an excellent starting point:

> Leadership is leaders acting—as well as caring, inspiring and persuading others to act—for certain shared goals that represent the values—the wants and needs, the aspirations and expectations—of themselves and the people they represent. And the genius of leadership lies in the manner in which leaders care about, visualize, and act on their own and their followers' values and motivations.

There are three key points to remember about this definition. First, leadership omits the use of coercive power. Leaders, rather, move others by caring, by inspiring, and by persuading. Tyranny and dictatorship are not only contradictory to the rights of human nature, they are contradictory to leadership itself. Second, leaders have a bias for action and a sense of urgency that are centered around shared goals. And third, leaders act with respect for the values of the people they represent—which are in concert with their own personal convictions.

True leadership, then, is very different from many theories of modern management that are centered around a command and control hierarchy. Furthermore, compromise, consensus, and teamwork vault to the forefront. Why? Because if leaders are to act for the people they represent, they must first listen, establish trust, discuss, debate, understand, and learn. Effective communication also becomes critical because it is the only way to inspire and persuade others.

There has always been difficulty in understanding and practicing real leadership. That's because it is more of an art than a science. There seem to be no set rules for leaders to follow— only guidelines and concepts, perceptions and ideas, abstractions and generalities.

So how do we learn to be effective leaders? We learn by observing successful individuals; by studying those who have demonstrated their abilities with tangible, visceral results. When studying great leaders of the past, consistent patterns begin to emerge; common skills become readily apparent; and certain personal traits appear and reappear time after time— from leader to leader, from century to century.

By careful observation, it becomes apparent that effective leadership requires specific skills and abilities. For example, good leaders are visionary and decisive. They are able to effectively communicate both their vision and their decisions to a wide array of people, in a variety of venues, with multiple methods. Effective leaders have an intuitive understanding of human nature that combines with the ability to care, establish trust, and build alliances. They are able to work in teams, which, in turn, leads to exceptional skills in fashioning consensus, compromising when necessary, and valuing diversity of thought, ability, and culture. Also, the best leaders have the know-how to successfully create and manage change.

In addition to these acquired abilities, truly great leaders tend to exhibit certain personal traits that are more a part of their character, more innate. They include high ethical standards in which a person consistently attempts to "do the right thing"; an unusually strong bias for action fueled by a high rate of personal energy and an almost uncontrollable desire to achieve; and a propensity for lifelong learning, curiosity, and continual improvement. Many leaders also possess an unwavering self-confidence that frequently translates into courage in the face of adversity, the willingness to take risks, and a sense of destiny—a personal belief that they are meant for something special, perhaps even greatness. This was certainly true of such leaders as George Washington, John Adams, Abraham Lincoln, and Winston Churchill.

Moreover, the study of great leaders has produced solid evidence that people can be predisposed to creative and effective leadership from childhood. For instance, many past leaders experienced a strong bond with their mothers. For some, this connection was accompanied by an overwhelmingly negative or virtually nonexistent attachment to their fathers—completing a true oedipal relationship.

Howard Gardner, in his book *Leading Minds,* noted that leaders often experienced "a contrasting set of relations with their parents" and that, at an early age, they displayed "confidence" and "a willingness to rely on oneself." Lincoln, for instance, had an exceptionally close relationship with his stepmother, Sarah Bush Johnston Lincoln, yet felt so negative in his paternal relationship that he refused to even attend his father's funeral. Franklin Roosevelt had a well-known attachment to his mother—and was frequently referred to as a mama's boy. Even Sigmund Freud, creator and leader of the psychoanalysis movement, received special attention from his mother while feeling ambivalent toward his father. He also had a motherly nanny who reinforced the message that he was somehow extra-special. This may have led, in part, to Freud's famous observation in *The Interpretation of Dreams:*

> I have found, that people who know that they are preferred or favored by their mother[s] give evidence in their lives of a peculiar self-reliance and an unshakable optimism which often seem like heroic attributes and bring actual success to their possessors.

Many future leaders also experienced the death of a loved one in their early, formative years. Mohandas K. Gandhi, Thomas Jefferson, and George Washington lost their fathers in adolescence. Lincoln lost his mother at the age of nine. Theodore Roosevelt's father died when he was nineteen and, six years later, his mother and wife died on the same day. Franklin Roosevelt was barely eighteen when his father passed away—and the death of his aunt in a fire when he was two years of age may have accounted for his lifelong fear of fire.

Sickness and death experienced by these well-known leaders may have led to a feeling that life is short; there's not much time to achieve; better make the most of it while you're here on this earth. Could this account for the fact that many of their contemporaries reported that great leaders always seemed to have more energy than the average person; that they were always busy, always in a hurry?

Many leaders, such as Lincoln, were super-sensitive as children, easily hurt, but also intelligent and introspective. Others grew up in a household that had a strong work ethic and high moral values—one where books and learning were not only encouraged but commonplace. Theodore Roosevelt's home was a place of habitual learning and constant reinforcement. Lincoln, when young, was rarely without a book. Harry Truman's parents admonished him to be good, urged hard work on the farm, and reinforced the belief that he could be anything he wanted to be. Many of these leaders, as did Gandhi and others, grew up in homes crowded with siblings, aunts, uncles, and grandparents.

Compare this profile with that of Martin Luther King, Jr.

He grew up in a household with his two parents, three siblings, and a grandparent. He was taught high moral values and a strong work ethic at an early age. His mother's father was a Baptist preacher who became an early leader in Georgia's NAACP and led a successful boycott against an Atlanta newspaper. Martin's father, also a preacher, was very active in Atlanta's civil rights movement—successfully leading an effort

to equalize teachers' salaries and eliminate segregated eleva-
tors in the city courthouse.

He also had a contrasting set of relations with his parents
that included a loving relationship with his mother. When
Martin was a preschooler and told that his little white friends
across the street could no longer play with him, it was his
mother who sat down, told him about slavery, the Civil War.
"You are as good as anyone," she said. "You must never feel
that you are less than anybody else. You must always feel that
you are somebody." Martin frequently told his college friends
that he had the "best mother in the world" and once wrote to
his brother: "Our mother was behind the scene setting forth
those motherly cares, the lack of which leaves a missing link in
life."

Conversely, when he was growing up, Martin was often
frightened of his father and tried to avoid provoking him. The
elder King had rough edges, tended to be intolerant and
tyrannical, and whipped Martin up to the age of fifteen. And
yet, Martin deeply loved and came to recognize his father's influence on him. "Perhaps my strong determination for justice
comes from the very strong and dynamic personality of my father," he noted in a 1964 interview.

In addition, Martin enjoyed an unusually close, loving relationship with his maternal grandmother, who lived with the
King family. Martin called her "Mama," and frequently went
to her for solace. Mama Williams would go off to another
room and cry when Martin was being whipped. "She was very
dear to each of us," he recalled in later years, "but especially
to me. I sometimes think I was her favorite grandchild."

When his beloved grandmother died of a heart attack when
Martin was twelve years old, the boy was so distraught that he
jumped out of a second-story window in an apparent suicide
attempt. Although unhurt from the fall, he cried for days and
would not be consoled. He had done exactly the same thing
a few years earlier when his brother, A.D., slid down a banis-
ter and knocked his grandmother to the floor. Believing that

Mama was dead, Martin ran upstairs and impulsively hurled himself out the window. When told that she was not hurt, he got up and simply walked off.

Moreover, when Martin was a child, adults noted that he was brighter than most kids his age, that he could understand things better, and that he often drove adults crazy with the questions he asked to satisfy his curiosity. His father remembered that Martin always "kept books around him" and "liked the idea of having them." He could recite long passages from the Bible before he turned six and entered school. As an adolescent, he'd spend hours reading alone in his bedroom—and often worried about poor people who didn't have enough to eat.

An extraordinarily intelligent individual, Martin graduated from high school at the age of fifteen. He went on to receive a bachelor's degree from Morehouse College and then spent three years at Crozer Theological Seminary where he graduated as valedictorian. He subsequently received his doctor of philosophy from Boston University's School of Theology.

When Martin was in college, one of his contemporaries described him as "quiet, introspective and introverted," with "a tendency to be withdrawn and not to participate." He also was known for his tremendous energy and activity. "I always had a desire to work," he once stated. "I had a paper route . . . worked up to become assistant manager of one of the paper's deposit stations. I was the youngest assistant manager the [paper] had at the time." In his career after graduation, Martin often worked twenty-hour days, rested on only a few hours of sleep a night, and traveled hundreds of thousands of miles a year while giving hundreds of speeches.

King's contemporaries also noted that he had a strong sense of destiny, as if he were preordained for some special work. That's one reason he chose the preacher's pulpit as his life's work. Not long after being notified he had won the

Nobel Peace Prize in 1964, he said to a friend: "History has thrust me into this position."

After completing his college education, Martin Luther King, Jr., could have pursued a career that might have been more financially promising than the ministry. He could have stayed in Boston where living conditions for African-Americans were better than those in the South.

But he chose to return to Atlanta.

"I had an opportunity to live in the North because I had one or two jobs offered," he recalled. "I went back south mainly because I felt that there were great opportunities there to transform a section of the country into something rich. I mean rich in spirit—and beautiful."

Perhaps Martin also went back home because he never got over the racial discrimination he had experienced—or because he never forgot the injustice of being treated as anything less than a human being. And maybe he went back because of a vow made to his mother when still a youngster. "You know," he told her, "when I get to be a man, I'm gonna hit this thing, and I'm gonna hit it hard. . . . Mother, there is no such thing as one people being better than another. The Lord made all of us equal, and I'm gonna see to that."

History has clearly demonstrated that especially effective leaders often tend to emerge during periods of great change. For every major turning point in American history, creative leaders—right for the times and uniquely suited to the task—assumed the mantle of leadership: the founding fathers during the American Revolution; Abraham Lincoln during the Civil War; Franklin Roosevelt during the Great Depression and World War II; Harry Truman in its aftermath. With time, history has judged all of these people to have been great leaders.

How is it, then, that Martin Luther King, Jr., another extraordinary leader, rose from the masses to successfully guide a nonviolent social revolution known as the American civil rights movement? What made him different from everybody else? What drove him? And why did people follow his lead—willingly, hopefully, passionately?

Part of Martin Luther King, Jr.'s, legacy is that of genuinely unselfish, compassionate, and action-oriented leadership. He was a remarkable human being whose lessons, principles, and philosophy can be a guide for those of us who hope to improve ourselves, our organizations, and the society in which we live.

# PART I

# PREPARING TO LEAD

*"Let nobody fool you, all the loud noises we hear today are nothing but the death groans of the dying system. The old order is passing away, the new order is coming into being. But whenever there is anything new there are new responsibilities. As we think of this coming new world we must think of the challenge that we confront and the new responsibilities that stand before us. We must prepare to live in a new world."*

MARTIN LUTHER KING, JR.,
AUGUST 11, 1956

> "I neither started the protest nor suggested it. I simply responded to the call of the people for a spokesman."
>
> Martin Luther King, Jr.,
> 1958

> "Montgomery is known as the Cradle of the Confederacy. It has been a quiet cradle for a long, long time. But now the cradle is rocking."
>
> Martin Luther King, Jr.,
> March 31, 1956

# 1 / First Listen: Lead by Being Led

As he reached the top of the steps, twenty-five-year-old Martin Luther King, Jr., must have paused to take a look around before entering the small two-story red-brick building for the first time. Looking to the east, he couldn't have missed the Confederate flag waving in the wind atop the old state capitol building—still there after having been unfurled for the first time nearly a century earlier. He probably would have noticed, too, that the American flag was positioned below the Confederate flag. Also from his position, he could have readily viewed the portico where, on February 18, 1861, Jefferson Davis had been sworn in as president of the Confederate States of America. As it was, Martin found himself standing smack dab in the middle of downtown Montgomery, Alabama—the "Cradle of the Confederacy"—the first national capital of the Confederate States. The building he was about to enter was Dexter Avenue Baptist Church—the parish for which he had just accepted the job of pastor. It was to be his first professional position after leaving Boston University, one he had taken despite the initial reluctance of both his father and his bride, Coretta Scott.

Martin's new church, with its all-black congregation, was created during Reconstruction after the Civil War—purposely erected in the shadow of the all-white capitol building as a symbol of the newly mandated freedom of former slaves. But in 1954, Montgomery was a bastion of racial segregation. It had been that way for generations—part of an ingrained southern culture that perpetuated a never-ending downward spiral of oppression and despair for African-Americans. People were used to it. That's just the way it was.

Black citizens and white citizens, for instance, were not allowed to sit together on a public bus. If a white person took a seat next to an African-American, the African-American was required to stand in the aisle. Even though 75 percent of the bus company's clientele were African-Americans, they were always directed to the back of the bus and, by city ordinance, violators were subject to fines and imprisonment. Bus drivers, all of whom were white, were given authority to enforce the rules. Such power, though, often resulted in heated arguments that resulted in the drivers calling passengers a variety of racial epithets, including "black cow," "ape," and "nigger." In one ugly episode, a fifteen-year-old named Claudette Colvin, who also happened to be unmarried and pregnant, was dragged from a bus for refusing to give up her seat to a white person. For her resistance, the young woman was charged with assault and battery along with violating city and state segregation ordinances. This incident occurred shortly after Martin King settled into his new home.

Interestingly enough, immediately upon his arrival, Martin placed the existing racial situation in a context that had not previously been articulated to local residents. "It is a significant fact that I come to Dexter at a most crucial hour of our world's history," he said in his first sermon, "at a time when the flame of war might arise at any time to redden the skies of our dark and dreary world. . . . At a time when men are experiencing in all realms of life, disruption and conflict, self-destruction and meaningless despair and anxiety."

For him, the human environment in Montgomery was part of a national crisis not to be tolerated. And Martin let it be known that he intended to do something about it—and that he also expected his parishioners to do something about it. "Dexter," he went on to say in that same sermon, "must somehow lead men and women to the high mountain of peace and salvation. We must give men and women, who are all but on the brink of despair, a new bent of life. I pray God that I will be able to lead Dexter in this urgent mission."

Montgomery's newest preacher hit the ground running. He joined the NAACP's local chapter and was quickly elected to its executive committee. He became a member of the Planned Parenthood Federation in an effort to assist and educate unwed young mothers. And, in an attempt to build alliances and broaden his understanding of cultural issues, he joined the only interracial organization in Montgomery, the Alabama Council on Human Relations. "From the beginning, I took an active part in current social problems," he told a reporter in later years. "I insisted that every church member become a registered voter and a member of the NAACP."

During Martin's second year in Montgomery, an incident occurred on a city bus that effectively ignited the American civil rights movement. On December 1, 1955, Mrs. Rosa Parks, a forty-two-year-old tailor's assistant, was commanded by a bus driver to give up her seat to a white male passenger who had just boarded. Mrs. Parks simply said, "No." She knew she was breaking the law, but she nevertheless refused to move. In response, the driver stopped the bus, called the police, and had her arrested. "I don't really know why I wouldn't move," she later commented. "There was no plot or plan at all. I was just tired. My feet hurt."

Rosa Parks, however, was no ordinary woman. For the previous twelve years she had been a civil rights activist with the NAACP and heavily involved in voter registration drives. She was well known in Montgomery's African-American community. And when she called home from jail, word of her arrest spread around town like wildfire. At that point, E. D. Nixon, a lawyer and former president of the local NAACP chapter, rushed downtown and secured Mrs. Parks's release on bond. After hearing the details of the incident, Nixon told Mrs. Parks that, if she was willing to be the lightning rod, they would try to take her case all the way to the United States Supreme Court while also instituting a boycott of the bus company. With some hesitation, Rosa Parks gave the okay to let her attorney move forward with his ideas.

That was all Nixon needed to hear. The next morning he telephoned every black leader in town to let them know what had happened, to inform them that there was already a spontaneously generated boycott of city buses taking place, and to call an emergency meeting for that evening. He was also asking everybody to support the boycott. When Nixon reached Martin King, he detected some reluctance in the young minister's voice—even though Martin had agreed to host the gathering in Dexter's basement meeting room. Nixon then called Ralph Abernathy (pastor of the First Baptist Church), who had become fast friends with King, and asked him to help persuade the young pastor to become fully committed to the boycott.

That evening, somewhere between fifty and seventy leaders of Montgomery's African-American community met at Dexter Avenue Baptist Church. Abernathy and Rev. L. Roy Bennett, president of Montgomery's Interdenominational Ministerial Alliance, ran the meeting. Anyone who wished to speak was allowed to do so. Martin, however, remained silent;

listening intently, whispering to those near him; pondering, thinking.

Two key decisions were agreed upon by the group. First, the ministers would launch at least a one-day boycott (starting on Monday, December 5) in a show of unity and support for Mrs. Parks's position. Second, they would hold a community-wide mass meeting that same evening in order to determine whether the public would support an indefinite extension of the bus boycott. After the meeting broke up, Martin and Ralph stayed at Dexter late into the night mimeographing flyers. The next day, hundreds of volunteers began spreading more than seven thousand notices all over town. Some of the ministers even went around to nightclubs to spread the word—and, at Sunday services, each alerted their congregation to the boycott and the upcoming mass meeting.

Over the next few days and weeks, Montgomery's African-American leadership team took five major steps that would result in the eventual success of their movement. These strategic actions would also become key elements in Martin Luther King, Jr.'s, future approach to leadership.

## 1. Set Goals and Create a Plan of Action

A specific plan of action was created to implement a long-term boycott of city buses where people would use any other method of transportation possible until government officials agreed to their proposals. In addition, three goals (or demands) were set that would be the basis for negotiation with the opposition for ending the boycott. First, no rider would have to stand when there was a vacant seat nor would anyone be compelled to give up a seat already occupied. Second, bus drivers would have to be courteous to all patrons. And, third, African-Americans could apply and be hired as bus drivers.

These goals and the overall plan were conceived by the three-person committee of Nixon, Abernathy, and Rev. Edgar

French (Hilliard Chapel AME Zion Church)—and later presented to, and approved by, the larger team of leaders.

## 2. Create a New Formal Alliance

The leadership group founded a formal organization that was specifically designed to administer the boycott. When Abernathy suggested the name Montgomery Improvement Association (MIA), it was immediately accepted. And then, to his surprise, Martin was nominated president of the new alliance. Those who supported him did so because he was well liked, highly educated, and an eloquent speaker. Also, because he was relatively new in town, he was not tied to any particular group and, therefore, had no known baggage or personal agenda. In essence, Martin Luther King, Jr., was something of a compromise, middle-of-the-road candidate. He accepted the position right off the bat. "Somebody has to do it," said Martin, "and if you think I can, I will serve."

## 3. Involve the People

A mass meeting at Holt Street Baptist Church was held in the evening of the first day of the boycott. Rather than riding the bus, over 99 percent of Montgomery's African-Americans walked, hitchhiked, rode mules and horses, or found some other way to get to work and back home again. Accordingly, the boycott started out as a tremendous success.

Thousands of people began assembling for the mass meeting several hours in advance. By the time it started, at least a thousand were in the church, spilling into the aisles, standing on the sides and in the back. An estimated four thousand more people were crowded together outside on the lawn and in the streets listening to what was being said from a loudspeaker that had been mounted on the church's roof.

The proceeding began with a prayer and scripture reading. Then Rev. King, as newly elected president of the MIA, rose to give a fifteen-minute opening speech. He spoke from an outline prepared less than an hour in advance. "We're here this evening for serious business," he began. "We are American citizens, and we are determined to acquire our citizenship to the fullness of its meaning." After portraying Rosa Parks as a great heroine and retelling her story, his voice rose in a melodramatic tone. "There comes a time when people get tired. We are here this evening to say to those who have mistreated us so long that we are tired—tired of being segregated and humiliated; tired of being kicked about by the brutal feet of oppression. We have no alternative but to protest," he said to thundering cheers from the crowd. Martin concluded by eloquently taking the cause to a higher level: "If we protest courageously, and yet with dignity and Christian love, when the history books are written in the future, somebody will have to say, 'There lived a race of people . . . who had the moral courage to stand up for their rights. And thereby they injected a new meaning into the veins of history and civilization.' "

Rufus Lewis, a business leader who had nominated King for president of the MIA, later commented that this speech was a "great awakening." "It was astonishing," he said. "[We] were brought face-to-face with the type of man that Martin Luther King was. . . ."

Rosa Parks was next introduced and the crowd gave her a standing ovation. They all knew that earlier in the day she had been convicted of her "crime" and fined $14. Then Rev. Abernathy went to the microphone and read a resolution calling for a boycott until the MIA's demands were met. When a voice vote was called for, the people in the audience unanimously thundered their approval.

In order to keep the citizens informed and up-to-date, similar mass meetings were held on a weekly basis and rotated to different churches. They were to become the chief form of two-way communication between the people and the movement's leaders.

## 4. Seek Dialogue and Negotiation

The next morning, a letter requesting formal negotiations, along with a copy of the people's three demands, was mailed to the bus company and to Montgomery city hall. That afternoon, the MIA leadership held a press conference to explain their goals. Two days later, a meeting was granted with city and bus company executives at city hall. At that gathering, however, King and the other black leaders were sternly informed that there would be no compromise, no meeting of demands, and no more discussions.

Although initially angry, Martin became more determined than ever in his quest, and philosophical concerning the reaction of the white majority. He recalled his study of the philosopher Friedrich Hegel, who wrote: "Growth comes through pain and struggle."

Over the course of the boycott, MIA leaders would seek additional negotiations. On occasion they spoke with those in positions of authority, but without substantial gain. An important lesson they learned was that the opposition would not yield on any issue unless absolutely forced to do so. Clearly, the boycott would have to go on for an indefinite period of time before any progress was made.

## 5. Innovate

The bus boycott created a major problem for Montgomery's African-American leadership. How would they get thousands of citizens to and from work without the benefit of the method of transportation to which people had long been accustomed?

Because they were faced with a new problem, one that had not been encountered before, it was obvious that they were going to have to generate some creative and imaginative solutions. Accordingly, the MIA set up a transportation committee to deal directly with the question to how to get people around town.

Someone came up with the idea of contacting all the taxi cab companies in town to work out some sort of a deal. Sensing a possible windfall in business, eight of Montgomery's taxi businesses agreed to transport people for the same fare as that charged on city buses—10 cents.

The committee also devised a clever car pool system with more than forty pickup and dispatch stations located strategically around the city. Hundreds of people volunteered automobiles and their time in order to make the car pool successful. People who did not work offered to drive any time of day (some drove all day long). Many who had jobs volunteered to drive before and after working hours. With generous donations, the MIA purchased a number of station wagons, dubbed them "rolling churches," and registered them as church property. Within a relatively brief period of time, more than three hundred automobiles were being dispatched in a well-thought-through system that efficiently moved people around town.

Where was Martin King during the implementation of these five steps? Even though elected president of the MIA, he was not as far out in front as most people naturally think a leader's place should be. He was, in fact, pretty much in the middle of the pack, perhaps even a bit to the rear.

Martin was something of a reluctant leader at first. He feared that he would take on too much for one person to handle and often related to others that he had been "suddenly catapulted into the leadership of the bus protest." "Everything happened so quickly," he said, "that I had no time to think through the implication of such leadership. . . . I neither started the protest nor suggested it," he admitted. "I simply responded to the call of the people for a spokesman." Having been asked to serve, however, he couldn't say no. "[So] we started our struggle together."

Naturally tentative at first, he followed the lead of others, worked in groups, and made no major policy decisions without the input and approval of other leaders in the MIA. Because he had not sought the point—and even hesitated at accepting it—Martin may have been the best possible leader for the movement to have had under the circumstances. To paraphrase Plato: "Only those who do not seek power are qualified to hold it." At that moment in time, the people of Montgomery involved in the bus boycott may have needed a leader whom they could trust to listen—one who rode *with* them—more than they needed someone who would simply tell them what to do.

While it's true that the people chose him to lead because, among other things, he had *no known agenda,* he had *a high rate of energy,* he was *perceived as someone who would try to do the right thing,* and he *could communicate effectively*—Martin, by his own admission, was "unprepared for the role." "This is not the life I expected to lead. But gradually you take some responsibility, then a little more. . . . You have to give yourself entirely. Then once you make up your mind that you are giving yourself, you are prepared to do anything that serves that Cause and advances the Movement. I have reached that point. I have given myself fully."

Early on in the Montgomery movement, Martin was gauging the wishes of the vast majority of people—following *their* lead. Essentially he was *listening.* And in doing so, he was gaining greater and greater trust from people as the months went by.

The best leaders realize that people want to know that their ideas and thoughts are being, at the very least, heard. Only then can there be a chance that those concerns may be acted upon. When leaders listen first, then speak, they are engendering trust in those who would follow. Furthermore, listening is not only an important aspect of leadership, it is an art. Like a painter in touch with his subject, effective listeners take in everything they hear, analyze it within the context of the environment, and then create an image for their minds to absorb. Stephen R. Covey, in *Principle-Centered Leadership*, wrote that leaders "listen to others with genuine empathy," and that they "seek first to understand, then to be understood." In essence, then, leaders simply must be good listeners. How else can they understand and act for *"certain goals that represent the values—the wants and needs, the aspirations and expectations—of the people they represent?"*

The desire for lifelong learning common to many creative leaders (including Martin Luther King, Jr.) also fosters an equally strong tendency to listen. That's because listening and learning go together. As the adage goes: "You can't learn anything if you are always talking." Deborah Tannen, in *You Just Don't Understand: Men and Women in Conversation,* noted that "listening is a way to show interest and caring" and that women "hear a language of connection and intimacy." With this realization, one can logically conclude that the art of listening—a decidedly more female characteristic than male—is a critical part of the language of connection. And connecting with people is something at which all leaders must excel if they are to be successful. As a matter of fact, listening itself is so critical in leadership that any leader who is not a good listener will be a failure.

In general, the skilled art of listening has four major benefits for any individual who desires to lead people. It 1) *builds trust,* 2) *facilitates understanding of the people's aspirations and expectations,* 3) *enables learning,* and 4) *fosters connection and rapport with others.*

Once Martin King formally assumed the mantle of leadership, he did not fail to step forward and take on responsibility for key management issues, and was proactive on a variety of levels. For instance, he oversaw the renting of office space and hiring of a small staff for the MIA. He constantly monitored the boycott's progress and effectiveness and, in response, worked with the leadership group to reevaluate and reset goals—and then create methods for implementation. Also, in an ongoing effort to keep the people informed, he increased the number of mass meetings held each week. At many of these gatherings, Martin took it upon himself to describe the movement as part of a much broader issue. In so doing, he inspired sustained involvement of a wide range of individuals.

"Our struggle here," he said a few months into the boycotts "is not merely for Montgomery but it is really a struggle for the whole of America." At other meetings, he merely expressed the feelings of the vast majority of participants. "As I look at it, I guess I have committed three sins. The first sin I have committed is being born a Negro. The second sin that I have committed, along with all of us, is being subjected to the battering rams of segregation and oppression. The third and more basic sin which all of us have committed is the sin of having the moral courage to stand up and express our weariness of this oppression." At most meetings a vote was held where the people unanimously agreed to continue the boycott.

As the cost of running the MIA and the boycott increased to $5,000 a month, Martin hit the road to give fund-raising speeches. Because the Montgomery movement had generated national attention, leaders of the MIA were in constant demand to tell their story. And because of his excellent speaking ability, Martin was the most popular of the group. Everywhere he went, he told the Montgomery story with eloquence, made it compelling to the audience, and constantly employed metaphor and drama. "Montgomery is known as the Cradle of the Confederacy," he'd say. "It has been a quiet cradle for a long, long time. But now the cradle is rocking. Dixie has a heart all right," he'd tell his audience. "But it's having a little heart trouble right now." Within a year of the beginning of the bus boycott, more than seven thousand individual contributions had been received from around the world totaling nearly $250,000.

The MIA needed every penny of that money to combat the resistance of the white establishment to the movement. The success of the boycott was evident early as the bus company quickly released a statement that it was losing twenty-two cents for every mile each bus traveled. As a result, a variety of methods were attempted to halt the movement. Bus runs in some of the black sections of town were canceled—but revenues went down even further. The police commissioner warned all taxi cab companies that they had better charge the legal minimum of forty-five cents per rider or they would be fined. That move effectively eliminated the use of taxis as a form of cheap transportation. At the same time, city policemen began harassing and dispersing groups of people waiting at pickup points for the car pool. And then one day, insurance policies on the MIA's station wagons were unexpectedly and mysteriously canceled—which prevented the vehicles from being used in the car pool transport system. Government leaders even attempted to settle the dispute with three African-American ministers who were not leaders in the MIA. When the city announced that a permanent settlement had been reached, MIA executives moved quickly to denounce the agreement as a farce. They confronted the black preachers, forced a retraction, and then announced publicly that the boycott would continue.

By the end of October 1956, Montgomery city attorneys finally devised a move that looked like it was going to end the movement once and for all. They petitioned the court to issue an injunction dissolving the MIA's car pool as a private enterprise operating without a permit. When a temporary injunction against the car pool was issued, MIA leaders stopped the project. As Martin later explained: "Many persons would have been arrested . . . cited for contempt of court and a lot of money would have been tied up and paid out. So, on [that] basis, as law-abiding citizens, we abided by the injunction."

At that point, things looked bleak for the protesters. They had managed to stay off the buses for nearly a year. But now their chief form of alternate transportation had been effectively eliminated and they were going to be tied up in court defending themselves against a city that also demanded $15,000 in punitive fines. Even though he had private doubts, Martin maintained an outwardly optimistic attitude. "The car pool is out of operation," he told the press. "[But] I don't believe any court would be ambitious enough to get an injunction against feet. . . . So we're going to continue to walk and share rides."

On November 13, Martin, as president of the MIA and chief defendant in the city's legal action, was sitting at the head table preparing for a long day in court, when he was handed a note. It informed him that the U.S. Supreme Court had just upheld a lower court decision that declared Alabama's laws on bus segregation unconstitutional. He immediately realized that the Court's decision meant victory for the Montgomery movement regardless of the city's current legal action. "The universe is on the side of justice," Martin declared euphorically. That night, MIA leaders held an executive session and agreed to call two simultaneous mass meetings to inform the people of the new development. In addition, they would recommend that the boycott be continued until the Supreme Court's order was formally mandated in Montgomery.

When Martin spoke at one of the mass meetings, he told his audience of the Supreme Court's decision and what it meant. The crowd was delirious with excitement, but he cautioned them: "I would be terribly disappointed," he said, "if any of you go back to the buses bragging. We won a victory. . . . But we must take this not as a victory over the white man but as a victory for justice and democracy. . . . Let us go back to the buses in all humility and with gratitude to Almighty God for making this decision possible." After his speech, the audience joyously and overwhelmingly voted to endorse the leadership's recommendations.

Five weeks later, when the Supreme Court order finally reached Montgomery, the MIA called two more mass meetings, distributed a leaflet entitled "Integrated Bus Suggestions," and released the following statement (written by Martin Luther King, Jr.) to the African-American community:

> This is the time that we must evince calm dignity and wise restraint. Emotions must not run wild. Violence must not come from any of us, for if we become victimized with violent intents, we will have walked in vain, and our twelve months of glorious dignity will be transformed into an eve of gloomy catastrophe. As we go back to the buses let us be loving enough to turn an enemy into a friend. We must now move from protest to reconciliation. . . . With this dedication we will be able to emerge from the bleak and desolate midnight of man's inhumanity to man to the bright and glittering daybreak of freedom and justice.

On December 21, 1956, at 6:00 A.M., Martin King, Ralph Abernathy, E. D. Nixon, Rosa Parks, and Glen Smiley (a white minister from Texas who had supported the boycott) waited at a corner bus stop near the King home. "I had decided I should not sit back and watch," remembered Martin, "but should lead them back to the buses myself."

When the bus pulled up, Martin was the first to board. "The bus driver greeted me with a cordial smile," he later wrote. "As I put my fare in the box he said: 'I believe you are Reverend King, aren't you?' I answered: 'Yes, I am.' 'We are glad to have you this morning,' he said." Martin thanked the driver, took a seat next to Glen Smiley as the others boarded the bus, and then the bus pulled out.

The Montgomery bus boycott lasted for over a year—381

days to be exact. Hundreds of thousands of dollars were spent on both sides. More than forty thousand people, as Martin Luther King, Jr., said, "expressed in a massive act of noncooperation their determination to be free. They came to see that it was ultimately more honorable to walk the streets in dignity than to ride the buses in humiliation."

It wouldn't be long before the rest of the South, and ultimately the rest of the nation, was embroiled in a social revolution—with periodic episodes of intense violence—that would last for more than a decade. In general most of the violent acts occurred as retaliation or revenge by the opposing side after some momentous advance.

In Montgomery, for instance, there was an immediate backlash in the wake of the Supreme Court's decision and the MIA's resulting victory. The Ku Klux Klan rose up and terrorized the African-American sections of town. Snipers began firing on buses and gangs of white racists attacked helpless passengers. A pregnant woman was shot in the leg while a teenage girl was savagely beaten. At least five black churches were bombed—two of which were completely destroyed. Several ministers' homes were also damaged by bombs, including Ralph Abernathy's and E. D. Nixon's. When Martin toured the ruins, he blamed himself for the suffering. "We are dealing with crazy people," he exclaimed. "I am to blame." But others near him assured King that the violence was not his fault and that they still supported him. "We are all together until the end," they told him.

People realized that, through the entire year of the movement, it had been Martin King among the leaders who had, perhaps, suffered most of all. He had received thirty threatening phone calls and letters a day. He was arrested for driving thirty miles per hour in a twenty-five-mile-per-hour zone. And he was indicted by a grand jury (along with eighty-nine other members of the MIA) for violating Alabama's boycott law and for "being party to a conspiracy." He was found guilty, and fined $1,000. Although released on appeal, he had become a convicted criminal in the eyes of the law.

Retaliation against him also took the form of serious physical violence. Someone fired a shotgun through the front door of the King home and, in two separate instances, threw bombs onto the front porch. One, with twelve sticks of dynamite, smoldered but did not explode. The other blew up the porch and a good portion of the front of the house while Coretta, their baby daughter, Yolanda, and a neighbor (all unhurt) were in the back kitchen.

After this act of violence, Martin's father, known as Daddy King, insisted that his son leave Montgomery and return to Atlanta for his own safety and that of his family. But with his wife, Coretta's, support, he stood up to Daddy King and refused to leave. He also took on the white establishment. "Tell Montgomery that they can keep shooting and I'm going to stand up to them," he said defiantly. "Tell Montgomery they can keep bombing and I'm going to stand up to them."

In addition, Martin encouraged the people involved in the protest, many of whom were afraid, not to back down—and to remember what they were fighting for: "This is a conflict between justice and injustice," he said at a mass meeting. "If we are arrested every day, if we are exploited every day, if we are trampled over every day, don't ever let anyone pull you so low as to hate them. . . . Let us not lose faith in democracy. For with all of its weaknesses, there is a ground and a basis of hope in our democratic creed."

After his own house was bombed, hundreds of angry people came over to survey the damage and retaliate. The policemen present, fearing the group would turn into a violent mob, asked King to come out and speak. When Martin stepped out onto what was left of his porch, he held up his hand and the agitated crowd grew silent. "Everything's all right," he said at first. "The police are investigating and nobody has been hurt."

Then he tried to calm the crowd. "I want you to go home

and put down your weapons. We cannot solve this problem through retaliatory violence," he told them. "We must love our white brothers, no matter what they do to us. We must make them know that we love them. . . . This is what we must live by. We must meet hate with love."

When Martin finished, everybody went back to their homes. And there was no further violence that night.

---

"As people began to derive inspiration from their involvement, I realized that the choice leaves your own hands. The people expect you to give them leadership. You see them growing as they move into action, and then you know you no longer have a choice, you can't decide *whether* to stay in it or get out of it, you *must* stay in it."

Martin Luther King, Jr.,
November 1956

---

"I had decided I should not sit back and watch, but should lead them back to the buses myself."

Martin Luther King, Jr.,
December 1, 1956

# MARTIN LUTHER KING, JR., ON LEADERSHIP

* Place your new situation in a context that has not previously been articulated to people in the organization.
* Let it be known that you intend to act—and that you expect others to act.
* When people nominate you for the lead, accept it. When you are asked to serve, you can't say no.
* Remember what Hegel wrote: "Growth comes through pain and struggle."
* Early on, stay in the middle of the pack—perhaps even a bit to the rear.
* Once you make up your mind that you are giving yourself, you must be prepared to do anything that serves your cause. You must give yourself fully.
* Listen and follow the lead of the people. Work in groups and make no major policy decisions without the input of other leaders in the organization.
* Step forward and take on responsibility for key management issues.
* Describe your movement as part of a much broader issue. Doing so will inspire sustained involvement of a wide array of individuals.
* Hit the road and garner support for your cause.
* When any major new development occurs, call the people together to inform them.
* Do not sit back and watch when victory is won. Personally lead people into the field.
* When you are confronted with violence, stand up to it. Meet hate with love.

"I had come to see early that the Christian doctrine of love operating through the Gandhian method of nonviolence was one of the most potent weapons available to an oppressed people in their struggle for freedom."

Martin Luther King, Jr.,
September 1958

"Our aim is to persuade."

Martin Luther King, Jr.,
July 19, 1962

# 2 / Persuade Through Love and Nonviolence

In the wake of the Montgomery movement, Martin Luther King, Jr., became an international celebrity. His picture appeared on the cover of *Time* magazine. He received dozens of job offers with salaries up to more than ten times what he was earning as pastor of the Dexter Avenue Baptist Church. And requests for him to speak around the world increased exponentially. Martin, however, turned down all the job offers and, initially, did not accept many speaking engagements. He wasn't so much interested in making money for himself as he was concerned about the future of the civil rights movement.

One invitation he did accept rather quickly, though, came from the new prime minister of Ghana. In March 1957, Martin and Coretta joined other American dignitaries and traveled to West Africa to attend ceremonies celebrating Ghana's recent independence from Great Britain. It was, at the time, a momentous event for Africans and people of African descent. For Martin, it symbolized success in a worldwide transformation toward freedom for oppressed people. On the return leg of their journey, the Kings visited other parts of Africa and Europe to see the sights, learn new things, and enjoy a much-needed vacation. When finally back home, Martin told friends that the trip to "the land of my father's fathers" had significantly rejuvenated him.

It was a good thing, too, because the nationwide civil rights movement was beginning to pick up steam. Various activist organizations were springing up across the South—and many northerners were also showing interest. Moreover, African-Americans in many southern cities were demanding total integration and, when they encountered resistance, were launching bus protests similar to the Montgomery effort.

Martin clearly wanted to be a part of the rising tide of social activism. So he went to New York to confer with A. Philip Randolph (president of the Brotherhood of Sleeping Car Porters) and Roy Wilkins (executive secretary of the NAACP). Together, the three hatched plans for a major national initiative—a "Prayer Pilgrimage for Freedom." It would be held on May 17, 1957—timed to celebrate the third anniversary of the Supreme Court's ruling in *Brown v. Board of Education*—at the Lincoln Memorial in Washington, D.C.

As had been done in the early days of the Montgomery protest, through a series of meetings the idea was presented to a larger group of leaders for their input and acceptance. Once approval was granted, a joint press conference was held with Randolph, Wilkins, King, and more than seventy other African-American leaders from around the country. There they announced the fivefold purpose of the Pilgrimage: 1) to demonstrate black unity; 2) to provide an opportunity for northerners to demonstrate their support; 3) to protest ongoing legal attacks on the NAACP by southern states; 4) to protest violence in the South; and 5) to urge the passage of civil rights legislation then being considered in Congress.

On May 17, more than twenty thousand people from all over the country gathered around the steps of the Lincoln Memorial. Several African-American leaders shared the podium, but it was Martin who garnered most of the attention from the national media. Even though he spoke for only ten minutes, his eloquence moved the crowd noticeably. "Our most urgent request to the President of the United States and every member of Congress is to give us the right to vote," he declared to the cheering throng. "Give us the ballot and we will transform the salient misdeeds of mobs into the good deeds of orderly citizens," he said. And in his closing comments, he echoed over and over again: "Give us the ballot . . . Give us the ballot . . . Give us the ballot. . . ."

The next morning, newspapers throughout the country ran his picture with the caption "Give us the ballot." In what was essentially his first nationwide address, Martin Luther King, Jr., had scored a smash hit. As a result, he become well known among the white community and even more popular with African-Americans everywhere.

Such recognition and adulation from the masses served to spur him on to take additional action. In early August, Martin hosted a conference in Montgomery with 115 African-American leaders. At that gathering, the group created a new formal organization, the Southern Christian Leadership Conference (SCLC). The purpose of the new alliance (based in Atlanta with a structure of local affiliates similar to that of the NAACP) was to encourage and coordinate Montgomery-type civil rights activity on a national scale—with special emphasis initially to be placed on voter registration.

Martin, in a unanimous vote, was again chosen president of a new formal alliance. This time, though, it was a position he expected to receive— from an organization he had conceived of himself. Over some objections, Martin insisted on having the word "Christian" as part of the organization's name. In

addition to promoting the obvious Christian doctrine of behavior, his intention was that the SCLC's base membership be
*from* the church and that it operate *through* the southern con-
federation of black churches.

Extensive detailed planning for the first major project of
the SCLC began immediately. The "Crusade for Citizenship"
was a massive voter registration drive that would take place
across the South beginning on February 12, 1958 (Abraham
Lincoln's birthday). On that day, dozens of mass meetings
were held in key southern cities. Martin spoke personally at
the Miami meeting and set the tone for the entire initiative.
"We want the right to vote now," he said. "We do not want
freedom fed to us in teaspoons over another 150 years. Under
God, we were born free. Misguided men robbed us of our
freedom. We want it back."

The overall mission of the Crusade was "to arouse the
masses of Negroes to realize that, in a democracy, their
chances for improvement rest on their ability to vote." With a
specific goal of registering 1.25 million new voters in a year,
the SCLC sent out thousands of people to walk door-to-door
in black neighborhoods urging residents to register. The organization also sponsored numerous voting clinics in an effort
to educate people who had never before registered or voted.

As events progressed, Martin was swept up into the rising
tide of activism faster than he had imagined it would happen.
It became clear to him at this point that he, Martin Luther
King, Jr., was going to be the major leader in the upcoming
period of social transformation. Accordingly, he needed to be
prepared. He needed to learn, organize, think through his
ideas, and be ready when the time came for him to stand at
the head of the pack on an ongoing basis.

One of the first projects he undertook was to write a book.
People had been pestering him to sit down and chronicle the
Montgomery movement so that others would be able to use
it as something of a blueprint for their future efforts. After a
publisher was secured—along with a small advance and a

deadline—Martin set out to research and write. But with his expanding duties as head of the SCLC, and his ongoing responsibilities at Dexter, he had quite a bit of difficulty finding the time to sit down and focus on his new project. At one point, he holed up in a motel room for a few weeks just to be able to write in a place where he could be away from the day-to-day distractions of his other jobs.

The entire process, though, provided Martin with an interim period to think and reflect on what had happened during the Montgomery movement. It was during this respite that he was able to judge what he had done right and what he had done wrong—what had worked well and what had not worked so well. With such reflection and analysis—not to mention a book to show for it—Martin was not only preparing a guide for others to adopt, he was preparing a blueprint for himself—one that he could utilize in his future leadership endeavors. While writing, Martin, in essence, became his own teacher. And, as the adage goes: "To teach is to learn twice."

The resulting book, titled *Stride Toward Freedom: The Montgomery Story,* turned out to be an informative and compelling narrative of the Montgomery protest movement. Martin chronicled the entire chain of events and took care to mention other leaders and give credit where credit was due. And he also touched on his developing philosophy of nonviolent direct action. "In the first days of the protest," he wrote, "none of these expressions [of nonviolence] were mentioned." That's because Martin was still formulating his philosophy. "The experience in Montgomery," he wrote in later years, "did more to clarify my thinking on the question of nonviolence than all of the books that I had read. As the days unfolded I became more and more convinced of [its] power. Living through the actual experience of the protest, nonviolence became more than a method to which I gave intellectual assent, it became a way of life. Many issues I had not cleared up intellectually were now solved in the sphere of practical action."

Martin's ideas surrounding nonviolent resistance were based on a combination of Mohandas K. Gandhi's actions and Christian values—both of which he had studied while in college. On one occasion, after attending a lecture at Crozer Theological Seminary about Gandhi's successful effort at leading the people of India to independence from Great Britain, Martin immediately went out and purchased "a half-dozen books on Gandhi's life and words." Before reading in detail about Gandhi, whom he had heard of in general terms, Martin believed that "the only way we could solve our problem of segregation was an armed revolt," and that Gandhi's success in India "did not mean that the pacifist approach would work everywhere." But, as he delved deeper and deeper into his new books, his mind began to change.

Martin learned, for instance, that Gandhi had taken as his inspiration Henry David Thoreau's essay on civil disobedience, in which Thoreau wrote, "We can no longer lend our cooperation to an evil system." Based on that idea, Gandhi created a new method of dealing with oppression that he termed "Satyagraha"—which, when translated literally, means "truth-force" or "love-force." The Satyagraha process involved such principles as *government by consensus, persuasion through discussion and reason, education of all members of the community, decisive action,* and *sincere compromise.* It also employed such nonviolent actions as strikes, boycotts, and protest marches. "Gandhi's goal," Martin noted, "was not to defeat the British in India, but to redeem them through love, so as to avoid a legacy of bitterness." And the truth is that, after the British finally left India, there was very little of the hatred and bitterness that so often follows a social revolution.

In addition, Martin began to notice a relationship between Gandhi's nonviolent methods and Christian teachings. Gandhi, for instance, had written, "The force of love is the same as the force of soul or truth," and that "complete non-violence is absence of ill will against all that lives. It is pure love." Martin's reflection on ideals such as these—combined with the inescapable parallels to Christianity's lessons of "love your enemies" and "turn the other cheek"—prompted him to write in *Stride Toward Freedom* that "Gandhi was probably the first person in history to lift the love ethic of Jesus above mere interaction between individuals to a powerful and effective social force on a large scale."

Martin was also inspired to think more deeply about the Christian concept of love—and exactly what it meant. To begin, he turned to the New Testament with its concept of "agape" love—and then, he called on the Greek language "to aid me at this point because there are three words in the Greek language for 'love.' One is 'eros,' which is sort of an aesthetic or a romantic love," he explained to one audience. "Another is 'phillia,' which is sort of an intimate affection between personal friends; this is friendship, it is a reciprocal love and on this level, you love those people that you like. And then the Greek language comes out with the word 'agape,' which is understanding, creative, redemptive good will for all men. It goes far beyond an affectionate response."

"Agape love," Martin would tell people, is about "understanding good will" and about a love "which seeks nothing in return." It is a love, he would say, that "loves the person who does the evil deed, while hating the deed that the person does." For him, agape love was "a higher type of love." It was "the love of God operating in the human heart." It was "the key that unlocks the door which leads to the ultimate reality."

The bottom line, though, for Martin *and* for Mohandas K. Gandhi, revolved around the idea that love was "a potent instrument for social and collective transformation." And the mere thought of combining love with nonviolent direct action convinced Martin that he had "discovered the method for social reform that I had been seeking for so many months." It's not surprising then, that when he had fully internalized the deep spiritual connection between Gandhi's teachings and the doctrines of Christianity, Martin decided to make a personal journey to India "before plunging too deeply once again into the sea of the southern segregation struggle."

Consequently, from February 2 to March 10, 1959, Martin, Coretta, and good friend Dr. Lawrence Reddick toured India. Upon their arrival, Martin made no secret as to why he was there: "To other countries I may go as a tourist, but to India I come as a pilgrim," he told the press. During the trip, the small group visited dozens of villages and towns where Gandhi had spent time. And they spoke personally with many of his relatives and close friends—listening intently, asking questions, taking it all in. "The three of us made up a sort of three-headed team," Martin noted, "with six eyes and six ears for looking and learning."

And so, Martin Luther King, Jr., not only read about Gandhi and reflected on Satyagraha, he also walked the very ground that the Mahatma had trod and spoke personally with the very people who had followed the great leader through India. This detailed study of Gandhi profoundly affected Martin—both in his general thinking about how to live life *and* in his developing leadership philosophy. He became convinced, for example, that true pacifism was "not simply nonresistance to evil, but nonviolent resistance to evil," and that Gandhi had not only been an active protester, he had "resisted with love instead of hate."

"I came to see for the first time," he wrote, "that the Christian doctrine of love, operating through the Gandhian method of nonviolence, is one of the most potent weapons available to an oppressed people in their struggle for freedom." It was clear that Martin not only looked to Gandhi as an important role model for effective leadership, but that he also revered Gandhi as someone who had been guided by providence. "I believe that in some marvelous way," Martin wrote, "God worked through Gandhi, and the spirit of Jesus Christ saturated his life. It is ironic, yet inescapably true that the greatest Christian of the modern world was a man who never embraced Christianity."

Moreover, it was not so much what Martin felt or *thought* about Gandhi as what he *did* once he understood what Gandhi had attempted and achieved: Essentially, Martin took the concept of nonviolence and applied it to his own situation—the American civil rights movement. But he didn't order people to employ nonviolence. He couldn't. People naturally wouldn't follow because they did not understand the idea. Rather he attempted to *persuade* others of its merit.

Martin instinctively realized that this element of persuasion is critical in leadership. He took it upon himself to inform people of what he had learned. He embraced the role of communicator—on a constant, direct, and emotional level. He spoke with people as often as he possibly could. At every opportunity he held a conversation, or told a story so that public opinion stayed on course—in the direction in which he felt it needed to go.

Not only did Martin give speeches and write articles as a method of communication, he also took time to compose letters or speak with people who disagreed with him. For instance, after receiving a letter from a woman who stated that "Negroes could never be equal to the whites—even the worst of them—that's God's decision not the white man's," Martin responded immediately with a respectful and eloquent letter of his own: "I must confess that I am in total disagreement with your position," he wrote. "I feel that segregation is totally un-Christian, and that it is against everything the Christian religion stands for. This, however, does not at all cause me to hate those who believe in segregation. I feel that we should seek to persuade the perpetrators of segregation through love, patience and understanding good will that it is wrong."

Toward the end of the Montgomery bus boycott, Martin also managed to get one threatening individual to listen to him. He later related the story in an article for *Liberation* magazine:

One anonymous phone caller, whose voice I have come to recognize, has been calling me for months to insult and threaten me and then slam down the receiver. Recently he stayed on the phone for half an hour, giving me the opportunity to discuss the whole underlying problem with him. At the end of the call he said: "Reverend King, I have enjoyed talking with you, and I am beginning to think that you may be right." This willingness to change deeply ingrained attitudes buoys us up and challenges us to be open to growth, also.

In the end, the only real power a leader may possess is the power to persuade—largely because the majority of people simply will not support a dictator. Recall that persuasion is also part of the definition of leadership (*leaders acting—as well as caring, inspiring, and persuading others to act*), so that when leaders begin to coerce or tell people what to do, they are essentially abandoning true leadership and embracing dictatorship.

Moreover, on a practical level, human nature is such that people will not follow a new leader unless they trust that individual and are persuaded that the course advocated is the right one to take. Upon assuming a new position, for instance, new leaders might find that their latest organization is like a large steamboat, filled with people, floating placidly on a wide river with turbulent rapids visible in the distance. If a new captain jumps on board and tries immediately to alter the course, the people may throw him overboard. They're used to the old riverboat pilot, whom they trust, who's been down the river before. The people on the boat would rather stick with the old captain even if he steers them into dangerous waters. A young pilot, one who wishes to alter the course of the boat, must first get on board—and then persuade the passengers that he knows what he's doing. While on the job, he must gain courage and learn how to navigate the rapids so as to ultimately steer the boat safely to its final destination.

The concept of nonviolence, largely because it is the preeminent tool of persuasion, fit perfectly into Martin Luther King, Jr.'s, idea of what leadership should be. It is a method of action and progress that avoids both the hopelessness of acquiescence and the tragedy of violence.

Martin strategically and intentionally set out to persuade others to take up the "weapon" of nonviolent direct action. At first, he explained the concept to people, preached it, advocated it as a technique to be utilized. Nonviolent direct action, according to Martin, was not a theory, it was "a method of action [employed] to rectify a social situation that is unjust." After all, what good is a theory if you can't apply it in some way. Accordingly, he promoted nonviolence as an agent of change. It was a "step forward," a "tool of achievement," a "weapon . . . the breastplate of righteousness, the armor of truth," he said.

The nonviolent resister, he noted, "is constantly seeking to *persuade* his opponent that he is wrong." "It is essential to understand that our aim is to persuade," Martin said in speech after speech and article after article. "We will try to persuade with our words, but if our words fail, we will try to persuade with our acts. . . . [We] must convince the white man that all [we] seek is justice, for both [ourselves] and the white man."

Martin also took the time to explain *why* nonviolence would work. For example, he noted that the tactic, once employed, had a profound impact on both the user and the target. Of the user, he noted: "It first does something to the hearts and souls of those committed to it. It gives them new self-respect; it calls up resources of strength and courage that they did not know they had." Of the target, he pointed out: "Under its banner, consciences are enlisted. . . . It exposes [the opponent's] moral defenses. It weakens his morale [while] it works on his conscience [so that] he does not know what to do."

Nonviolence, according to Martin's ongoing explanation to the people, also was a method for raising awareness in the community—which, coincidentally, is the first step in a massive change initiative—and then ultimately driving the opposition to deal with the situation of the oppressed. "Often the oppressor goes along unaware of the evil involved in his oppression so long as the oppressed accepts it," he wrote in *Stride Toward Freedom*. A few years later, while sitting in jail, he also wrote that "Nonviolent direct action seeks to create a crisis and foster a tension [so] that a community which has constantly refused to negotiate is forced to confront the issue. It seeks so to dramatize the issue that it can no longer be ignored. . . . We know through painful experience that freedom is never voluntarily given by the oppressor, it must be demanded by the oppressed."

In addition, Martin always took care to point out that his methods did not seek "to defeat or humiliate the opponent—but to win his friendship and understanding," or to "bring about a transformation and change of heart." Nonviolence, he said, seeks to "defeat the unjust system, rather than the individuals who are caught in that system."

Furthermore, the man who as a college student had once firmly believed that the only solution to segregation was through armed revolt now constantly lectured *against* violence of any sort. "Civilization and violence are antithetical concepts," he argued. "Through violence you may murder a murderer, but you can't murder murder," he said. "Through violence you may murder a liar but you can't establish truth. Through violence you may murder a hater, but you can't murder hate. Darkness cannot put out darkness. Only light can do that."

And he was quick to point out some of the historical lessons he had learned through his studies and preparation—such as the fact that "riots are not revolutionary" because "they cannot win"; and that a violent confrontation in the United States was impractical:

No internal revolution has ever succeeded in overthrowing a government by violence unless the government had already lost the allegiance and effective control of its armed forces. Anyone in his right mind knows that this will not happen in the United States. In a violent racial situation, the power structure has the local police, the state troopers, the National Guard and, finally, the army to call on—all of which are predominantly white. Furthermore, few if any violent revolutions have been successful unless the violent minority had the sympathy and support of the nonresistant majority.

No, said Martin to anyone who would listen, violence was not the path they should take. There was a better way—"a way as old as the insights of Jesus of Nazareth and as modern as the methods of Mahatma Gandhi." And contrary to popular opinion, "nonviolence was not a way for the weak and cowardly but for the strong and courageous. . . . That is why Gandhi often said that if cowardice is the only alternative to violence, it is better to fight."

Rather, the path of nonviolence was not only a better way, according to Martin, it was a *higher* road—morally and ethically. In 1963, while speaking to a large audience, he illustrated this belief through a vivid story:

I remember some years ago, my brother and I were driving from Atlanta to Chattanooga, Tennessee. For some reason the drivers that night were very discourteous or they were forgetting to dim their lights, and every time we passed a car for some reason the lights stood there with all their force. And finally A.D. looked over at me and said, "I'm tired of this now, and the next car that comes by here and refuses to dim the lights, I'm going to refuse to dim mine." And I said, "Wait a minute, don't do that.

Somebody has to have some sense on this highway. If somebody doesn't have sense enough to dim the lights, we'll all end up destroyed."

And I'm saying the same thing for us here. We're moving up a mighty highway toward the City of Freedom. There will be meandering points. There will be curves and difficult moments, and we will be tempted to retaliate with the same kind of force that the opposition will use. But I'm going to say to you, "Wait a minute. Somebody's got to have some sense."

For Martin Luther King, Jr., nonviolent direct action was the "guiding light of our movement." It was a "way of life." He preached this idea to anyone who would listen over more than a decade of active leadership. "The ultimate weakness of violence," he said, is "that it multiplies evil and violence in the universe. It doesn't solve any problems." Rather, he urged people to "meet the forces of hate with the power of love. . . . We've got to learn not to hit back," he said. "We must learn to love the white man."

On September 20, 1958, Martin Luther King, Jr., was on tour in New York City promoting his just-released book, *Stride Toward Freedom*. After several speeches and media appearances, he went to Blumstein's department store in Harlem for a book signing. As he was writing an inscription, an ordinary-looking forty-two-year-old woman came up to the table and asked him if he was Martin Luther King. When he replied yes, while continuing to write, the woman reached into her purse, pulled out a seven-inch letter opener, and stabbed him in the chest.

Bystanders quickly grabbed the woman and called for help. And when emergency medical personnel arrived a few minutes later, they found Martin calmly sitting upright in his chair with the letter opener still sticking out of his chest. He had

had the wherewithal to remain motionless and wait for assistance.

Martin was transported to Harlem Hospital where he immediately underwent emergency surgery to remove the sharp-edged metal. Afterward, the doctor who had performed the operation told him that the tip of the blade had been resting against his heart. "If you had sneezed," the doctor said, "your aorta would have been punctured and you would have drowned in your own blood."

Martin subsequently developed pneumonia and remained in the hospital for two weeks. When told that the woman who stabbed him had a serious mental illness, he said that he felt "no ill-will." "Don't do anything to her," he told the authorities. "Get her healed."

Earlier that month, Ralph Abernathy had been assaulted in Montgomery and spent several days in the hospital himself. When the day came for the trial of the assailant, Martin and Coretta, in a show of support, attempted to accompany Ralph to court.

On the courthouse steps, however, they were met by two policemen, one of whom yelled, "Boy, if you don't get the hell away from here, you will need a lawyer yourself." When Martin paused and tried to explain that he had business there, the two officers raced up and grabbed him. "Boy, you done done it. Let's go," yelled one of the officers. They twisted his arm behind his back and forced him to the jail around the corner. "The police tried to break my arm," Martin later recalled. "They grabbed my collar and tried to choke me." He was immediately arrested on charges of loitering and refusing to obey an officer. The police then gruffly frisked him and took him to a dirty jail cell. "When they got me to the cell," Martin told some friends, "they kicked me in."

A few days later, the incident came to trial. The presiding judge hastily announced a guilty verdict and presented him with the choice of paying a fine of $10 plus court costs or serving fourteen days in jail.

Martin chose jail.

"Your Honor," he told the judge, "I could not in all good conscience pay a fine for an act that I did not commit and for brutal treatment I did not deserve. . . . The time has come when perhaps only the willing and nonviolent acts of suffering by the innocent can arouse this nation to wipe out the scourge of brutality and violence inflicted upon Negroes who seek only to walk with dignity before man and God."

———————

"Through violence you may murder a murderer but you can't murder murder. Through violence you may murder a liar but you can't establish truth. Through violence you may murder a hater, but you can't murder hate. Darkness cannot put out darkness. Only light can do that."

Martin Luther King, Jr.,
March 4, 1967

———————

"Along the way of life, someone must have sense enough and morality enough to cut off the chain of hate and evil. The greatest way to do that is through love."

Martin Luther King, Jr.,
May 1956

# MARTIN LUTHER KING, JR., ON LEADERSHIP

★ Create a blueprint for yourself—one that you can utilize in your future leadership endeavors. Become your own teacher.

★ Remember that many issues you have not cleared up intellectually may be solved in the sphere of practical action and experience.

★ Love is a potent instrument for social and collective transformation.

★ Power without love is reckless and abusive—and love without power is sentimental and anemic.

★ Take time to compose a letter or speak on the phone with people who disagree with you.

★ Your aim should be to persuade through love, patience, and understanding good will.

★ If your words fail, persuade with your acts.

★ Take the time to explain why your ideas will work.

★ Seek to create a crisis and foster a tension so that a community which has constantly refused to negotiate is forced to confront the issue.

★ Remember that freedom is never voluntarily given by the oppressor, it must be demanded by the oppressed.

★ Never seek to defeat or humiliate an opponent. Try to bring about a change of heart.

★ Remember that only light can put out darkness.

★ Meet the forces of hate with the power of love.

★ The reason you should not follow the old eye-for-an-eye philosophy is that it ends up leaving everybody blind.

"There were weaknesses in Albany. . . . Each of us expected that setbacks would be a part of the ongoing effort. [Human beings] must make mistakes and learn from them, make more mistakes and learn anew. They must taste defeat as well as success. Time and action are teachers."

Martin Luther King, Jr.,
1963

"When we go into action and confront our adversaries, we must be as armed with knowledge as they."

Martin Luther King, Jr.,
1967

# 3 / Learn, Learn, Learn

Toward the end of 1959, pressure was mounting on Martin to spend more of his time managing and directing the Southern Christian Leadership Conference. The organization was without adequate funding ("We don't have enough money to pay salaries," he told his wife) and, consequently, its Crusade for Citizenship was falling significantly short of target goals. Martin was also being pulled in so many different directions that he was not able to achieve much in any one particular area—especially in his full-time job at Dexter Avenue Baptist Church—and he felt guilty about the situation. "The demands of the movement were getting so great," Coretta later explained, "he really didn't feel that he was doing an adequate job of pastoring."

It was at this point that Martin Luther King, Jr., made a decision that would change the course of his life. He decided to move his family back to Atlanta where he could be at the main office of the SCLC on a regular basis. "I have been under extreme tension for four years because of my multiple duties," he explained in his letter of resignation. "The time has long since come for me to shift gears."

A few months later, a farewell gathering held at Dexter was filled with sadness and sentiment from both the members of the congregation and their departing preacher. Martin tearfully apologized for having not served the church as well as he should have. He also mentioned that he had "a sort of nagging conscience that someone will interpret my leaving Montgomery as a retreat from the civil rights struggle. Actually, I will be involved in it on a larger scale. I can't stop now. History has thrust [a responsibility] upon me from which I cannot turn away."

The Kings' relocation to Atlanta was not only a change in scenery for Martin, it was a major career move. No longer would his principal profession be that of a Baptist minister. Now he would primarily be the leader of a major social movement—the president of a nonprofit organization for which he would accept only $1 per year in salary. Martin would also serve as co-pastor, along with his father, of the Ebenezer Baptist Church, for which he would earn a salary. But it was Daddy King who would handle the majority of work at the parish because Martin had plans for the future of the civil rights movement—big plans. "The time has come for a broad, bold advance of the Southern campaign for equality . . ." he wrote. "Not only will it include a stepped-up campaign of voter registration, but a full-scale approach will be made upon discrimination and segregation in all forms."

Martin spent most of his first full year back in Atlanta organizing and mobilizing. He traveled extensively giving speeches in an attempt to raise money and increase publicity for his new organization. He began to build a team of energetic, skilled individuals who could operate effectively in the field. He encouraged and sought the active participation of students and other young people in the civil rights movement. And he journeyed frequently to Washington, D.C., in attempts to coordinate the SCLC's efforts with those of the NAACP.

The national civil rights movement was also forging ahead. In Greensboro, North Carolina, for example, students from North Carolina A&T College walked into a Woolworth department store, sat down at the "whites only" luncheonette counter, and refused to leave until they were served. Almost immediately thereafter, sit-ins began taking place all over the South as a weapon in the protest movement.

Also, in 1960, the U.S. Supreme Court extended to terminals its 1946 ruling that banned segregation on interstate modes of mass transportation. Shortly afterward, the Interstate Commerce Commission issued an order banning segregation in all interstate travel facilities. In response, the Congress of Racial Equality (CORE) decided to conduct "Freedom Rides"—where demonstrators would ride buses and trains across state lines, disembark into terminals, and effectively test whether the facilities were, indeed, segregated. Since most facilities in the South simply ignored the Supreme Court's ruling, the Freedom Rides tended to cause major confrontations that often led to violent acts on the part of white citizens.

In another significant event, students from southern black colleges banded together to form a new organization, the Student Nonviolent Coordinating Committee (SNCC), with headquarters initially in Atlanta. The group had become active in response to the Greensboro sit-ins and now intended to mobilize students across the nation in nonviolent protest. Martin supported the students by raising money for them, serving on their advisory board, and giving them office space at SCLC headquarters.

In one of their first projects, the students set up a local office in Albany, Georgia, with the intention of protesting against segregation in train and bus terminals. Located approximately ninety miles south of Atlanta, Albany had a population of fifty thousand (half of which was African-American) and had been a center for the slave trade prior to the Civil War.

When SNCC first entered the town and announced its plan to target a Freedom Ride there, they did not receive a warm welcome. Many local leaders in the old-guard African-American community were resistant to outsiders from the national civil rights movement. Other than having a local NAACP office, they weren't much interested in changing anything at all. In addition, the national office of the NAACP would not support any civil rights activity by another organization. Only if activity was coordinated through them would they help.

Younger, more aggressive men and women in Albany, however, who were not in significant leadership roles, were receptive to the SNCC initiatives. Students at Albany State College quickly stepped forward to become Albany's core activists. Accordingly, in November 1960, several students purchased bus tickets, went into a segregated white waiting room, and then tried to obtain service from a "no Negroes" lunch counter. For their efforts, they were arrested, thrown in jail, and fined.

The next month, several more riders tested the new ICC rules in a train ride from Atlanta to Albany. Upon arrival, they were all arrested by Albany Police Chief Laurie Pritchett for blocking traffic. Unlike the first group, this time all the students refused bail and stayed incarcerated. The next morning, more than 250 students marched on city hall in protest—and Chief Pritchett arrested and jailed all of them. As the first of the trials began, hundreds more protesters marched downtown and they, too, were arrested. Consequently, by December 14, more than 470 people filled the jails in Albany and surrounding rural communities.

It was at this point that Dr. William G. Anderson, a local

physician and one of the more progressive African-American leaders, appealed to Martin Luther King, Jr., and the SCLC to get involved. Feeling that he couldn't refuse the request, Martin agreed to go to Albany with Ralph Abernathy (the SCLC treasurer and a friend of Anderson's) and Wyatt Tee Walker (the SCLC's new executive director). "I can't stand idly by while hundreds of Negroes are being falsely arrested simply because they want to be free," said Martin. The three subsequently hopped in the car and drove down to Albany—without a toothbrush, an overnight bag, or any prepared strategy.

Upon arrival, they found that a boycott of white businesses had already been initiated—and that an inflamed African-American community had picked up the pace of demonstrations. Albany's black leadership had also asked for negotiation talks, even offering to halt all protests if the bus and train terminals were desegregated and amnesty was granted to those arrested. But city leaders absolutely refused to even consider the requests.

On December 15, 1961, a mass meeting was held at Albany's Shiloh Baptist Church to welcome King, Abernathy, and Walker. When they entered the church, hundreds of people enthusiastically began chanting "Freedom, Freedom." Energized by the crowd, Martin delivered a passionate speech. "How long will we have to suffer injustice?" he asked. "How long will justice be crucified and truth buried? Don't stop now," he encouraged them. "Walk together. Don't you get weary."

The next morning, King, Abernathy, Walker, and Dr. Anderson led several hundred people in a protest march into downtown Albany. The entire group was arrested for parading without a permit and blocking traffic—and now the total number of jailed protesters numbered more than seven hundred. King and Abernathy were hustled into a cell together. Martin vowed that he would not accept bond and, if convicted, would refuse to pay the fine. "I expect to spend Christmas in jail," he said. "I hope thousands will join me."

With Martin Luther King and so many other people locked up, both black leaders and white leaders saw the necessity of starting a round of talks. In relatively short order, city representatives offered a three-point settlement that included: 1) jailed persons released without having to post a cash bond; 2) cessation of all protests over the next thirty days; and 3) creation of a biracial committee to address problems. Black leaders accepted these terms even though the mayor of Albany refused to put anything in writing or grant formal recognition of the local African-American leadership.

When informed of the settlement, Martin was concerned that it had no teeth and that no concessions were given regarding the elimination of segregated practices. Yet he still left jail because he felt it was a contingency of the already-arrived-at agreement. He then spoke at Shiloh Baptist once again and traveled home to Atlanta. Shortly thereafter, Albany officials let it be known that they had no intention of giving in one iota on the issue of segregation. In response, the boycott of white businesses resumed—including a full-fledged bus boycott with a car pool system similar to that in Montgomery. Increased protest activity also included sit-ins at lunch counters, marches, and local picketing.

In mid-July, Martin and Ralph were summoned back to Albany where they were found guilty of the December charges. They received a sentence of forty-five days in jail or a $178 fine. In demonstration of unity and defiance, both men chose the jail term. After one day in prison, however, Chief Laurie Pritchett released them on orders from the mayor—although he told King and Abernathy that an anonymous donor had paid their fines.

Albany's white leadership had astutely realized that to keep Martin King in jail for a month and a half would generate national attention that would only put pressure on the city's representatives to loosen their grip on segregation—which, of course, is exactly what King and Abernathy hoped to achieve. Martin protested his release vigorously: "I do not appreciate the subtle and conniving tactics used to get us out of jail," he told the press. A few days later, he noted the irony of the situation to a larger audience. "We have witnessed persons being ejected from lunch counters during the sit-ins," he said, "and thrown into jails during the Freedom Rides. But for the first time, we witnessed persons being kicked out of jail."

Leaders in the Albany movement next issued a demand for direct negotiations. When city officials again refused, another mass demonstration was scheduled. The morning of the march, however, a temporary restraining order was issued by a federal judge against any such protests in Albany. Martin felt that the court order had to be obeyed and he canceled the march. But members of SNCC criticized the decision and argued heatedly that the judge's order should be ignored and the march held. They also complained that Martin was being too passive, that he didn't say what he meant or do as he said, that his actions did not mirror his words. As a result, they told him, the excitement generated from his first speech was gone and students from Albany State College were no longer motivated to demonstrate.

Furthermore, other local black leaders also became so disenchanted that they actually made an offer to Chief Pritchett that, in return for direct talks, Martin Luther King would leave town and go back to Atlanta. When asked his opinion of the offer, Martin responded: "I'd be happy to leave if I stand in the way of any negotiations which would be held in good faith."

Meanwhile, the economic boycott of Albany was beginning to have a noticeable impact on local white businessmen, who were complaining that their income had dropped by more than half. In addition, a legal appeal against the federal restraining order was successful and the marches were allowed to resume. The next day, people marched and they were again arrested. This time, however, some of the participants turned to violence by throwing rocks at the police and causing some serious injuries.

Black leaders then watched helplessly as Chief Pritchett cleverly and adeptly maneuvered the press with misinformation, schmoozing, and criticism of Dr. King. How did Martin Luther King explain those "nonviolent rocks"? the chief asked the press. As a result, national media coverage painted Pritchett as the good guy—and members of the movement as violent "outside agitators."

At this point, Martin was not only stung by the vilification, he was also terribly alarmed by the eruption of violence. Could it be that the two were related? That because he had failed to keep the people motivated and enthused that they had turned to throwing rocks in desperation? Feeling he needed to act to correct the situation, the next day Martin walked into black Albany's pool halls, which were traditional gathering places for local youth, and spoke out against further violence. "Nothing could hurt our movement more," he preached. "It's exactly what our opposition likes to see."

Eventually, Albany city leaders accepted the offer to hold direct, face-to-face negotiations with local movement leaders if the SCLC left town. But after King and Abernathy went back to Atlanta, Albany closed its public parks and libraries rather than integrate them. The bus company, too, simply shut down—effectively leaving the town with no form of public transportation.

After that, local African-American leaders, in effect, gave up. They no longer had the will or drive to continue protesting nor did they feel that direct negotiations with the city would yield any meaningful results. Rather, with the help of the SCLC, regional efforts began to focus on the long-term solution of voter registration. That news prompted Police Chief Pritchett to euphorically announce that "Albany is as segregated as ever."

The entire chain of events in Albany was viewed as a major defeat for the civil rights movement, the SCLC, and, Martin Luther King, Jr., in particular. In effect, the city of Albany had granted the African-American community nothing. Asked why he had gotten involved in Albany in the first place, Martin responded, "The people wanted to do something they would have done with or without me, but having preached the effectiveness of going to jail for one's rights, I could hardly do less than they."

Even though Martin was steeped in defeat and burned with heated criticism, he remained hopeful and optimistic. "Albany," he stated, "has proved how extraordinary was the Negro response to the appeal of nonviolence. Approximately 5 percent of the total Negro population went willingly to jail. Were that percentage duplicated in New York City, some fifty thousand Negroes would overflow its prisons. If a people can produce from [their] ranks five percent who will go voluntarily to jail for a just cause, surely nothing can thwart its ultimate triumph."

One might wonder how Martin King could have been so confident and upbeat after such a negative outcome. But the truth is that he was not only an optimistic individual (as most great leaders are), he was also persistent, determined, and had an eye focused on the future. Even more important, however, is the fact that Martin was a lifelong continuous learner. He constantly learned from experience—so that he could do better the next time around. "I subject myself to endless self-analysis," he once said in an interview. "I question and soul-search constantly into myself to be as certain as I can that I am fulfilling the true meaning of my work, that I am maintaining my sense of purpose, that I am holding fast to my ideals, that I am guiding my people in the right direction."

The people closest to him often noted Martin's personal quest to *do* better—and to *be* better. Coretta King, for instance, mentioned that he "criticized himself more severely than anyone else did," that he was the first to say, "Maybe I made a mistake." She also noted that Martin never felt adequate to his position. "That is why he worried so much," she said, "worked so hard, and studied constantly—long after he had become a world figure."

Interestingly enough, Martin also studied constantly long *before* he became a world figure. From an early age, it was apparent that he had an innate drive to learn, a tremendous capacity for personal growth. And as he grew, his skills and abilities became better—and more noticeable.

In college, he exposed himself to a vast amount of culture. He diligently studied all the classic social philosophers, such as Plato, Aristotle, Rousseau, Locke, Thoreau, Kierkegaard, and Sartre. He investigated the great religions, including Christianity, Judaism, Hinduism, Buddhism, Taoism, and Confucianism, to name a few. He delved into the details of history and of such figures as Caesar, Augustine, Aquinas, Lincoln, William Cullen Bryant, James Russell Lowell, and, of course, Gandhi. One person who knew Martin well in college commented about the long hours that he spent alone with his nose in a book. He was "very studious," noted the friend, and spent "a lot more time on his lesson assignments than most of us did."

During his early years in the civil rights movement, Martin continued with the same general demeanor—studying, listening, and learning. In formulating his strategy for the Montgomery protest, for instance, Martin's studies led him to call for advice from Rev. Theodore Jemison in Baton Rouge, who had led a successful boycott back in the early 1950s. Later in the movement he was well aware that, after World War II, CORE had directed little known Freedom Rides and stand-ins. And, in formulating his basic theory of nonviolence, Martin's study of African-American history, including Nat Turner's murderous and unsuccessful rebellion, persuaded him that it was impossible for an armed revolution in the United States of America to succeed.

As he began to be pulled in many different directions, Martin craved time alone—often going off by himself so that he could read and think. Along those lines, he made good use of the time he spent incarcerated. During his stint in the Albany jail, for example, Martin wrote one of his weekly *People in Ac-*

*tion* columns and entitled it *A Message from Jail.* "Every time I go [to jail], it's a spiritual experience," he noted. "You can get a lot of things done that you need to do and you can't get done in the hurly-burly of everyday life. You can think about things."

Noticing his penchant for being alone, some people thought Martin almost too quiet, too shy—and that he kept people at an arm's length. With time, however, he warmed up and became more outgoing. In essence, as he gained more knowledge and experience, his confidence grew. As a matter of fact, with a kind of gradual assertiveness, he began influencing people in the civil rights movement with his personal philosophy on learning. "Education is more than ever the passport to decent economic positions," he preached. "When we go into action and confront our adversaries, we must be as armed with knowledge as they," he advised. "Help us to see the enemy's point of view," he wrote, "to hear his questions, to know his assessment of ourselves. For from his view we may indeed see the basic weakness of our condition, and if we are mature, we may learn and grow and profit from the wisdom of the brothers who are called the opposition."

It's a proven maxim that learning and leadership go hand in hand; so much so, in fact, that a poor learner cannot possibly be a good leader. Harry Truman once perceptively noted that "Not all readers can be leaders. But all leaders must be readers." More recently, modern leadership theory has emphasized the need for continuous learning. Stephen Covey, for example, wrote in *Principle-Centered Leadership* that "principle-centered [leaders] seek . . . to continually expand their competence, their ability to do things," and that "most of this learning and growth energy is self-initiated and feeds upon itself." Peter Senge, author of *The Fifth Discipline,* also emphasized the need for continuous learning—especially in the business world. "Leaders," he wrote, "are responsible for building organizations where people continually expand their capabilities to understand complexity, clarify vision, and improve shared mental models—that is, they are responsible for learning."

Nearly all past presidents of the United States who were even remotely deemed good leaders were, like Truman, avid lifelong learners. Abraham Lincoln, for example, taught himself nearly everything he ever learned. With his own private book collection, Thomas Jefferson personally replenished the Library of Congress after it was burned by the British during the War of 1812. And John F. Kennedy, a writer before becoming a politician, once wrote that it was "vital for a presidential aspirant to have a deep sense of history."

Many well-known leaders of the past suffered severe setbacks that resulted in long periods of quiescence where they were either out of power or out of favor. But the best of them made good use of that downtime. Lincoln, for instance, took a hiatus from politics and the Illinois state legislature in the 1850s to prepare himself to run for the U.S. Senate against Stephen A. Douglas. Even though he lost that election, it paved the way for his successful campaign for the presidency. Much later, and halfway around the world, Mohandas K. Gandhi used political "downtime" to travel throughout India, meet people, and understand their wants and needs, their hopes and aspirations. Moreover, when Gandhi later pleaded guilty to sedition and was sentenced to six years in prison, he spent his term reflecting on the past and preparing for the future. During those years, Gandhi read widely, thought deeply, and laid the foundation for a plan that, when implemented, eventually separated India from Great Britain.

Howard Gardner, in his book *Creating Minds*, noted several personal attributes and tendencies common to creative leaders. Many were "curious about everything" and "sought to improve performance through self-study and self-observation." Some read widely and "displayed a protean ability to absorb information from a gamut of disciplines and a galaxy of other individuals. . . ." Others kept a childlike view of the world their entire lives. Upon formulating the theory of relativity, for instance, Albert Einstein did not allow all the "noise" of popular physics and conventional wisdom to get in the way. "Einstein," wrote Gardner, "was able to effect a breakthrough precisely because he did not simply accept as given the paradigms and agendas of the physics of his time."

Children look at the world without prejudiced views because they are seeing things for the first time—and because they have not lived long enough to have their views prejudiced by personal experiences or the opinions of others. The world's greatest creative leaders somehow hold on to that childlike quality, which allows them to view the world in more simple and basic terms—so that they do not automatically accept as given the paradigms and agendas of their time. Such an outlook on life allows individuals the ability to come up with creative ideas that the vast majority of the population cannot conceive—because there are no prejudicial "cataracts" clouding their vision.

Martin Luther King, Jr., not only possessed such a childlike view of the world, he understood its importance. And, with a deft eye toward the future, he took that understanding one step further by advocating that children be educated about values—or, as he termed it, so as to "forge the priceless qualities of character," while they were still in their early learning modes. "You should teach your children at an early age that it is both morally wrong and psychologically harmful to hate anyone," he advised one individual. "Parents should be involved in the schools to a much greater extent," he wrote to others. "How shall we turn the ghettos into a vast school?" he asked in 1967. "How shall we make every street corner a forum, not a lounging place for trivial gossip and petty gambling, where life is wasted and human experience withers to trivial sensations? How shall we make every house worker and every laborer a demonstrator, a voter, a canvasser and a student?"

Martin also grasped the necessity of continual communication and learning in any leadership situation. Early in the

Montgomery movement, for instance, he noted that "The boycott must be sustained over a period of several weeks and months to assure results. This means *continuous education* of the community in order that support can be maintained."

In general, great leaders anticipate setbacks. They expect to make mistakes because they understand that when an individual is out in front making things happen, events will not always turn out perfectly. People who are not continuous learners tend to keep making the same mistakes. And when that happens, nothing of value is ever achieved. The innate capacity for continual learning is, in fact, a tool for achievement. And *achievement* must be part of a leader's constitution because people will not long listen to or follow an individual who is unable to accomplish something over the long term.

It was precisely for this reason that it became standard operating procedure for the SCLC to conduct a "postmortem" analysis of every major campaign in which they became involved. As president of the organization, Martin insisted on it. He had done one on his own in the aftermath of the Montgomery bus boycott—looking at what had gone right and what had gone wrong. From this critique, he prepared a list of what he had learned, and then shared it with other members of the organization. Even though Montgomery had a successful outcome, there were still mistakes made that he wanted to avoid in the future.

With the unsuccessful outcome of the Albany movement, however, Martin realized there was more need than ever for an intelligent examination of what had happened. As a result, the SCLC's postmortem analysis of Albany revealed the following mistakes or problems, which would be corrected in future campaigns:

1. There was divisiveness and internal fighting. The NAACP didn't get along with SNCC, whose leaders, in turn, didn't get along with the SCLC. The "old guard" also didn't want to work with the students.

2. Movement leaders did not make their original agreement with the city of Albany a formal document. In other words, they did not get it in writing.
3. There was no help from the federal government whatsoever.
4. They obeyed the federal court injunction, which, Martin concluded, had "broken our backs."
5. They were not adept at using the press.
6. The SCLC had no major comprehensive plan when it entered Albany. They didn't know how to mobilize people en masse. Their efforts were "centered on segregation in general, and no form of segregation in particular." The main tactical error, Martin pointed out, was that "the leadership did not center on some particular phase of segregation so that you could win a victory there and give the people the kind of morale lift that they needed."
7. The marches in Albany concentrated on city hall where they had little leverage and no votes. "All of our marches in Albany," said Martin, "were to the city hall trying to make them negotiate, where if we had centered our protests at the businesses in the city, [we could have] made the merchants negotiate. And if you can pull them around, you pull the political power structure because the political power structure listens to the economic power structure."
8. The fact that Martin left jail hurt the movement. As a matter of fact, Martin's constant travels back and forth to Atlanta had also done some damage because the local leaders couldn't get as many people out to march when he wasn't in town.

"There were weaknesses in Albany," Martin wrote upon further reflection. "Each of us expected that setbacks would be a part of the ongoing effort. There is no tactical theory so neat that a revolutionary struggle for a share of power can be won merely by pressing a row of buttons. Human beings with all their faults and strengths constitute the mechanism of a social movement. They must make mistakes and learn from them, make more mistakes and learn anew. They must taste defeat as well as success. Time and action are teachers."

"If I had that to do it again," he admitted at another time, "I would guide the community's Negro leadership differently than I did." Meanwhile, the lessons of Albany "would serve as a guidepost for other communities."

It shouldn't be ignored that Martin and the SCLC didn't wait until after the campaign was over to make changes. They tried to learn from their mistakes as they went along. By the end of the Albany movement, for instance, the SCLC had already implemented a four-pronged strategy that would be the basis for future endeavors. It included: *direct action, lawsuits, boycotts,* and *voter registration.* They also learned to anticipate violent retaliation from the opposition in the wake of any campaign, successful or unsuccessful. Shortly after the movement subsided, the Ku Klux Klan dynamited four African-American churches in communities surrounding Albany. Martin drove down from Atlanta and recalled that "tears welled up in my heart and in my eyes" as he walked through the bombed-out rubble and spoke with local parishioners.

It had been a tough year for Martin Luther King, Jr. Yet, with all the setbacks and criticism, he was determined to get better. Every step of the way in Albany he tried to learn from his mistakes and acted to correct them as soon as he could.

A week after being kicked out of jail, for instance, Martin, Ralph Abernathy, and two friends went down to the Albany city hall unannounced and demanded to speak with city commissioners. Authorities informed them that there would be no meeting and that if they did not leave right away they would be arrested. When the four kneeled down in an attempt to hold a prayer vigil, they were quickly hauled off to jail. Again Ralph and Martin were thrown into a cell together. After Coretta was informed, she brought the three King children down to the police station for a visit. It was the first time the little ones had seen their daddy in jail.

A few hours after they departed, Police Chief Pritchett sent a deputy down to the jail with a request that Dr. King come upstairs to see him for a few minutes. Martin said no. This time he refused to leave the jail cell.

---

"Help us to see the enemy's point of view, to hear his questions, to know his assessment of ourselves. From his view we may indeed see the basic weakness of our condition, and if we are mature, we may learn and grow and profit from the wisdom of the brothers who are called the opposition."

> Martin Luther King, Jr.,
> 1968

---

"How shall we turn the ghettos into a vast school? How shall we make every street corner a forum, not a lounging place for trivial gossip and petty gambling, where life is wasted and human experience withers to trivial sensations? How shall we make every house worker and every laborer a demonstrator, a voter, a canvasser and a student?"

> Martin Luther King, Jr.,
> 1967

---

"In order to love your enemies, you must begin by analyzing yourself."

> Martin Luther King, Jr.,
> November 17, 1957

# MARTIN LUTHER KING, JR., ON LEADERSHIP

- ★ Don't be afraid to shift gears and make a major career move.
- ★ When you fail to keep people motivated and inspired, they may complain or "throw rocks" in desperation.
- ★ Subject yourself to endless self-analysis so as to be certain that you are fulfilling the true meaning of your work, maintaining your sense of purpose, holding fast to your ideals, and guiding people in the right direction.
- ★ Self-criticism is a sure sign of maturity—and the first step toward eliminating any personal weakness.
- ★ Study constantly even after you leave high school and college.
- ★ Make good use of downtime. Go somewhere so that you may think about things.
- ★ When you go into action and confront your adversaries, you must be as armed with knowledge as they.
- ★ Analyze your adversaries' point of view so that you may see the basic weakness of your condition—so that you may learn and grow from the wisdom of the opposition.
- ★ Forge the priceless qualities of character. Teach your children values at an early age.
- ★ Ensure continuous education of the community in order that support can be maintained.
- ★ Conduct a postmortem analysis of every major endeavor. Share it with other members of your organization. Make a list of things to be done better and use it as a blueprint for future action.
- ★ You must make mistakes and learn from them, make more mistakes and learn anew. You must taste defeat as well as success.
- ★ Remember that time and action are teachers.
- ★ Take action after sober reflection. Learn from bitter experience.

> "We must not overlook the fact that, in the final analysis, the greatest channel of publicity for the organization is the existence of a positive, dynamic, and dramatic [public relations] program."
>
> Martin Luther King, Jr.,
> September 29, 1959

> "A leader has to be concerned with semantics."
>
> Martin Luther King, Jr.,
> June 1966

> "I spoke from my heart."
>
> Martin Luther King, Jr.,
> 1963

# 4 / *Master the Art of Public Speaking*

In the summer of 1956, Almena Lomax, editor of the *Los Angeles Tribune,* went to hear Martin Luther King, Jr., speak at an event in Los Angeles. It was during the heat of the Montgomery bus boycott and Martin was in town to drum up support for the movement. After the speech, she wrote him a letter to say that she had been so moved by his remarks as "to become an associate member of your church [despite having been] an agnostic since the age of 12."

Mrs. Lomax was not the only person to have been inspired to take some sort of action after hearing Martin King speak in public. There were, in fact, reports that he once roused an austere, mostly white group of union workers to stand up and passionately cheer him—and that he regularly moved audiences to tears and frenzied states of emotion. Some witnesses to his oratory commented that it was like being transcended to a different time and place and that, when he was behind a podium, he became charismatic. Others noted that he could move people not only to vote the way he asked them to, but to act on their own initiative. People also reported being fascinated with his frequent use of many different kinds of quotations—from the Bible, from history, and from philosophy. During one of his speeches, a woman without a great amount of formal education was overheard to say: "I don't know what that boy is talkin' about, but I sure like the way he sounds."

Modern scholars have acknowledged Martin Luther King, Jr., to be one of the great orators in American history—and have ranked his "I have a dream" speech with Lincoln's Gettysburg Address and Patrick Henry's "Give me liberty or give me death" speech. Interestingly enough, Martin's unique speaking ability was revealed at a very early age. As a child, he started following in his father's footsteps at the Ebenezer Baptist Church where he would read the scripture during mass, lead discussions in Sunday school, even preach to the congregation on occasion. And according to Daddy King, "Martin held his [audiences] spellbound when he talked."

It was not uncommon for a black minister's son to so participate in church functions—although Martin seemed to have a bit of an extra flair for it. Oratory in African-American history was a tradition on a par with storytelling—where past events were passed down through the generations. Public speaking was especially common in the church where audiences usually participated in the form of talking, shouting, and applause. The church was *the* social gathering place for the community, a rallying point where people could renew their strength and courage. Moreover, the preacher was the leader of the community—a political as well as a spiritual mentor.

Martin's roots in the church went deep. Not only was his father a God-fearing preacher, but so were his grandfather and great-grandfather. So he grew up in an environment where speaking in public was natural to him, where it was expected of him, and where he did it often enough that he honed and perfected his skill. When the time came, then, for him to choose a career, it's not surprising that he informed his father he wanted to become a Baptist minister so he could "convince white folks that all black folks are not dumb." And for all that he would later do and become, throughout his life Martin constantly referred to himself as simply a preacher.

The time he spent behind the pulpit in his youth came in very handy when he was an adult. Every year that he was leader of the American civil rights movement, for instance, he traveled hundreds of thousands of miles crisscrossing the country to deliver sometimes up to 450 speeches. At first, he did so out of necessity. With the fledgling Southern Christian Leadership Conference in financial crisis, Martin hit the road early to raise funds not only for administration purposes but for bail bond money as well to secure the release of arrested protesters.

He gave commencement speeches at black colleges, spoke at specially organized fund-raising rallies, at a Billy Graham Crusade, at local churches or union meetings—wherever he could gain the ear of willing donors to the movement. And "the preacher" had no qualms about asking for monetary support. He'd beseech everyone to "go down in our pockets and give big money for the cause of freedom." Everywhere he went—Chicago, Detroit, Louisville, New York City—he tended to draw large crowds. In one day alone he raised more than $50,000 after speaking to 25,000 people in Los Angeles. But Martin King wasn't looking only for cash donors. He was also seeking future participants in the movement. In each speech, at every opportunity, he would remind the audience what the movement was all about, tell people where they had been and where they were going, and stress the importance of becoming involved.

During the early years of the movement, Martin spent a great deal of time organizing and preparing his sermons and speeches. He would write out the entire text, practice in front of the mirror at home, and then deliver his remarks from memory. But as time progressed and his schedule became more hectic, Martin had difficulty securing the time to practice and memorize. "I find myself so involved I hardly have time to breathe," he mentioned to a friend. In addition, he complained about losing his "freshness and creativity" because he was giving so many speeches. "I cannot write speeches each time I talk, and it is a great frustration to have to rehash old stuff again and again."

Yet public speaking had become so second nature to him he was able to employ, through habit and without thinking about it, all the skills and techniques he had mastered. For instance, it took no preparation for him to continue speaking in simple common language—as if he were engaged in a casual conversation. And when he explained concepts or articulated goals, he almost always did so with easily understandable wording. "The nonviolent resisters can summarize their message in the following simple terms," he once said: "We will take direct action against injustice without waiting for other agencies to act. We will not obey unjust laws. We will do this peacefully." Clearly, everyone could understand a message with such basic wording—whether they had a Ph.D. or no formal education at all. Although he used a lot of esoteric quotations, Martin King also spoke in the shared language of the community—which helped him establish common ground with his audience. In turn, people were put at ease with the feeling that he was one of them—so his ideas and messages were more easily received.

Moreover, Martin was a gifted storyteller who liberally filled his speeches and sermons with anecdotes and parables.

Of course, as a Baptist minister, he frequently used stories from the Bible and was adept at employing biblical symbols and imagery. He often compared people in the movement to the "David of truth" set out against members of the oppressive establishment, whom he labeled as "the Goliath of injustice and neglect." He used the Old Testament story of the Exodus as a comparable analogy to the African-American quest for freedom. "The Bible tells the thrilling story of how Moses stood in Pharaoh's court and cried, 'Let my people go.' This was an opening chapter in a continuing story. The present struggle in the United States is a later chapter in the same story."

Taking his message a step further, in one sermon Martin also portrayed the miracle of the opening and closing of the Red Sea as symbolic of the forces of good over evil. "There is a Red Sea in history that ultimately comes to carry the forces of goodness to victory," he told his congregation, "and that same Red Sea closes in to bring doom and destruction to the forces of evil. This is our hope and conviction that all men of goodwill live by."

The telling of stories also provided a mechanism for freshness and creativity in Martin's addresses—which was helpful when he was giving the same speech over and over on fundraising trips. He also often peppered his prepared remarks with news of what had happened to him as he traveled. In one instance, he told of trying to board a train through the white waiting room in Nashville only to be told by a local policeman that he'd be killed if he tried to do it again. Another time, he related to a New York City audience an experience he had flying from Montgomery to Virginia with a scheduled stop in Atlanta. "In Atlanta," he said, "the plane developed a little motor trouble, [so] they gave all of us tickets to go in the airport and have lunch." As the only African-American on the plane, Martin explained that he was led away from the other white passengers to a dingy room in the back of the dining area where he could eat but not be seen. But he refused to be treated in such a manner. "I went on back and took a seat in the main dining room with everybody else," he said, "and I waited there but nobody served me. So finally I asked for the manager."

"Now, Reverend," the manager said to Martin, "this is the [state and city] law. We can't serve you out here. But now, everything is the same, everything is equal back there. You'll get the same food, you will be served on the same dishes, and you'll get the same service as everybody out here."

But Martin refused to be isolated, and his response to the manager was simple and heartfelt. "I just don't like sitting back there," he said. "It makes me almost angry, and I know that I shouldn't be . . . but when you put me back there something happens to my soul so that I confront inequality in the sense that I have a greater potential of the accumulation of bitterness."

This one simple story informed the audience that discrimination was actually sanctioned by state and city law in the South—which was not the case in New York—a fact that many people probably did not know. In telling it, Martin also related his feelings and emotions—emotions that anyone caught in the same position would have felt. As such, he was able to connect with the audience in a way that more formal rhetoric might not.

Another way he got through to people was by consistently telling stories of individual acts of sacrifice and courage. More than once, for example, he passed on the words of one elderly woman who told reporters why she was participating in the Montgomery bus boycott: "I'm doing it for my children and for my grandchildren," she said. And he also often related the story of an elderly, "toil-worn woman in Montgomery" who began her "slow, painful four-mile walk" to work. "It was the tenth month of the Montgomery bus boycott," Martin said. "The old woman's difficult progress led a passerby to inquire sympathetically if her feet were tired. Her simple answer became the boycotters' slogan. 'Yes, friend, my feet is real tired,' she said, 'but my soul is rested.' " In fact, it was Martin Luther King, Jr., who made that simple answer the boycotters' slogan, by telling the story every chance he got.

Later, during the Birmingham movement, Martin witnessed one particular touching exchange between a white police officer and a small black child. It also became a story he would tell many times over—and one that never failed to move the audience. "A child of no more than eight walked with her mother one day in a demonstration," he said. "An amused policeman leaned down to her and said with mock gruffness, 'What do you want?' The child looked into his eyes, unafraid, and gave her answer. 'F'eedom,' she said. She could not even pronounce the word," he concluded, "but no Gabriel trumpet could have sounded a truer note."

The musical parallel used at the end of this story was not uncommon in Martin's speeches. In fact, it was quite the norm as he frequently made extensive use of metaphors, similes, and metaphorical imagery. For example, African-Americans were not simply oppressed; according to Martin they were "lost in the thick fog of oblivion," or were "smothering in an airtight cage of poverty in the midst of an affluent society." Segregation wasn't just a bad thing, it was "a cancer in the body politic which must be removed before our democratic health can be realized." And injustice, before it could be cured, had to be exposed, "like a boil that must be opened with all its ugliness, to the natural medicines of air and light."

Martin also used metaphors to express hope and courage. After seeing demonstrators assaulted in Birmingham with high-pressure water hoses, for instance, he pointed out that the police failed to realize that the protesters "had a certain kind of fire that no water could put out." Another time, he asserted that "the plant of freedom is only a bud and not yet a flower"—and that freedom "is like life," and cannot be "given in installments" like so many slices of bread. "You cannot be given breath but no body, nor a heart but no blood vessels," concluded Martin. "Freedom is one thing. You have it all, or you are not free."

Furthermore, implicit in his speeches and writings regarding the national civil rights movement and its participants were constant references to a journey not only from "despair to hope" or "oppression to freedom"—but one from the "the valley to the mountaintop" and from "darkness to light." More than once he stated things like "It is midnight in our world, and the darkness is so deep that we can hardly see which way to turn." And then he pointed out that "at midnight colors lose their distinctiveness and become a sullen shade of gray," which he compared to "moral principles that have lost their distinctiveness." And, in both speeches and writings, he often issued calls to action similar to this one: "Now is the time to rise from the dark and desolate valley of segregation to the sunlit path of racial justice. Now is the time to lift our nation from the quicksands of racial injustice to the solid rock of brotherhood."

In nearly all of his speeches, Martin also employed techniques that were obvious to the audience. He used simple themes, for instance, such as good triumphing over evil, or the traditional slavery theme of liberation and deliverance. He also used the method of contrasting myth versus truth. "One myth is that the Negro is going ahead too far, too fast," he'd say. "A more enduring myth is that the Negro has waited so long that any improvement will satisfy him." Martin would then proceed to debunk the myth by giving all kinds of examples as to what the truth really was.

While such methods were fairly obvious to all who listened, he also applied more subtle devices that enhanced the overall impact of his addresses. These techniques—such as rhythm, cadence, alliteration, and anaphora—were not quite so obvious to people in the audience. Anaphora (the repeated use of words or phrases), for instance, was used so often by Martin that one gets the impression that it was as natural to him as blinking his eyes. Recall that in his first national address at the

Prayer Pilgrimage for Freedom, the press picked up on his repetition of the phrase "Give us the ballot. . . . Give us the ballot. . . ." Near the end of his "I have a dream" speech, Martin repeated "Let freedom ring . . ." nearly a dozen times: "Let freedom ring from the mighty mountains of New York. Let freedom ring from the heightening Alleghenies of Pennsylvania. But not only that. Let freedom ring from Stone Mountain of Georgia." Such repetition focuses the attention of the listener during the speech—similar to calling out a person's name several times before they take notice. It also works on the mind of the listener—making the theme and words more memorable.

In some rare instances, Martin made his speeches almost unforgettable to the audience by combining anaphora with an audience participation "call and response." At the end of the march in Selma, Alabama, in 1965, for example, Martin ended his address with a stirring repetition of the rhetorical question "How long?"

"How long?" he asked.

"Not long!" the audience responded.

"Not long," Martin echoed, "because no lie can live forever."

"How long?" he asked again.

"Not long!" roared back the audience.

"Not long," he said again, "because the arm of the moral universe is long but it bends toward justice."

Everyone who heard the speech that day will never forget it—just as nearly everyone who has ever heard Martin Luther King, Jr.'s, speech in front of the Lincoln Memorial on August 29, 1963, will never forget the constant repetition of "I have a dream, today."

Martin's physical gestures were also important in his impact on the audience. He would extend his arms, wave his hands over his head, shake his head, vary the rate of his words and the intonation of his melodious baritone voice—and the audience would respond by shouting, cheering, raising their hands and stamping their feet. However, such enthusiastic audience response was not purely the result of charisma or varied oratorical techniques. It was also due to the fact that Martin Luther King, Jr., with sincerity, seriousness, and simplicity, always spoke about the hopes and aspirations of African-Americans everywhere. He became the acknowledged leader of the civil rights movement, in large part, because he combined a deep-seated compassion and empathy with oratorical skill. People were not used to seeing one of their own speak with such eloquence about exactly what they were feeling inside. They could not do what he could do. They trusted him because of what he said and what he did. And therefore the people allowed him to speak for them—and they followed his lead.

"We're here this evening for serious business," he said in his very first mass meeting in Montgomery. "We are here because of our deep-seated belief that democracy transformed from thin paper to thick action is the greatest form of government on earth. . . . If we are wrong, the Supreme Court of this nation is wrong. If we are wrong, the Constitution of the United States is wrong. If we are wrong, God Almighty is wrong."

For Martin, the civil rights movement was not simply a series of protest marches. He took it to a higher level and portrayed it as the continuation of a long struggle that began with the Declaration of Independence and extended beyond the Civil War. "Our destiny is bound up with the destiny of America," he said over and over again.

Recent studies in the field of leadership have stressed the importance of public speaking and effective mass communication. James MacGregor Burns, in his book *Leadership,* wrote that "the leader's fundamental act is to induce people to be aware or conscious of what they feel—to feel their true needs so strongly, to define their values so meaningfully, that they can be moved to purposeful action." But there is more to communication than just motivation and value-shaping.

"Leaders," wrote Warren Bennis and Burt Nanus in *Leaders,* "articulate and define what has previously remained implicit or unsaid; then they invent images, metaphors, and models that provide a focus for new attention. By so doing they consolidate or challenge prevailing wisdom."

Of all human senses, sound is the primary intellectual stimulant—while vision is secondary. A speech combines both sound *and* vision and, therefore, can be an unusually effective method of communication to a mass audience. Moreover, telling stories during an address may serve to enhance and make the speaker's remarks that much more memorable.

Abraham Lincoln, who effectively employed storytelling as a leadership tool, noted that he had "learned from long experience that people are more easily influenced through the medium of a broad and humorous illustration than in any other way." Tom Peters and Nancy Austin, in *A Passion for Excellence,* noted that "stories are memorable . . . they teach . . ." and that "human beings reason largely by means of stories, not by mounds of data."

Stories also provide a means of connecting and bonding with people. "For most women," noted Deborah Tannen in *You Just Don't Understand,* "the language of conversation is primarily a language of rapport: a way of establishing connections and negotiating relationships. For most men, talk is primarily a means to preserve independence and negotiate and maintain status in a hierarchical social order. This is done by exhibiting knowledge and skill, and by holding center stage through verbal performance such as storytelling, joking, or imparting information." It's clear, then, that stories and conversation impact both men and women with equal intensity—although in different ways.

From the positive reactions of his audiences, Martin certainly sensed the powerful impact of his stories. He also realized the importance for a leader to travel and get out in front of members of his organization. Certainly, he worked hard at his public speaking, at thinking carefully before answering questions, and at choosing his words. "A leader has to be concerned with semantics," he once said.

When a person gets up and speaks in front of people, it enhances the speaker's role as that of a leader. As a matter of fact, simply being up there on stage makes an individual appear more courageous than others who are unwilling to take the risk. It has to be done, however, because in the end, a leader must have followers—and the only way people will follow for any extended length of time is to be well informed of the direction in which the organization is heading and the reason for going there.

In general, there are five main reasons for a leader to master the art of public speaking:

1. To articulate, reinforce, and intensify the values and beliefs of the organization.
2. To educate, persuade, and sell people on new ideas.
3. To ensure and inform members of the organization on what action the leader is taking.
4. To build support and enthusiasm.
5. To inspire people to take action.

In addition to personal public speaking appearances, Martin also encouraged the use of songs and slogans to achieve effective communication. That's one reason freedom songs—such as "Go Down Moses," "Ain't Gonna Let Nobody Turn Me Around," and "We Shall Overcome"—were sung at mass meetings. "Songs are the soul of a movement," Martin once explained. "[They] bind us together, give us courage together, help us to march together. Songs add hope to our determination."

"We Shall Overcome" also became an important *slogan* of the American civil rights movement. "We must have slogans during any revolution," noted Martin, "in order to fire people, motivate them, and get them moving."

Moreover, after Albany, the Southern Christian Leadership

Conference consciously used the mass media to raise awareness and get across the organization's messages. In print media, good use was made of everything from church newsletters to the *New York Times*. And virtually every major and intermediate-sized magazine, such as *Time, The Nation, The Saturday Evening Post,* and *Christian Century,* printed articles, stories, and interviews with movement leaders. The SCLC also purchased space in local newspapers and wrote numerous articles to make certain their true intentions were communicated accurately to members of white communities.

Martin himself had a syndicated newspaper column that evolved from the title of *Advice for Living* to *People in Action.* He also authored a half dozen books, hundreds of articles, essays, and letters, and gave personal interviews whenever time permitted. His books, written in the years 1958, 1959, 1963, 1964, 1967, and 1968, chronicled key events in the decade-long civil rights movement and articulated his changing and growing leadership style. Taken together, they reached millions of people all over the world. *Stride Toward Freedom* alone sold several hundred thousand copies within five years and was translated into a dozen languages.

When his books came out, Martin ordinarily embarked on a nationwide book tour—appearing on radio and television talk shows. In addition, he frequently appeared on national shows such as *Meet the Press, Face the Nation, Today,* and others whenever there was a major event taking place. It was all part of his communications philosophy. In an early meeting with the SCLC, he recommended that "a person be employed to carry out the all-important task of placing the organization before the public through intelligent publicity. . . . We must not overlook the fact," Martin continued, "that, in the final analysis, the greatest channel of publicity for the organization is the existence of a positive, dynamic, and dramatic [public relations] program."

\*   \*   \*

During the first several weeks of September 1962, Martin King had mounted his own personal public relations campaign in New York City—giving speeches, appearing at events around town, raising money for the movement in the wake of the failed effort in Albany, Georgia. At the end of the month, he traveled to Birmingham, Alabama, to attend the SCLC's fall convention where, on the final day, he delivered his scheduled presidential address in front of more than a thousand delegates.

During his speech, a tall, heavyset twenty-four-year-old white member of the Nazi party jumped from his seat in the first few rows, rushed up to the podium, grabbed Martin by the scruff of the neck, and then punched him in the face several times. But Martin just straightened his back and took it. He made no move to recoil or fight back. Rather, he attempted to reason with the young man.

A policeman and several witnesses emerged from the stunned and silent crowd to subdue the youth and pull him away. Martin, however, asked that his attacker be allowed to take his seat again. "This system that we live under creates people such as this youth," he said after the meeting. "I'm not interested in pressing charges. I'm interested in changing the kind of system that produces this kind of man."

In this one incident, Martin Luther King, Jr., the leader who for years had been advocating nonviolence, practiced *exactly* what he preached. Under direct assault, in front of hundreds of members of his own organization, he had literally turned the other cheek.

---

"These songs bind us together, give us courage together, help us to march together."

Martin Luther King, Jr.,
1964

---

"We must have slogans during any revolution in order to fire people, motivate them, and get them moving."

Martin Luther King, Jr.,
1967

## MARTIN LUTHER KING, JR., ON LEADERSHIP

★ In your public addresses, speak in simple common language—as if you were engaged in a conversation.

★ Speaking in the shared language of the community helps establish common ground with your audience.

★ Relate stories of individual acts of sacrifice and courage by people in the organization.

★ Make extensive use of metaphors, similes, and metaphorical imagery.

★ Apply subtle devices—such as rhythm, cadence, alliteration, and anaphora—that enhance the overall impact of a speech.

★ Remember that repetition of words and phrases works on the mind of the listener—making your theme and words more memorable.

★ Always speak about the hopes and aspirations of the people in your organization with sincerity, seriousness, and simplicity.

★ In your oratory, take your cause to a higher level.

★ As a leader, you must be concerned with semantics.

★ Every revolution must have songs and slogans to add hope to determination—and to fire people, motivate them, and keep them moving.

★ You should consciously use the media to raise awareness and get across your key messages.

★ The greatest channel of publicity for your organization is the existence of a positive, dynamic, and dramatic public relations program.

★ Practice what you preach.

# PART II

# GUIDING THE MOVEMENT

*"We can choose either to walk the high road of human brotherhood or to tread the low road of man's inhumanity to man. History has thrust upon our generation an indescribably important destiny—to complete a process of democratization which our nation has too long developed too slowly. The future of America is bound up in the present crisis. If America is to remain a first-class nation, it cannot have a second-class citizenship."*

MARTIN LUTHER KING, JR., 1959

"Human progress is neither automatic nor inevitable. Every step toward the goal of justice requires sacrifice, suffering, and struggle; the tireless exertions and passionate concern of dedicated individuals. Without persistent effort, time itself becomes an ally of the insurgent and primitive forces of irrational emotionalism and social destruction. This is no time for apathy or complacency. This is a time for vigorous and positive action."

Martin Luther King, Jr.,
1959

"Injustice anywhere is a threat to justice everywhere."

Martin Luther King, Jr.,
December 1960

# 5 / Awaken Direct Action

On the evening of May 4, 1960, Martin borrowed a car to drive Lillian Smith, the acclaimed southern novelist, to the Emory University hospital on the outskirts of Atlanta for treatment of an ailment. As they neared their destination, a De Kalb County policeman pulled them over because he noticed a white woman and a black man sitting in the front seat together. Unfortunately for Martin, the license plates on the vehicle had expired and he was still driving with an Alabama driver's permit—long past the ninety-day grace period the state granted to obtain a Georgia driver's license. After issuing a citation, the officer (who no doubt recognized who he had just stopped) allowed the two to continue on their way. It was one of the rare times that Martin's notoriety actually eased him through a difficult situation. He was, however, later fined and placed on twelve months' probation.

At about this time, a Montgomery grand jury had also indicted him on two felony perjury counts—for falsifying his 1956 and 1959 Alabama state income tax returns. It was the first time the state had ever prosecuted an individual on such a charge. Martin was arrested, extradited, released on bond, and then placed on trial back in Montgomery. Fortunately, an all-white jury found him not guilty.

In the meantime, Martin's hometown of Atlanta began to feel the impact of the spreading civil rights movement. Local African-Americans were growing increasingly intolerant of the "separate but equal" rest rooms, water fountains, parks, theaters, and restaurants. And, inspired by the Greensboro sit-ins, Atlanta members of SNCC began to hold spontaneous sit-ins of their own at downtown department store lunch counters. Members of the older established African-American leadership, however, discouraged the students and openly advocated that such demonstrations were improper and endangered the peaceful coexistence with whites that had been established under their regime. As a result, support for the sit-ins lagged through the spring and summer months.

But when students came back to college for the fall session, SNCC leaders, who were outraged at the old guard's passivity, planned a comprehensive major initiative aimed at all downtown Atlanta department stores. Central to their plan was to involve Martin Luther King, Jr. So the day before the scheduled launch date, a small group called on King to ask him to participate in the sit-ins—and go to jail with them, if necessary. Finding Martin initially hesitant, the students appealed to his sense of honor as the "spiritual leader of the movement" and reminded him of his previous admonitions to take action and "fill the jails." Martin then decided to make a stand with the young people because, as he later said, "I felt a moral obligation" to do so and "had to practice what I preached."

On the morning of October 19 then, right on schedule, students from local black colleges began their protest with sit-ins and picket lines at most of downtown Atlanta's big stores. In short order, Martin and thirty-five protesters were arrested on trespassing charges at Rich's department store when they refused to leave the lunch counter without receiving service. The entire group of protesters were subsequently taken to the Fulton County jail, booked, and incarcerated. When offered his release, Martin refused to pay the $500 bond and resolved to "stay in jail ten years if necessary."

His initial hesitation at joining the protest was twofold. First, he was in the process of making other plans that would have to be scrapped if he were in jail for any length of time—and the students' request was on pretty short notice. Second, and more important, however, was the fact that Martin simply didn't like being locked up. "Jail going wasn't easy for him," explained Coretta, "because he never liked to be alone. He could never stay away from people for long periods."

Overriding Martin's natural resistance to being alone were a couple of other factors that were just as innate, just as deeply a part of his inner being. He not only cared a great deal about the civil rights movement, he had a strong conscience. If Martin was advocating a position for others to take, he did not feel he could do less himself. That's one reason the heartfelt appeal from the students helped him decide to join their protest. Furthermore, in *Stride Toward Freedom,* Martin provided a clue to a far more determining reason that moved him. It was there he wrote the credo of nonviolent direct action, which began with the statement: "We will take direct action against injustice without waiting for other agencies to act. We will not obey unjust laws or submit to unjust practices." The key message is contained in the first five words, "We will take direct action."

Martin Luther King was an extraordinarily action-oriented

individual. He was always busy, always striving to achieve, always ready to get something done. This one innate, natural desire usually won out over any internal conflicts he may have had with his other natural tendencies. In essence, he would rather try to achieve *something*—even if it meant being isolated in a jail cell—than do *nothing* at all. As a matter of fact, Martin could not abide total pacifism. That was unacceptable for him, contrary to his nature, and very obvious to anyone who knew him. In an early sermon at Dexter Avenue Baptist Church, for instance, he had said: "It is true that if the Negro accepts his place, accepts exploitation and injustice, there will be peace. But it would be a peace boiled down to stagnant complacency, deadening passivity; and if peace means this, I don't want peace."

What's more, there was something inside the man that would not allow him to remain silent when he saw somebody being wronged. As a child, he had told his mother that "there is no such thing as one people being better than another. The Lord made all of us equal, and I'm gonna see to that." That same innate sense of justice was a major part of his leadership demeanor when he became an adult. "If peace means keeping my mouth shut in the midst of injustice and evil, I don't want peace," he said in that same Dexter sermon.

Keeping quiet when seeing somebody wronged, or being docile or complacent in regard to obtaining goals or results, are not characteristics of great leaders. As a matter of fact, many of history's most successful leaders possessed a deep, driving need to achieve. It was part of their physical and chemical makeup. It's what set them apart from the crowd. And, in many cases, it was much more than a simple inclination to get things done—it was almost an uncontrollable obsession.

Several well-known presidents of the United States were able to accomplish a great deal in the midst of significant crises. When Franklin Roosevelt took over from Herbert Hoover during the Great Depression, for example, he had an overwhelming mandate from the people to take action. As a result, the Congress passed nearly every initiative he proposed during his first six months in office. "Such breathtaking, fundamental changes," Martin King once noted of FDR's accomplishments, "took place because a leadership emerged that was both determined and bold, that rejected inhibitions imposed by old traditions and habits." Similar to Roosevelt, Abraham Lincoln did not receive much resistance from what was left of the Congress as he moved forcefully to prepare for civil war.

Both FDR and Lincoln fit the pattern of being great leaders who had an innate drive to achieve. Furthermore, the circumstances under which they assumed leadership roles enhanced their ability to accomplish things. However, for leaders who are not involved in a crisis situation—one where the vast majority of people clearly recognize and support the need for immediate action—achievement of vision and goals can prove to be a much more daunting challenge. Hence, the innate drive to achieve in a leader is even more important in a normal situation—one where there is no crisis—simply because people are not as motivated to act.

Mohandas Gandhi was successful in achieving his vision of liberating India from the autocratic arms of Great Britain. But where Lincoln won the Civil War in only four years, it took Gandhi nearly forty to achieve his dream. For Gandhi, the inner desire to achieve was the core of his being. "While he was not always loved, he was widely respected for the dogged yet calm way in which he pursued his ends," wrote Howard Gardner in *Creating Minds*. Gandhi himself often said: "Action is my domain." Clearly, the great Indian Mahatma achieved much even though he did not assume power during a crisis situation.

The same can be said of Theodore Roosevelt. "I felt a pleasure in action," the energetic Rough Rider once wrote. "My blood seemed to rush warmer and swifter through my veins; and I fancied my eyes reached to a more distant vision." It's

interesting to think that Theodore Roosevelt's natural inclination toward action may have, in some way, fostered his ability to lead, as his statement suggests—at least for that
important part of leadership that involves creating a vision.
Often, a leader like Roosevelt, who possessed an unusually
high level of physical energy, also has an equally high intellectual capacity. That combination, in turn, results in the ability
to create a wide-ranging philosophy that provides context in
which to pursue many initiatives at once. Moreover,
Theodore Roosevelt's tremendous physical energy resulted in
his becoming something of a whirlwind president—with more
activity, more initiatives, more decisions, more problem-
solving, more of everything a leader does. He also advised
others to use the "bully pulpit" of public speaking—knowing
full well that it often inspired people to take action on their
own initiative—without waiting for him to proceed.

In general, a leader's strong desire to achieve often results
in the deployment of many other well-recognized qualities of
effective leadership, including persistence, a sense of urgency,
innovation, creativity, the process of renewal, and a willingness to compromise and learn. Leaders with an action-
oriented nature also tend to empower and delegate more as
well as convene task forces and facilitate teamwork because, in
the long run, they are able to realize increased results.

Overall, the life of a leader is consumed with activity. In
*Principle-Centered Leadership,* Stephen Covey noted that the
best leaders "are amazingly productive," and that "their spirit
is enthusiastic." Bennis and Nanus, in *Leaders,* wrote that effective leaders are "reliable and tirelessly persistent" and that
they are "the most results-oriented people in the world." In
essence, great leaders try to get up every morning and make a
little progress. Or, as Theodore Roosevelt once said, "In life,
as in a football game, the principle to follow is: 'Hit the Line
Hard.' "

Clearly, Martin Luther King, Jr., fit the profile of a high-
energy, action-oriented leader. His mission was to institute

massive transformation in the social order of America. "What is needed is a strategy for change," he said, "a tactical program that will bring the Negro into the mainstream of American life as quickly as possible." And because Martin realized that action is a necessary ingredient in any recipe for change, he stressed that "This is no time for romantic illusions and empty philosophical debates about freedom. This is a time for action."

Because leaders cannot do everything themselves, they must find ways to awaken action in others. Martin's methods for achieving movement were designed not only to create positive activity from the opposition, but to inspire others to act on their own initiative. "Only when the people themselves begin to act are rights on paper given lifeblood," he said in August 1962.

Overall, there were at least four general strategies employed by Martin Luther King to motivate, inspire, and persuade people to act.

## 1. Place Events in Context

True inspiration to perform comes from within the heart and mind of each individual. Good leaders realize this fact and attempt to tap into the internal desires of the people they represent. One way to make that happen is to place the organization's vision and goals in context with history and current events. Doing so creates understanding as to why the movement is important—and that, in turn, allows each individual to decide what the vision means to them personally.

Martin placed the American civil rights movement in the context of a much broader struggle. It wasn't just a group of people protesting for their civil rights, it was a resumption of the "incomplete revolution of the Civil War." And it was the continuation "of that noble journey toward the goals reflected in [the Declaration of Independence], the Preamble to the Constitution, the Constitution itself, the Bill of Rights and the Thirteenth, Fourteenth, Fifteenth, and Nineteenth Amendments to the Constitution."

There was also a "revolution occurring in both the social order and the human mind," and it was "no overstatement to characterize these events as historic." What had happened in Montgomery, Albany, and Atlanta was "part of a world-wide movement" that was bigger than any single event. "This is not only a nation in transition," said Martin, "but a world in transition. . . . [And] one day historians will record this movement as one of the most significant epics of our heritage."

To illustrate his concept, Martin would sometimes refer to Washington Irving's tale of Rip Van Winkle—how the main character had fallen asleep in the Catskill Mountains of New York when the American colonies were still part of Great Britain; and how he woke up twenty years later to find a fellow he had never heard of (George Washington) president of the country he lived in—now renamed the United States of America. "The most striking thing about the story of Rip Van Winkle," Martin pointed out, "is not merely that Rip slept for twenty years, but that he slept through a revolution . . . one that would alter the course of human history."

After mentioning this little-remembered facet of Washington Irving's story, Martin then made his point: "One of the great liabilities of history," he said, "is that all too many people fail to remain awake through great periods of social change. Every society has its protectors of the status quo and its fraternities of the indifferent who are notorious for sleeping through revolutions. But today our very survival depends on our ability to stay awake, to adjust to new ideas, to remain vigilant and to face the challenge of change."

By placing world events in context with history, Martin was able to mobilize great numbers of people in a common cause. "Wake up," he essentially told everybody. Not only was there a revolution going on, but it was time to "complete the process of democratization," because "democracy is one of the grandest forms of government ever conceived by the minds of men. . . . If the American dream is to be a reality, we must work to make it a reality and realize the urgency of the moment. . . . We must make a massive move toward self-determination and the shaping of our own destiny. . . . The hour is late; the clock of destiny is ticking out; we must act now before it is too late. . . . We must remain awake through a great revolution. . . ."

## 2. Appeal to Ethics and Morality

Throughout his speeches, writings, and conversations, Martin built in themes based on such values as brotherhood, justice, human rights, and human dignity. He advocated action by appealing to people's highest standards of ethics and morality. "We can choose either to walk the high road of human brotherhood," he said, "or to tread the low road of man's inhumanity to man."

In the Montgomery movement, Martin believed very strongly that people banded together over a long period of time because "nonviolence was presented to them as a simple expression of Christianity in action." Consequently, he continued to preach: "Let us be Christian in all of our actions." And he also pointed out that "action is not in itself a virtue; its goals and its forms determine its value."

So, for Martin Luther King, Jr., action simply had to be taken, but everything must be done for a reason and under a legitimate banner of virtuous purpose. "We must do it because it is right to do it," he preached. "Freedom is not only from something, but to something . . ." he said. "True peace is not merely the absence of some negative force, it is the presence of some positive force [such as] justice, good will and brotherhood." And he told everyone that they should "stand up until justice comes our way," because "injustice anywhere is a threat to justice everywhere."

Adversaries often urged him to slow down, to be patient, to wait. But Martin refused to sit back. "We can't afford to slow up because we have a date with destiny," he said. "We must keep moving. We must keep moving." Moreover, his response to such advice usually took the form of an appeal involving basic human dignity. Nowhere is that more eloquently illustrated than in the famous letter he wrote and had smuggled out of the Birmingham jail in 1963:

> Perhaps it is easy for those who have never felt the stinging darts of segregation to say, "Wait." But when you have seen vicious mobs lynch your mothers and fathers at will and drown your sisters and brothers at whim; when you have seen hate-filled policemen curse, kick and even kill your black brothers and sisters . . . when you take a cross-country drive and find it necessary to sleep night after night in the uncomfortable corners of your automobile because no motel will accept you; when you are humiliated day in and day out by nagging signs reading "white" and "colored"; when your first name becomes "nigger," your middle name becomes "boy" (however old you are) and your last name becomes "John," and your wife and mother are never given the respected title of "Mrs."; when you are harried by day and haunted by night by the fact that you are a Negro, living constantly at tiptoe stance, never quite knowing what to expect next, and are plagued with inner fears and outer resentments; when you are forever fighting a degenerating sense of "nobodiness"—then you will understand why we find it difficult to wait. . . .

Constantly, fervently, passionately, Martin King portrayed the racial problems of his day as an attempt by the entrenched establishment to perpetuate an outdated, oppressive, and feudalistic plantation social system in the midst of a modern democracy. He pointed out that such an order was at odds with not only the very meaning of the Constitution of the United States, but the very highest principles of humanity, as well.

It was an extraordinarily effective and impressive argument because it appealed to people's basic sense of right and wrong. And in fact, Martin often portrayed the movement as just that—not simply a conflict between white people and black people, but a struggle between "justice and injustice," between "the forces of light and the forces of darkness." In Martin's mind, it was a "quest for freedom and human dignity."

"Why is it so difficult to understand that the Negro is sick and tired of having reluctantly parceled out to him those rights and privileges which all others receive upon birth or entry in America?" he asked. "[We] no longer will be tolerant of anything less than [our] due right and heritage. . . . Now is the time to lift our national policy from the quicksand of racial injustice to the solid rock of human dignity. . . . If America is to remain a first-class nation, she can no longer have second-class citizens. . . . We must all learn to live together as brothers, or we will all perish as fools."

## 3. Disseminate Facts and Advocate Specific Initiatives

In order to awaken action, a leader has to make people aware of current events as they stand. One way Martin highlighted injustice was by simply making it public. In doing so, he set the tone for others to stand up and tell it the way it was. "More and more southerners are speaking out," he said in 1963, "telling plain truths to the bitter and the blind."

Martin continually set forth information about the plight of everyday African-Americans—such as the fact that unemployment among "Negro youth averages 33 percent. In some of the northern ghettos," he said, "[it is] 50 percent. These figures of unemployment dwarf even those of the depression of the 1930s." In his 1967 book, *Where Do We Go from Here,* Martin also eloquently cited a series of stunning facts that would cause any compassionate individual to take notice:

> Of the good things in life, [the Negro] has approx-imately one-half of those of whites; of the bad he has twice those of whites. Half of all Negroes live in substandard housing. Negroes have half the income of whites . . . and there are twice as many unem-ployed. The rate of infant mortality among Negroes is double that of whites. There were twice as many Negroes as whites in combat in Vietnam at the be-ginning of 1967, and twice as many Negro soldiers died in action in proportion to their numbers in the population. . . . In elementary schools Negroes lag one to three years behind whites. One-twentieth as many Negroes as whites attend college, and half of those are in ill-equipped southern institutions. . . . Of employed Negroes, 75 percent hold menial jobs.

After mentioning facts like these in his speeches and writings, Martin would inevitably place responsibility squarely on the back of the federal government. "The law pronounces [the Negro] equal," he would say, "but his conditions of life are still far from equal to those of other Americans." And he would contrast modern technological advancement with inaction on civil rights. "We have created scientific and industrial miracles," he'd say. "Man-made instruments guide missiles millions of miles into space, measuring and analyzing the components of other worlds. Yet in a luncheonette in a southern town, the government cannot make the Constitution function for human rights." Martin also matter-of-factly pointed out that the federal government was the nation's "highest investor in segregation." Billions of tax dollars, he said, "have gone to support housing programs and hospital and airport construction in which discrimination is an open and notorious practice. Private firms which . . . totally exclude Negroes . . . receive billions of dollars annually in government contracts. The federal government permits elections and seats representatives in its legislative chambers in disregard of the fact that millions of Negro citizens have no vote."

If adversaries would ask him, "Well, what do you suggest we do about it?" or "What would you do?" Martin was always prepared to answer. In what is the mark of a true leader, he was always making recommendations and offering specific proposals. To the U.S. Congress, he suggested a variety of initiatives, including a "Bill of Rights for the Disadvantaged" and a new "Voting Rights Bill" that explicitly included eliminating varying standards and undue discretion on the part of state registrars, abolition of literacy tests, and enforcement by federal registrars appointed by the president.

As for the president of the United States, Martin urged using the office for "moral persuasion" to set a clear example "for Americans everywhere, of every age, on a simple, easily understood level." He advised John F. Kennedy to "personally exert executive leadership in the desegregation of public education in the Southern states of this nation." Specifically, he wanted Kennedy to form a "Committee on Fair Employment," to issue an order prohibiting segregation in government-financed housing, and to direct the Secretary of Health, Education, and Welfare "not to approve grants to states whose plans authorize segregation or denial of service on the basis of race." He even audaciously asked the new president to appoint a secretary of integration—and to issue an executive order outlawing the practice of segregation once and for all—similar to what Harry Truman had done with the armed forces after World War II and Abraham Lincoln had done with slavery during the Civil War.

"Mr. President," King told Kennedy in the White House,

"I'd like to see you stand in this room and sign a second Emancipation Proclamation outlawing segregation, one hundred years after Lincoln's. You could base it on the Fourteenth Amendment." JFK asked Martin to prepare a detailed document for him to consider, which he did. While Kennedy never issued such an executive order, with time he did initiate many of Martin King's suggestions which, in turn, led to substantial progress for the American civil rights movement.

## 4. Provide Ongoing Encouragement and Set a Good Example

Leaders are always providing people regular reminders to act. They are continually giving a little encouragement when things are going well—and a *lot* of encouragement when things are *not* going well. They provide a constant, ongoing message to move forward, not to slow down, to make progress. Martin King did so, not once or twice, but throughout the entire decade of his leadership in the movement.

"Press on and keep pressing," he said during the midst of the Montgomery crisis. "If you can't fly, run; if you can't run, walk; if you can't walk—CRAWL." Eight years later, when he was asked by a white reporter if he was going to call for a cooling-off period in the movement, Martin's response was unhesitating. "I don't think we can even think in terms of cooling off . . ." he said. "We've [already] cooled off all too long. If we continue this, we'll end up in a deep freeze."

At times, when there were setbacks, Martin offered the people comfort and reassurance. "No lie can live forever," he'd say. "Truth pressed to earth will rise again. . . . The arm of the moral universe is long but it bends toward justice." He would remind them that "sometimes it's necessary to go backward in order to go forward" or that "a final victory is an accumulation of many short-term victories." And always, Martin would employ his rousing and inspiring oratorical skills to fire people up. "We are on the move now," he said while engaged in the midst of the struggle in Selma, Alabama. "The burning of our churches will not deter us. We are on the move now. The bombing of our homes will not dissuade us. We are on the move now. The beating and killing of our clergymen and young people will not divert us. We are on the move now."

When Martin went to jail with other protesters, when he chose to remain incarcerated by refusing bail, or when he was punched in the face by a white man and, in response, turned the other cheek—he was setting an example. People will respect and follow leaders who do what they advise others to do, who display courage in the face of adversity, who act and behave as they are expected to. The fact is that a leader's actions tend to inspire others to act similarly. It's that simple—and Martin knew it. "Affirmative action," he stressed, "can guide [public opinion] into constructive channels."

The whole idea in this action-oriented aspect of leadership is to keep making progress—to "keep on keepin' on." Martin clearly understood this principle, as is illustrated in the way he ended a speech in 1963: "I say good night to you," he concluded, "by quoting the words of an old Negro slave preacher, who said, 'We ain't what we ought to be and we ain't what we're going to be. But, thank God, we ain't what we was.' "

The Atlanta department store protests that left Martin King and dozens of SNCC students in jail quickly resulted in direct negotiations with leaders in the white community. In short order, a settlement was agreed upon where all store facilities (including lunch counters and rest rooms) would be desegregated one month after public school integration began—in September 1960. All demonstrations would subsequently cease and all jailed persons would be released with charges dropped. It was a complete victory for the movement and, this time, the white government and business leaders kept their word, as desegregation went smoothly and success-fully. In addition, the ripple effect across the South was pro-found. Within a year's time, lunch counters in virtually every southern city were integrated.

Martin Luther King, however, paid a significant personal price for the victories achieved.

When it came time for him to be released with the Atlanta SNCC protesters, the white leadership had another surprise in store for him. As the students were marching out of jail, Mar-tin was told that he was being held for violation of his one-year probation for the traffic infractions he had incurred while driving Lillian Smith to the Emory University hospital six months earlier.

A judge quickly found him guilty and handed down a four-month sentence at hard labor. The next day, prison officials awoke Martin at 3:30 A.M., handcuffed him, placed him in leg irons, and informed him that it was time for a "little trip." Worried and terribly frightened that he was going to be taken on the same type of "midnight trip" that so many jailed African-Americans had never returned from, King sat silently in the back of a squad car for more than four hours—not knowing what his final destination would be.

Just after dawn, the car pulled up at the Reidsville, Geor-gia, state prison—several hundred miles from Atlanta. There Martin was issued a striped prison uniform and led down to a cold, solitary, roach-infested cell. For the moment, neither Coretta, nor any of his friends, nor anyone in the SCLC knew where he was. Martin was completely alone—and it was here that he would begin to serve his prison sentence.

"The most striking thing about the story of Rip Van Winkle is not merely that Rip slept for twenty years, but that he slept through a revolution . . . one that would alter the course of human history. . . . We must remain awake through a great revolution."

Martin Luther King, Jr.,
March 31, 1968

"Press on and keep pressing. If you can't fly, run; if you can't run, walk; if you can't walk—CRAWL."

Martin Luther King, Jr.,
March 31, 1956

# MARTIN LUTHER KING, JR., ON LEADERSHIP

★ Take direct action without waiting for other agencies to act.

★ If keeping the peace means keeping your mouth shut in the midst of injustice and evil, you should not keep the peace.

★ The best leaders are determined, bold, and reject inhibitions imposed by old traditions and habits.

★ Stay awake, adjust to new ideas, remain vigilant, and face the challenge of change.

★ Do it because it is right to do it.

★ Always be prepared to answer the question "What would you do?"

★ Sometimes it's necessary to go backward in order to go forward. That's an analogy for life.

★ A final victory is an accumulation of many short-term encounters.

★ Affirmative action can guide public opinion into constructive channels.

★ Never allow the theory that it is better to remain quiet and help the cause to become a rationalization for doing nothing.

★ Remember that the chance to act is today. The time is now.

★ Nothing will be done until people of good will put their bodies and their souls in motion.

★ You must substitute courage for caution.

★ Leadership never ascends from the pew to the pulpit, but invariably descends from the pulpit to the pew.

> "Any real change in the status quo depends on continued creative action to sharpen the conscience of the nation and establish a climate in which even the most recalcitrant elements are forced to admit that change is necessary."
>
> Martin Luther King, Jr.,
> March 14, 1965

> "In a new era, there must be new thinking."
>
> Martin Luther King, Jr.,
> February 4, 1961

# 6 / Encourage Creativity and Innovation

In 1942, a young man named James Farmer, working for African-American civil rights in Chicago, helped found the Congress of Racial Equality (CORE). Five years later, in response to the Supreme Court's decision that segregated seating was unconstitutional in all interstate transportation facilities, CORE came up with an innovative idea to test the new ruling. They launched an integrated bus ride—which was called "Journey of Reconciliation"—through a few cities in the South. The endeavor proved a failure, however, as the ride was halted and several of the passengers were arrested and sent to serve short prison terms.

Then, in the early '60s, when the Interstate Commerce Commission issued new regulations prohibiting segregation in interstate travel facilities, James Farmer remembered CORE's earlier attempts to test the law. He decided to resurrect the idea and combine it with the new sit-in technique that had been initiated successfully by college students in Greensboro, North Carolina. He planned to test federal regulations in a half dozen deep South states by having both blacks and whites sit in "whites only" bus station waiting rooms and try to obtain service at segregated lunch counters. Essentially, Farmer announced that CORE was going "to put the sit-ins on the road." And this time, they would be called "Freedom Rides."

Because the same idea had proven unsuccessful in 1947, Farmer performed extensive preliminary preparations—thinking of every possible contingency, building as much support as he could. He sent letters to the executive and judicial branches of the federal government notifying them of CORE's intentions. He contacted the two bus companies that might be used. And he placed a personal phone call to Martin Luther King, Jr., in Atlanta to ask for the support of the SCLC—and to request that Martin serve as the chairman and chief spokesman for the newly created Freedom Ride Coordinating Committee.

Martin not only agreed to serve in that capacity, he arranged for the SCLC to train the Freedom Riders in nonviolent direct action techniques. He also met frequently with the participants—inspiring them to move forward, reinforcing their determination to stand strong, and constantly reminding them of the purpose of the Freedom Rides and the movement itself.

Prior to the launch of the first ride, for instance, Martin reasserted that the purpose was to "test the use of transportation facilities, according to federal law; to encourage others to demand use of the facilities; and to direct the spotlight of public attention to areas which still segregate." He also told them that they "must develop the quiet courage of dying for a cause. We would not like to see anyone die," he said. "We all love life and there are no martyrs here—but we are well aware that we may have some casualties." And to the SCLC staff,

Martin made certain to give credit where credit was due. "CORE started the Freedom Ride," he reminded everyone, "and should get the credit. We will play a supportive role."

On May 4, 1961, thirteen well-trained passengers departed Washington, D.C., in one bus with a schedule of stops that would take them through various cities in the deep South—finally arriving in New Orleans two weeks later. As they traveled through Virginia, North Carolina, and South Carolina, they encountered no major clashes—only a few minor scuffles and a couple of arrests. When the bus arrived in Atlanta, Martin and Wyatt Walker, the executive director of the SCLC, met with the Freedom Riders, had dinner with them, and saw them off the next morning as they split up and boarded two buses for the drive to their next destination—which was Birmingham. It was when they left Georgia and entered Alabama that events began to take a turn for the worse.

On May 10, when the first bus pulled up in Anniston, Alabama (which was the only scheduled stop before reaching Birmingham), an angry mob of two hundred whites swarmed over the Freedom Riders. The bus's windows were smashed and the tires slashed. A Molotov cocktail was thrown through the rear door and the bus burst into flames. As the passengers fled, they were stoned and beaten. Meanwhile, the driver of the second bus, having seen the violence, traveled on to Birmingham. But there was another angry mob waiting there. As the Riders emerged, they were attacked and beaten with chains, baseball bats, and lead pipes. Most of the passengers were seriously injured, bloodied, and battered. One Freedom Rider was even paralyzed for life. National news accounts and pictures described the events on television and in newspapers around the world—creating tremendous publicity and sympathy for the movement and for the plight of the Freedom Riders.

With one bus destroyed and many of the participants hospitalized, it looked as if the Freedom Ride was all but stopped. But ten college students from Nashville, Tennessee, decided to drive down to Birmingham, fill in for the injured demonstrators, and continue the route. As soon as they arrived, though, Commissioner of Public Safety Eugene "Bull" Connor arrested and threw them all in jail. Then, they were rousted in the middle of the night, driven two hours north to the Tennessee state line, and abandoned on the side of the road. After some considerable negotiation by U.S. Attorney General Robert F. Kennedy with the governor of Alabama, the new group of Nashville reinforcements—along with some of the original Freedom Riders who had recovered enough to resume their mission—were allowed to board the bus in Birmingham and continue on their way to New Orleans via Montgomery.

The Freedom Ride was clearly an innovative and creative tool—one of which most people had never heard before. While it had been attempted unsuccessfully fourteen years before, the decision by James Farmer to resurrect the concept was clearly risky. But by 1961, it seemed to be an idea that fit in perfectly with the general philosophy of the civil rights movement.

Initiative, creativity, and innovative thinking were a major part of Martin Luther King's leadership strategy. Why? Because Martin was trying to lead a social revolution—one where the great majority was entrenched and recalcitrant; and one where the minority was essentially without significant economic and political power. Most of American society's conventional methods for seeking change were largely unavailable to African-Americans. The local and federal court systems were controlled largely by hostile white judges. Court actions were time-consuming, seeming to take forever—and they were also complicated, which created another disadvantage because there were far fewer black lawyers than there were white lawyers. In addition, the national television and print media industries were all controlled by the white establishment. Therefore, the leaders of the civil rights movement had to create newsworthy events of which the media would take note.

In general, African-Americans, if they hoped to make any significant progress, simply had to think and act anew. Martin King made this point over and over again. "[We] must shun the very narrow-mindedness that in others has so long been the source of our own afflictions," he counseled. Constantly, he advocated that people should seek new ways to achieve fundamental change. "We're faced with an extreme situation," he said, "and therefore our remedies must be extreme." To accomplish the movement's goals, Martin advised people to first transform themselves; to "cease imitating and begin initiating." "The necessity for a new approach," he warned, "is not a matter of choice."

One of the most important and obvious of Martin's new approaches was the entire concept of nonviolent resistance—which had never before been attempted in the United States on a massive scale. It had been done with great success by Gandhi over a forty-year period in India. But it was new and innovative when applied to the American civil rights movement. For Martin, nonviolence was not simply a tool to be used for persuasion, it was a "creative contribution"—an "imaginative and bold constructive action."

Such creative concepts came not only in the form of broad, general philosophies such as nonviolent direct action, but also appeared—sometimes spontaneously—in the form of specific techniques that could be applied on a day-to-day basis. For example, the concept of mass demonstrations began in Albany, Georgia, when more than three hundred black marchers decided to march downtown and then, after being arrested, to remain in jail rather than post bonds. Martin was extremely impressed with the initiative of the people in Albany and pointed out that such demonstrations served "the purpose of bringing the issues out in the open." It was a concept that was quickly picked up and imitated. "Our reliance on mass demonstrations," Martin later noted, "[was] intended to isolate and expose the evil-doer."

In turn, the mass demonstrations themselves led to more strategic marches—on city halls, on police stations, on libraries, and so on. At the end of the marches, people crowded into department stores, halls and corridors of public buildings, streets, sidewalks, and other public places—and just stayed there. In most cases, public officials didn't know what to do because they had never quite encountered these situations before. On a much larger scale, massive youth marches in the late '50s were staged to demand integrated schools nationwide. They attracted tens of thousands of young people who, in turn, collected and presented half a million signatures on petitions. During the entire decade of the civil rights movement, mass demonstrations ranged from a dozen people marching up to a public lunch counter to the historic March on Washington, which included more than 200,000 people.

And then there were the famous sit-ins first staged by four college students in Greensboro, North Carolina, on February 1, 1960. In what proved to be an instant success because it embarrassed managers and scared away customers, the sit-in idea spread rapidly. The next day there were two dozen students at that same lunch counter; and the next day fifty. Within a week, the sit-ins had spread across North Carolina—to Raleigh, Durham, Winston-Salem, and Charlotte. Within two weeks, similar protests were taking place in South Carolina and Virginia. And by the fall of that year, more than seventy thousand people had taken part in sit-ins across the nation. Moreover, the general concept of sit-ins led, in turn, to swim-ins at all-white beaches, stand-ins, wade-ins, kneel-ins, prayer vigils, and even insurance-ins against white insurance companies.

Insurance-ins were also part of a larger creative strategy to target the business and economic world rather than only the political realm. From that broad concept, newer, more specific ideas arose. The Montgomery movement, for instance, initiated an overwhelmingly effective economic bus boycott that eventually forced the local bus company out of business. In addition, the boycotting of specific stores and products grew into an important method of protest. "The innovation for this year," King announced in 1964, "will be large-scale selective buying programs aimed at the giants in the consumer industry." Such techniques were extraordinarily successful in forcing businesses into open hiring practices and eliminating "whites only" facilities. They were so successful, in fact, that by 1968 Martin was urging a selective buying campaign against national companies judged to be discriminatory. "We are asking you to go out and tell your neighbors not to buy Coca-Cola . . . not to buy Sealtest milk . . . or Wonder Bread," he advised people in Memphis, Tennessee.

And there were tremendously innovative and creative methods employed by local citizens when, at times, there seemed to be no other options—when it seemed as though failure was imminent. Recall, for instance, in the midst of the Montgomery movement, when taxis were enjoined from transporting citizens to and from work for a small fare, people not only walked, they rode mules, bikes, and talked their employers into picking them up and dropping them off. In addition, they devised an ingenious car pool system that included more than forty dispatch and pickup stations scattered throughout the city. And they purchased as church property a fleet of station wagons that they dubbed rolling churches.

Martin and the movement also developed many creative ways to communicate with each other. Mass meetings, for instance, originated in Montgomery and continued throughout the decade of the movement. Early on, two meetings a week were needed, on Mondays and Thursdays, because Montgomery did not have a black-owned radio station or newspaper. The Montgomery Improvement Association (MIA) also created a communications committee which produced pamphlets and circulars that were delivered door-to-door by volunteers.

Because the boycott "had to be sustained over a period of several weeks and months to assure results," Martin advocated continuous education of the community through continuous communication. "We had to use our mass meetings to explain nonviolence to a community of people who had never heard of the philosophy and in many instances were not sympathetic with it."

"People will work together and sacrifice if they understand

clearly why and how this sacrifice will bring about change," he said at another time. "We can never assume that anyone understands. It is our job to keep people informed and aware." It was in this vein that Martin and his team employed a strategic and creative utilization of the media to get the movement's mission across. Massive publicity generated sympathy for people who were attacked and brutalized—whether it was Freedom Riders being attacked and beaten in Anniston or children being bitten in Birmingham by police dogs.

All told, the utilization and employment of creative new techniques during the American civil rights movement proved tremendously effective for a minority group that had meager resources, insufficient finances, and minuscule numbers compared to the larger, wealthier, and more powerful white majority. In reality, if people in the African-American community were to achieve their dreams, they had no other choice but to innovate. Martin King not only knew this was necessary, he constantly worried that complacency in his own ranks would inhibit such creativity. For instance, he expressed concern that some older blacks had "so conditioned themselves to the system of segregation that they have lost that creative something called initiative. So many," he said, "have used their oppression as an excuse for mediocrity."

On the other hand, Martin admired and promoted the innovative actions of the younger, more energetic college students—termed them "daring," "imaginative," and "bold." "Today the imitation has ceased," he wrote. "The Negro collegian now initiates. Groping for unique forms of protest, he created the sit-ins and freedom rides. . . . Very few adhere to the established ideology or dogma. . . . All understand the need to take action. . . . This may be their most creative collective insight." "In sitting down at the lunch counters," he also said of the students, "they are in reality standing up for the best in the American Dream."

In leadership, as in life, innovation and creativity are tools designed for sustaining action, achievement, and change. "Any real change in the status quo," King noted, "depends on continued creative action to sharpen the conscience of the nation and establish a climate in which even the most recalcitrant elements are forced to admit that change is necessary." People become interested when something new is presented or attempted. And once their attention is drawn to a new idea, especially one that seems to work (as, for instance, the sit-ins did), they are more likely to try it themselves. In many of his speeches, Martin highlighted this point by quoting Ralph Waldo Emerson's famous line: "If a man can write a better book, or preach a better sermon, or make a better mouse trap than his neighbor . . . the world will make a beaten path to his door."

As a leader, Martin considered one of his primary roles to be a seeker and a seller of new ideas. He searched for "new ways and means" to achieve; he advocated a more "vigorous and creative use of power." And, like the Freedom Rides that had failed in 1947 only to succeed in 1961, he reminded people of Victor Hugo's admonition that "There is no greater power on earth than an idea whose time has come."

Martin also realized that encouraging innovation as he did meant that more mistakes would be made. So he warned people not to be discouraged when their risky ventures were not successful. "We will err and falter as we climb the unfamiliar slopes of steep mountains," he said, "but there is no alternative, well-trod, level path. There will be agonizing setbacks along with creative advances."

While innovative actions can be risky, they can also pay great dividends in teamwork and mobilization of the masses. Creative new endeavors, for instance, also serve to bring people together, to unify them in a common mission, and to keep them focused on productive measures—and away from other actions that might harm the cause. This was a concept that Martin articulated in a 1968 article in which he noted that mass demonstrations had "brought blacks and whites together," and that the crime rates during the Montgomery bus boycott had gone down "sixty-five percent for a whole year."

"Anytime we've had demonstrations in a community," he wrote, "people have found a way to slough off their self-hatred, and they have had a channel to express their longings and a way to . . . get at the power structure."

Moreover, the ability to be innovative helps a leader to break people out of the narrow confines and closed-minded thinking of established tradition. "[Many people] fail to see the necessity of creative protest," Martin once remarked to a large audience. "But I say to you that I can see no way to break loose from an old order and to move into a new order without standing up and resisting the unjust dogma of the old order."

Great leaders clearly understand that creative endeavor is essential in a changing environment—especially in times of revolution where new problems are encountered, where new goals must be set, where new trails must be blazed. "Whenever anything new comes into history it brings with it new challenges and new opportunities," noted Martin. "In a new era," he also said, "there must be new thinking." "Nothing could be more tragic," he warned, "than for men to live in these revolutionary times and fail to achieve the new attitudes and the new mental outlooks that the new situation demands."

Effective leadership sets the tone for people in the organization. A good idea gets around quickly and people will follow their leader when something new is proven effective. In this regard, the students who launched the sit-ins were themselves leaders. And Martin King was practicing true leadership, not only when he spread the word about such creative forms of protest, but when he suggested new ones.

And what did all the innovative techniques employed during the American civil rights movement achieve? Well, the Montgomery bus boycott effectively ended segregated seating in virtually every city where it was still practiced. Within a year, the Greensboro sit-ins eliminated segregated lunch counters in more than 150 cities across the South. And the Freedom Rides, which continued throughout the summer of 1961, eventually ended Jim Crow practices in bus stations everywhere. The Interstate Commerce Commission also quickly reaffirmed its policy and issued additional regulations prohibiting discrimination not only in bus stations, but in train stations, and for all other forms of transportation.

But the cost for all this progress was high. Many people were beaten, bloodied, pummeled, or worse. It was courage and determination that won the day. It was also leadership—the kind of leadership that Martin Luther King, Jr., demonstrated when the Freedom Riders who had left Birmingham were greeted by riotous mobs in Montgomery, Alabama.

On May 20, 1961, one week after the first Freedom Ride was attacked in Anniston and Birmingham, a reinforced group of twenty-one people, black and white, boarded two new Greyhound buses to continue the journey from Birmingham to their final destination of New Orleans. As the buses pulled up to the Montgomery bus terminal, an angry mob of several hundred white segregationists began throwing bricks and bottles at them. Then, as the passengers stepped off the buses, they were viciously attacked amid shouts of "Kill the niggers! Kill the niggers!" The first white man off the bus was clubbed particularly savagely. An aide to President Kennedy, who had been following the bus in a car, was also mauled and knocked unconscious. In response, Attorney General Robert Kennedy then dispatched several hundred federal marshals to the city to protect the Riders in what was quickly turning into a full-scale riot.

Hearing of the crisis, Martin dropped everything in Atlanta and flew to Montgomery. Upon arrival he immediately went to Ralph Abernathy's church to address a mass meeting. As darkness fell, several thousand segregationists, who were being held off by the federal marshals, surrounded the church. "Now, we've got an ugly mob outside," Martin said to the several hundred people huddled in the church. "They have injured some of the federal marshals. They've burned some automobiles. But we are not giving up."

At four in the morning, the church was still under siege when the mob began to pelt the federal marshals with rocks and bricks. In turn, the marshals fired tear gas canisters into the crowd—and fiercely defended themselves as the mob attacked. Hand-to-hand combat then broke out in the streets and on the church grounds. As some of the tear gas drifted into the church and began to choke the people inside, Martin rose to the podium and spoke once again: "The first thing we must do here tonight," he said to the frightened group, "is to decide we are not going to become panicky. That we are going to be calm, and that we are going to continue to stand up for what we know is right. . . . Alabama will have to face the fact that we are determined to be free. The main thing I want to say to you is fear not, we've come too far to turn back. . . . We are not afraid and we shall overcome."

---

"Nothing could be more tragic than for men to live in these revolutionary times and fail to achieve the new attitudes and the new mental outlooks that the new situation demands."

Martin Luther King, Jr.,
1967

---

"We must use time creatively."

Martin Luther King, Jr.,
April 16, 1963

# MARTIN LUTHER KING, JR., ON LEADERSHIP

★ Give credit where credit is due.

★ You must shun the very narrow-mindedness that has been the source of your organization's past afflictions.

★ When faced with an extreme situation, your remedies must be extreme.

★ People will work together and sacrifice if they understand clearly why and how the sacrifice will bring about change.

★ Never assume that anyone understands. It is your job to keep people informed and aware.

★ Any real change in the status quo depends on continued creative action.

★ There will be agonizing setbacks with creative advances. Be tolerant of mistakes.

★ Creative new endeavors bring people together, unify them, and keep them focused.

★ In a new era there must be new thinking.

★ A good idea will spread quickly.

★ When an emergency ensues and people are in danger—rush to the scene.

★ Innovative actions may serve as unifying forces in any movement.

★ Creative power can pull down mountains of evil and level hilltops of injustice.

★ You must use time creatively.

"Our most powerful nonviolent weapon is . . . organization. To produce change, people must be organized to work together in units of power. These units might be political; they may be economic; or they may be laboring units of persons who are seeking employment and wage increases."

Martin Luther King, Jr.,
October 1966

"The biggest job in getting any movement off the ground is to keep together the people who form it. This task requires more than a common aim: it demands a philosophy that wins and holds the people's allegiance; and it depends upon open channels of communication between the people and their leaders."

Martin Luther King, Jr.,
1959

"In a multi-racial society, no group can make it alone."

Martin Luther King, Jr.,
March 31, 1968

# 7 / Involve Everyone Through Alliances, Teamwork, and Diversity

In 1954, a young man named James Meredith, anticipating his graduation from high school, applied for admission to the all-white University of Mississippi. His application was rejected for no other apparent reason than the fact that he was of African-American descent. After serving a stint in the air force, Meredith enrolled at Jackson State, one of Mississippi's all-black colleges, and began building a solid academic record—one that was strong enough to gain any white person easy admission to the larger, state-sponsored University of Mississippi.

Not one to easily give up on his dreams, Meredith began to lay the foundation for another attempt to become the first African-American to enter Ole Miss. He received enthusiastic and reliable aid from Medgar Evers, the NAACP's field secretary in Mississippi, who helped him make contact with Thurgood Marshall, head of the NAACP Legal Defense Fund in Washington. Then, in the spring of 1961, after also securing the support of local NAACP lawyers, James Meredith reapplied for admission to the University of Mississippi. His application was once again summarily rejected, but the following week the NAACP filed suit claiming that Meredith was refused admission "solely because of his race." That action was to set off a chain of legal events that would last more than a year and culminate in a major decision from the Supreme Court of the United States.

Prior to Martin Luther King, Jr., arriving on the scene, the National Association for the Advancement of Colored People was the only major coalition with the means, talent, and organization to effectively help a person with a goal similar to that of James Meredith. Other national groups, such as the National Urban League or the Congress of Racial Equality (CORE), were more localized in their efforts or, in the early 1950s, even somewhat dormant. After Martin became active, however, a flurry of new formal organizations were born. Creation of the MIA (Montgomery Improvement Association), for example, gave birth to the PIA (Petersburg Improvement Association) and a variety of other groups dedicated to aiding local movements. In addition, there was the formal incorporation of larger associations such as the Student Nonviolent Coordinating Committee (SNCC), the Committee on the

Appeal for Human Rights (COAHR), the Summer Community Organization and Political Education Project (SCOPE), the Gandhi Society for Human Rights, the Southern Christian Leadership Conference (SCLC), and the Western Christian Leadership Conference.

All this alliance-building activity, coupled with the natural progression of the civil rights movement, correspondingly resulted in rejuvenation and renewed activity for the National Urban League, CORE, and, most importantly, the NAACP. Martin's hope was that all the civil rights organizations would form a united front and work together "in many different ways" for the good of the cause. However, initial reaction to the SCLC from the deeply entrenched NAACP was antagonistic and even a bit hostile. But Martin realized such a response was part of human nature. After all, there had been only one leading association in the civil rights movement for more than a half century. As such, the leaders of the NAACP considered themselves *the* leaders of the African-American cause in the United States. Accordingly, Martin King's emergence as a national leader was met with all the natural human emotions of jealousy, apprehension, and distrust—even in his own hometown.

In response, Martin strategically set out to establish trust and build personal relationships with the leaders of the national civil rights groups. He traveled to New York often to confer with NAACP secretary Roy Wilkins, for instance, to assure him that the work of the SCLC supported and complemented NAACP plans and goals. He proposed joint activity and asked for guidance, support, and advice. In addition, Martin included other leaders in his plans on a variety of initiatives and, through constant communication, made sure that they were informed of the SCLC's plans.

Why did Martin Luther King, Jr., work so diligently to build trusting relationships, to form his own alliances—and then advocate the creation of even more organizations devoted to his cause?

First of all, he believed that African-Americans, in general, were behind the curve in this area. History, he felt, indicated they had been "slow to organize because they had been traditionally manipulated" and that "the leadership neither planned ahead nor maintained itself at all times." Martin pointed out that African-Americans "lack experience because ours is a history of disorganization" and he advocated that they should "shun the very narrow-mindedness that has so long been a source of [our] own afflictions" and that "the ability to enter alliances is a mark of strength, not of weakness."

Second, Martin understood that, in isolation, a minority group would not be able to achieve a major social transformation. "Ten percent of the population cannot by tensions alone induce ninety percent to change a way of life," he said. "We aren't going to be free anywhere in the United States until there is a committed empathy on the part of the white [majority]."

So Martin advocated the creation of alliances of many kinds—political, social, religious, intellectual, economic, and cultural. In general, he regularly articulated five major advantages that resulted from such alliance-building:

1. *The banding together of individuals creates energy, enthusiasm, and courage.*
   "We shall have to have people tied together in a long-term relationship instead of evanescent enthusiasts who lose their experience, spirit and unity because they have no mechanism that directs them to new tasks."

2. *In contrast to individuals working alone, people gain more power and strength in formal organizations.*
   "Through group identity, determination and creative endeavor [ethnic minorities] have gained power. . . . Negro solidarity is a powerful growing force which no society may wisely ignore."

*3. Major social change is best achieved in groups.*

"To attempt radical reform without adequate organization is like trying to sail a boat without a rudder. . . . The future of the deep structural changes we seek . . . lies in new alliances of Negroes, Puerto Ricans, labor, liberals, certain church and middle-class elements . . . cities of the North and black belts of the South."

*4. Alliances effectively expand contacts and networks of communication.*

"Many segments must band together . . . to create a consensus and a political force for the democratization of this nation. . . . The only truly responsible consensus will emerge when grass roots people know the issues, articulate their demands, and become a part of the democratic process."

*5. Alliances allow more results to be achieved.*

"We begin to glimpse tremendous vistas of what it might mean for the world if [we] succeed in forging an even wider alliance of today's awakened youth."

Not only did Martin advocate alliance-building, he strategically set out to build a variety of affiliations—with "every alliance considered on its own merits." He wanted to involve everyone in the civil rights movement if he could. But he was astute enough to realize that "the art of alliance politics" is "complex" and "intricate"; that a great deal of time had to be expended gauging the critical issues and interests of the potential partner, determining the right people to approach, and then planting the seeds of a fruitful, ongoing relationship. "A true alliance," said Martin, "is based upon some self-interest of each component group and a common interest into which they merge. For an alliance to have permanence and loyal commitment from its various elements, each of them must have a goal from which it benefits and none must have an outlook in basic conflict with the others."

Accordingly, Martin pushed for "a grand alliance of Negro and White." "The economically deprived condition of the Negro will remain," he said, "unless the Negro revolution builds and maintains alliances with the majority of the white community." He reminded everyone that "there exists a substantial group of white Americans who cherish democratic principles above privilege . . . [who] are just as determined to see us free as we are to be free ourselves." And he eloquently pointed out to multiracial audiences that "the black man needs the white man and the white man needs the black man. We are bound together in a single garment of destiny," he said. "The language, the cultural patterns, the music, the material prosperity and even the food of America are an amalgam of black and white." By early 1963, after years of hard work in forging relationships with the white majority in the South, some progress had been made. "Georgia, on the basis of a Negro-white de facto alliance," reported Martin, "elected a moderate governor, a moderate mayor in Atlanta, a moderate congressman from the most populous county, and sent a Negro to the state senate for the first time in nearly a hundred years."

Martin also set out to build a strategic relationship with organized labor unions across the country. "Labor and the Negro have identical interests," he said. "This unity of purpose is not an historical coincidence. Negroes are almost entirely a working people. Our needs are identical with labor's needs; decent wages, fair working conditions, livable housing, old age security, health and welfare measures, conditions in which families can grow, have education for their children and respect in the community."

In a 1965 television interview, when asked who he believed were the best African-American leaders in the nation, Martin—in addition to naming Roy Wilkins of the NAACP, Whitney Young of the National Urban League, and John Lewis of

SNCC—made a point to mention A. Philip Randolph, founder of the Brotherhood of Sleeping Car Porters and chairman of the Negro American Labor Council (NALC). Martin not only courted Randolph, but George Meany of the AFL-CIO, Walter P. Reuther of the United Automobile Workers, and Jimmy Hoffa of the Teamsters Union. "Labor needs far more political leverage than it presently possesses to attain its minimum legislative goals," he told union leaders. "Therefore, labor too like the Negro needs more ballots to have more respect. We must unite our efforts and our resources to effect this change. We are together a great reservoir of liberal power, and if we are conscious of our potentialities we can shift political alignments until they become truly responsive to our needs."

In the long run, Martin was able to persuade many white labor leaders that black America was their ally. As a result, many began to accept African-American members. By the mid-1960s, for example, nearly every member union in the AFL-CIO had eliminated discriminatory guidelines and integrated their organizations. Not only did organized labor provide a powerful ally for securing African-American goals, it donated hundreds of thousand of dollars to advance the aims of the civil rights movement.

In the area of fund-raising, Martin built strategic relationships with a number of northern philanthropic organizations that, in turn, funded many SCLC initiatives, including the massive Voter Education Project targeted throughout the South. Also, he became a close friend of singer Harry Belafonte, who was a tireless leader in raising vast amounts of revenue during the decade of the movement. For example, when Martin was accused of perjury in regard to his Alabama state income tax returns, it was Belafonte (along with A. Philip Randolph) who participated in a "Committee to Defend Martin Luther King" by raising funds through a series of benefit concerts. Over the years, he also gathered friends in the entertainment business—such as Frank Sinatra, Joan Baez, and

Sammy Davis, Jr.—to put on concerts that raised bail money for jailed protesters and for administration expenses of the SCLC.

Furthermore, Martin set out to build and solidify black relationships with various government entities. "We shall have to master the art of political alliances," he said. "Negroes should be natural allies of many white reform and independent political groups." More specifically, he wanted to "bring pressure on the federal government for protective action on our behalf," and to have the government "drive a wedge into the splitting south, spreading it open."

In the late 1950s, Martin sent frequent letters to President Dwight Eisenhower—and secured meetings with Vice President Richard Nixon and an array of congressmen and senators in an effort to raise awareness and build support. But he was unable to gain an audience with Eisenhower until after the autumn of 1957, when the president decided to nationalize the Arkansas National Guard and dispatch a thousand army paratroopers to ensure integration of Central High School in Little Rock, Arkansas. Several months later, Martin and a few other black leaders, including Roy Wilkins and Whitney Young, met with Eisenhower at the White House. They presented the president with a nine-point action list detailing exactly what they expected from the executive branch of the federal government. Eisenhower politely offered his thanks and assured the men that he would consider their recommendations.

Two years later, in June 1960, Martin secured a private meeting with presidential candidate John F. Kennedy to discuss the civil rights movement and support of his candidacy. While Martin was impressed with the candidate, he did not offer a public endorsement. However, when Senator Kennedy, in October, intervened to obtain Martin's release from the four-month prison sentence at Reidsville, nearly the entire African-American population voted Democratic in the November election—which Kennedy won by the smallest margin in history.

After Kennedy took office, Martin made it a point to build a strong personal alliance with the new president. He and other black leaders met frequently at the White House to plan and lobby for effective civil rights legislation. These early meetings, with both the president and Attorney General Robert Kennedy, eventually led to such important action as appointment of African-Americans to significant posts in the executive branch, new bills presented to Congress, and future federal intervention and support. Moreover, in the wake of President Kennedy's assassination, Martin developed a relationship with Lyndon Johnson and eventually supported the new president's War on Poverty initiative.

It must not be overlooked that Martin King, in addition to fashioning formal alliances, also spent a great deal of his time bringing together a strong team—and then, in turn, building personal relationships with each member of that team. At the SCLC, for instance, he assembled a group of aggressive, dedicated individuals to run the day-to-day operations in Atlanta and to guide general activities across the nation. For the position of executive director, Martin first choose Wyatt Tee Walker, an action-oriented native of Massachusetts who had two college degrees and eight years of field experience attempting to integrate public facilities. He also selected energetic and bright young people for his general staff and the SCLC's "direct action team"—the mission of which was to go into the field wherever necessary to prepare, mobilize, and train the masses, and then to institute a specific plan of protest action. Hosea Williams, C. T. Vivian, Bernard Lee, James Bevel, Andrew Young, Jesse Jackson, Walter Fauntroy, and others were strong leaders in their own right—with a variety of talents that complemented one other.

Martin not only had enough self-confidence to surround himself with the best people he could find, he was humble enough to listen to them—and talented enough to keep them all together, which is a major task in and of itself for any leader. "The biggest job in getting any movement off the ground," Martin wrote, "is to keep together the people who form it. This task requires more than a common aim: it demands a philosophy that wins and holds the people's allegiance; and it depends upon open channels of communication between the people and their leaders."

Martin's methods for teamwork were simple and basic. He would hold regular retreats, usually several days in length, with no more than a dozen staff members. The place of the small conference was always "secured" and "conducive to deep thinking and serious discussion." As the leader of the team, he would begin each retreat with an opening statement that set the general direction and tone. "Now, I want this to be informal," Martin said at one group discussion. "After my remarks, we will have a discussion period. And I hope there will be give and take, very honest give and take."

During serious sessions, Martin would ask questions, try not to take sides, let everyone debate and discuss—and then attempt to arrive at a consensus. "No parliamentary rules were necessary," he recalled in one of his books. "The rule of the majority was tacitly accepted." He also constantly advocated dialogue rather than monologue. "The greatest channel to peace" he said, "[involves] talking about problems. . . . For as long as we have men, we are going to have differences. And it seems to me we can disagree without being disagreeable."

Once a course of action was agreed upon, committees were set up to ferret out details and then carry out the action plan. This was a procedure Martin employed from his earliest days in Montgomery—as both a leader of the bus boycott and as a Baptist minister. One of his first initiatives for the church, for instance, was to set up a "serious evangelistic campaign" that would be carried on throughout his first full year. "This campaign," he wrote in a letter of recommendation, "shall be carried out by 25 evangelistic teams, each consisting of a captain and at least three other members. Each team shall be urged to bring in at least five new members within the church year. The team that brings in the highest number of members shall be duly recognized at the end of the church year. Each captain shall call his team together at least once a month to discuss findings and possibilities."

King's strategy of surrounding himself with strong, talented, and action-oriented individuals was a mark of strong leadership. And clearly, such a philosophy is not unprecedented in the annals of history. Many great leaders of the past were known for their appointments of "field generals" who would act on their own initiative. Harry Truman had George Marshall, FDR had Dwight Eisenhower, and Abraham Lincoln had Ulysses S. Grant. Each of these leaders also had a healthy dose of self-esteem. They possessed a broader ability and willingness to listen and accept other people's ideas. And they were willing to listen to the people surrounding them.

Every good leader, past or present, usually possesses a powerful sense of self-confidence—so powerful sometimes that it borders on arrogance and is often perceived as such by contemporaries. Theodore Roosevelt, Thomas Jefferson, George Washington, and Abraham Lincoln, for instance, were all supremely self-confident. But they were also vilified in their own time as supercilious and conceited. Moreover, many well-known innovative leaders and creators from professions other than politics have also been noted for possessing a peculiar self-confidence that may have helped them succeed in life. Scientist Albert Einstein "was certain" that his general theories on relativity were correct. Physician Sigmund Freud had "no doubts" about his interpretations surrounding psychoanalysis. Composer Wolfgang Mozart "never made a mistake" in his handwritten musical compositions. And inventor Thomas Edison knew that if he "perspired" long enough, he could create an effective incandescent electric light bulb.

Martin Luther King, Jr., also had confidence in himself—and in the belief that he could make a difference by working in a team-oriented environment. He knew that by employing effective teamwork, rather than allowing people to work only individually, he could achieve more definitive and comprehensive results in the long run. Modern research and practical experience clearly confirm this philosophy. For example, Jon R. Katzenbach and Douglas K. Smith, authors of *The Wisdom of Teams,* noted several reasons why teams perform better than individuals. The four most important advantages are:

1. Teams bring together a broader mix of skills that exceed those of any single individual.
2. Teams jointly develop and strive toward clear goals.
3. Teams can adjust with greater speed and effectiveness.
4. Trust and confidence are more easily built in teams.

Katzenbach and Smith further noted that "Teams are more flexible because they can be more quickly assembled, deployed, refocused, and disbanded, usually in ways that enhance rather than disrupt more permanent structures and processes. . . . Teams and performance are an unbeatable combination."

The teamwork process involves many working members of an organization. As a result, when a final initiative is put in place, there are more supporters to champion the cause, more people to actually put the plan into action—which can be a major factor in overcoming an organization's natural resistance to change. It also gives reinforced meaning to the adage "People support what they help create." It is precisely because active members of an organization are involved that teamwork vaults to the forefront of leadership. Recall the definition of leadership itself: *Leaders act for the wants and needs . . . of the people they represent.* As teams are comprised of people in the organization, a team may become the perfect vehicle for a leader to discern goals, values, and aspirations. Furthermore, teamwork provides a major link to the role of empowerment in leadership. A leader has to let other people be part of his or her team; to trust them enough to let them have the ball and run with it; to let them make mistakes; and to give them credit for success.

Also going hand in hand with teamwork is diversity—diversity of thought, skill, culture, and ideas. Whether in business, government, or private organizations, it does little good to have a team where all members look, think, and act exactly the same. A variety of opinions and perspectives invariably results in greater productivity, quicker problem-solving, and better decisions.

This was a concept that Martin Luther King, Jr., clearly understood. In addition to advocating the formation of "interracial coalitions," and "organizations representing a wide variety of interests," he pushed hard for diversity in his own associations—not only because it was effective, but because it sent the right message. "Every time a Negro in the slums of Chicago or the plantations of Mississippi sees Negroes and whites honestly working together for a common goal, he sees new grounds for hope," Martin stated in a 1959 interview. "This is why I always have in the past and will in the future insist that my staff in the SCLC be interracial. By insisting on racial openness in our organizations, we are setting a pattern for the racially integrated society toward which we work." True to his word, Martin strategically appointed whites to the board of the SCLC and noted that "our staff was small but what it lacked in quantity, it more than made up in versatility." In addition, he sought to bring together people of strong character. "In the nonviolent army," he said, "there is room for everyone who wants to join up. There is no color distinction. [People] are called upon [only] to examine their heart, their conscience, their courage and their sense of justice."

Assembling people with a diversity of skills and backgrounds was a strategy he employed from the inception of the civil rights movement. Because of the broad mix of individuals in Montgomery, for example, Martin was able to set up his smaller teams with a diverse group of men and women. It was not at all uncommon, for instance, to see professors, businessmen, and lawyers sitting around the committee table with taxi drivers, maids, and construction workers. That type of diversity was particularly evident for all to see in the regularly held and well-attended mass meetings. "Physicians, teachers, and lawyers sat or stood beside domestic workers and unskilled laborers," wrote Martin in *Stride Toward Freedom.* "The Ph.D's and the no 'D's' were bound together in a common venture. The so-called 'big Negroes' who owned cars and had never ridden the buses came to know the maids and the laborers who rode the buses every day. Men and women who had been separated from each other by false standards of class were now singing and praying together in a common struggle for freedom and human dignity."

Martin constantly preached that "in a multi-racial society, no group can make it alone," that "our world is a neighborhood," that "all will benefit from a color-blind land of plenty," and that "integration is an opportunity to participate in the beauty of diversity." And he pointed out to African-Americans who tended to be isolationist or more inclined toward violence that they would be "living tomorrow with the very people against whom [they are] struggling today." To illustrate his point, Martin also quoted John Donne on several different occasions: "No man is an island entire of itself. Every man is a piece of the continent— a part of the main. . . . Any man's death diminishes me because I am involved in mankind. Therefore never seek to know for whom the bell tolls; it tolls for thee."

The freedom and human dignity that people were struggling for during the American civil rights movement, according to Martin, was not only to be administered at the national and state levels, but at local levels—all the way down to the way people interacted with each other on a daily basis. As such, he set the example in his own organizations by instituting "a real sharing of power and responsibility" because, as he said, "Freedom is participation in power."

True teamwork, then, is an effective technique for any leader to share power with members of the organization. It allows everyone who wants to be involved to participate in the process. Furthermore, teamwork raises hopes, expectations, and energy—all of which serve to mobilize and inspire people to act toward the achievement of goals. Well-implemented diversity also adds great power to any organization—whether a small committee or a global business corporation. For as Charles Darwin noted in *On the Origin of Species:* "Diversity in the gene pool creates strength and survivability in any species."

On June 25, 1962, the Fifth Circuit Court of Appeals in New Orleans, in a 2–1 decision, issued an injunction forcing the University of Mississippi to admit James Meredith as a full-fledged student. Three months later, after the Supreme Court upheld that decision, Meredith arrived on campus accompanied by four U.S. marshals. But the governor of the state, Ross Barnett, was waiting to greet the group. In dramatic fashion, surrounded by a multitude of local police, Barnett—who had been designated acting registrar by the Ole Miss board of trustees—informed James that his application had been rejected and he would not be admitted. Meredith and the marshals turned around and went home.

The next day, however, after the Fifth Circuit Court of Appeals threatened to hold the governor in contempt, university trustees agreed to the enrollment. Two days later, back came Meredith and the marshals. Only this time they were greeted by a snarling Lieutenant Governor Paul Johnson, who categorically refused to admit the African-American under any circumstances. Once again, James Meredith walked away peacefully.

Within a few days, however, President Kennedy got involved. He federalized the Mississippi National Guard, sent additional U.S. marshals to the Oxford, Mississippi, campus, and, together with Attorney General Robert Kennedy, pressured Governor Barnett to back down. By this time, however, not only were troops, marshals, and police pouring into Oxford, so were thousands of white segregationists—armed and ready to do battle.

Everyone knew there was going to be a showdown.

On September 30, President Kennedy addressed the nation and urged restraint but, at the same time, was firm in his position. "Americans are free . . . to disagree with the law, but not to disobey it," he said. "For in any government of laws and not of men, no man, however prominent and powerful, and no matter however unruly and boisterous, is entitled to defy a court of law. . . ."

Just about the time the president was speaking to the nation, the Mississippi Highway Patrol was ordered to withdraw from campus. On that cue, the crowd of white separatists turned into an angry mob and began throwing rocks, bricks, and Molotov cocktails at the federal troops. In response, the chief federal marshal ordered his troops to fire tear gas into the mob. At that point, the battle turned into a full-scale riot as shots rang out, screams sounded, and blood flowed in the streets.

When the dust had finally settled, two people had been killed, 375 were injured, and nearly a hundred were arrested. More than 180 of the wounded were U.S. marshals who had either been shot or beaten.

Despite the resistance, the riots, and the resolve of the segregationist state government, on October 1, 1962, James Meredith was quietly enrolled as a freshman at the University of Mississippi.

James Meredith achieved his dream, in large part, because Martin Luther King, Jr., had made it a point to build a personal alliance with President John F. Kennedy.

"The meetings cut across class lines. The vast majority present were working people. Physicians, teachers, and lawyers sat or stood beside domestic workers and unskilled laborers. The Ph.D.'s and the no D's were bound together in a common venture."

Martin Luther King, Jr.,
1959

"Our world is a neighborhood. . . . We are tied together in the single garment of destiny, caught in an inescapable network of mutuality. And whatever affects one directly affects all indirectly."

Martin Luther King, Jr.,
March 31, 1968

# MARTIN LUTHER KING, JR., ON LEADERSHIP

★ The only truly responsible consensus will emerge when grass-roots people know the issues, articulate their demands, and become a part of the democratic process.

★ Every alliance must be considered on its own merits.

★ A true alliance is based upon some self-interest of each component group and a common interest into which they merge.

★ Keeping people together in a team depends upon open channels of communication between the people and their leaders.

★ Hold regular retreats (with no more than a dozen people) in a place that is conducive to deep thinking and serious discussion.

★ During serious discussions, ask questions, try not to take sides, let everyone debate and discuss—and then attempt to arrive at a consensus.

★ People are going to have differences. You should be able to disagree without being disagreeable.

★ In a multi-racial society, no group can make it alone.

★ Remember, you may be living tomorrow with the very people against whom you are struggling today.

★ Don't forget that winning allies is more difficult in the absence of facts.

★ A destructive minority can poison the wellsprings from which the majority must drink.

★ When one person stands up, he may be run out of town. But when a thousand stand up together the situation is drastically altered.

★ Life at its best is a creative synthesis of opposites in fruitful harmony.

★ Laws only declare rights, they do not deliver them.

"We will reach the goal of freedom in Birmingham and all over the nation, because the goal of America is freedom. Abused and scorned though we may be, our destiny is tied up with America's destiny."

Martin Luther King, Jr.,
April 16, 1963

"We began to prepare a top-secret file which we called 'Project C'—the 'C' for Birmingham's *Confrontation* with the fight for justice and morality in race relations. . . . In preparation for our campaign, I called a three-day retreat and planning session with SCLC staff and board members at our training center near Savannah, Georgia. Here, we sought to perfect a timetable and discuss every possible eventuality."

Martin Luther King, Jr.,
1963

"[We] can differ and still unite around common goals."

Martin Luther King, Jr.,
1967

# 8 / Set Goals and Create a Detailed Plan of Action

After the September 1962 SCLC convention in Birmingham, Alabama—the one that ended with Martin being punched in the face during his keynote address—Fred Shuttlesworth, leader of the SCLC's Birmingham affiliate, placed

154

a call to headquarters in Atlanta. It seemed that Birmingham's white merchants had gone back on a promise.

When the SCLC first announced it would hold its fall convention there, Shuttlesworth, who had already launched a boycott of downtown department stores, was approached by local business executives. They offered to desegregate their lunch counters immediately if the SCLC would not hold demonstrations in the downtown department stores. A cautiously optimistic Shuttlesworth agreed to the deal and, in a show of good faith, halted the existing downtown boycott. But after the SCLC convention ended and all the delegates left town, the department store executives decided to again segregate their lunch counters.

Although he had hoped for the best, Fred Shuttlesworth was used to such treachery. As pastor of the Bethel Baptist Church and a senior leader in the African-American community, he had worked for years to desegregate Birmingham's public facilities. For his efforts, he was thrown in jail a half dozen times, beaten by the Klan, his wife stabbed, his home bombed, and he was forced into bankruptcy when the city filed a $3 million lawsuit against him.

But Shuttlesworth wouldn't give up. He kept coming back. And now he was making a personal appeal to Martin Luther King, Jr., to get involved in Birmingham in a big way. "If you want a victory for the civil rights movement," he told Martin, "come to Birmingham. We can win."

Such a statement was optimistic, indeed—and Martin knew it because he observed that white Birmingham had been fighting back tenaciously against even the slightest hint of integration. Not only had attacks been made on Shuttlesworth and other African-American leaders, but everything had been done, from stopping black music being played on radio stations to murdering, castrating, and mutilating the body of a young man who had simply been standing on a street corner. Martin King himself had termed Birmingham "the most thoroughly segregated city in the country." It was a community, he said, that apparently had "never heard of Abraham Lincoln, Thomas Jefferson, the Bill of Rights, the Preamble to the Constitution, the Thirteenth, Fourteenth and Fifteenth Amendments, or the 1954 decision of the United States Supreme Court outlawing segregation in the public schools."

The fact is that Birmingham was one of the most entrenched segregationist cities in the entire South. And although Martin was initially cautious at the plea of Fred Shuttlesworth, he also knew that a success there could serve as a symbol for the rest of the nation and might effectively ignite the movement with a much-needed victory.

Martin's first step in the Birmingham campaign was to call a retreat with his SCLC staff and board members. It was held in mid-January 1963 at an out-of-the-way facility in Dorchester, Georgia, on the eastern side of the state. The location was far enough from Atlanta that participants would not be interrupted, nor would they be easily tempted to return home until the few days of meetings were ended.

Initial discussions centered around the telephone conversation between Shuttlesworth and King—and focused on the obvious question Martin posed to the group. "Should we go to Birmingham?" he asked. They all knew that this particular city would be a tough nut to crack. But if it could be done there, it could be done everywhere in the South. The group also reached a consensus that some sort of action needed to take place. The nation was simply too complacent in regard to civil rights. Just the previous year, for instance, President Kennedy had submitted a civil rights bill that languished and then died in Congress because no one took any interest in it. Everyone agreed that if the SCLC went to Birmingham, the ultimate goal would not be to desegregate the city, but to "awaken the moral conscience of America" and produce federal legislation that would force desegregation everywhere.

Now that was a noble mission around which everyone could rally. And, indeed, a consensus was reached to move forward. Discussion then turned to creating a detailed plan of

action—which the group collectively named "Project C"—
the "C" standing for "Confrontation."

Remembering that in Albany they had scattered their efforts too widely, the group chose to focus on one facet only—
the business community rather than the city government. "We
decided to center the Birmingham struggle," wrote Martin,
"on the economic power structure [because] we knew
that . . . Negroes had enough buying power to make the difference between profit and loss in almost any business."

Specific goals were then proposed and agreed upon for
Project C. The primary objectives included desegregation of
department store facilities and all other public facilities; establishment of fair hiring practices for local business and government; dismissal of all charges against demonstrators; and
creation of a biracial committee to monitor and enforce the
implementation of city desegregation.

Next, a precise timetable for action was defined—along
with specific methods and techniques to be employed, such as
mass meetings, boycotts and sit-ins, mass marches, and
enough arrests to fill up the jails in and around Birmingham.
Overall, the plan was designed to precipitate a crisis or "a creative tension," as Martin liked to call it, that would force the
recalcitrant majority to the negotiating table.

At that point, it was time to begin the implementation
phase. First, the direct action team was deployed to Birmingham. Once there, its members established a general office at
the Gaston Motel, Room 30. And central headquarters for
the entire local movement was designated to be the conve-
niently located 16th Street Baptist Church on the edge of
downtown.

The team immediately set to work on a variety of fronts.
They reviewed all the local laws regarding marching, picketing, and demonstrating. They carried out preliminary detailed
footwork involving such things as investigating the department stores that were to be targeted—right down to the number of stools at each lunch counter. Preliminary groundwork

was also laid for mobilizing the media. Part of the SCLC's strategy here was to have local, national, and international news coverage—especially television coverage—of everything that happened in Birmingham.

Recruitment of demonstrators also began in force. Once enough people volunteered to serve, the SCLC sponsored free workshops to train all recruits in nonviolence and direct action techniques. In short order, two hundred fifty volunteers were trained and ready to go into action. At the end of their training, all the recruited demonstrators were required to sign the following "Birmingham Pledge":

I HEREBY PLEDGE MYSELF—MY PERSON AND BODY—TO THE NONVIOLENT MOVEMENT. THEREFORE I WILL KEEP THE FOLLOWING TEN COMMANDMENTS.

1. MEDITATE daily on the teachings and life of Jesus.
2. REMEMBER always that the nonviolent in Birmingham seek justice and reconciliation—not victory.
3. WALK and TALK in the manner of love, for God is love.
4. PRAY daily to be used by God in order that all men might be free.
5. SACRIFICE personal wishes in order that all men might be free.
6. OBSERVE with both friend and foe the ordinary rules of courtesy.
7. SEEK to perform regular service for others and for the world.
8. REFRAIN from the violence of fist, tongue, or heart.
9. STRIVE to be in good spiritual and bodily health.

10. FOLLOW the directions of the movement and of the captain on a demonstration.

Martin subsequently became directly involved in the preliminary planning by focusing his efforts primarily on personal communication with potential allies. "We were seeking to bring about a great social change which could only be achieved through unified effort . . ." he wrote in his 1963 book, *Why We Can't Wait.* "It was decided that we would conduct a whirlwind campaign of meetings with organizations and leaders in the Negro community, to seek to mobilize every key person and group behind our movement."

So, along with members of the SCLC staff, Martin hit the road. In New York, they briefed Roy Wilkins of the NAACP and asked for help. In Washington, D.C., they made contact with their allies in the federal government to let them know what was going to occur. And, most importantly, Martin went to Birmingham to meet with Fred Shuttlesworth and other local leaders. In a concentrated effort to drum up support, he scheduled dozens of meetings where he met with hundreds of ministers, professional people, and businessmen. As Martin remembered it, most of the meetings began with an atmosphere that was "tense and chilly." For that reason, he would immediately go to the point. "I pleaded for the projection of strong, firm leadership. . . . I asked how the Negro would ever gain his freedom without the guidance, support and inspiration of spiritual leaders. . . . I spoke from my heart, and out of each meeting came firm endorsements and pledges of participation and support."

Martin Luther King realized the strategic importance of starting a major initiative carefully and cautiously. He devised a long-term, detailed strategy and then sought to build support and consolidate forces. He also painted the reason for his entrance into Birmingham in the bright colors of ethics, values, and integrity. "I am in Birmingham," he said simply, "because injustice is here."

Regardless of the rhetoric, however, everyone knew that the Birmingham campaign would not be a picnic. George Wallace had just taken the oath of office as governor of the state of Alabama and virtually the first words out of his mouth were: "Segregation now! Segregation tomorrow! Segregation forever!" Moreover, Martin himself had issued a stern warning on the final day of the planning conference: "I want to make a point that I think everyone here should consider very carefully and decide if he wants to be with this campaign," he said. "I have to tell you that in my judgment, some of the people sitting here today will not come back alive from this campaign. And I want you to think about it."

That statement was, in a way, indicative of how the SCLC's planning retreats were conducted: straight talk; everyone could speak their mind; no stone left unturned. It had always been that way and that's the way it would always be. Even before the SCLC was formed, Martin assembled Montgomery Improvement Association strategy committees frequently in various members' homes. The Montgomery movement, he wrote, "did not spring into being full grown as Athena sprang from the head of Zeus; it was the culmination of a slowly developing process." Later, he expanded the SCLC annual meetings from one to two, in part to allow for "more long range, detailed planning on the part of the staff." And, over the years, he constantly preached that everyone "must commit themselves to a whole long-range program."

For every major initiative during the decade of the civil rights movement there were frequent planning and strategy sessions held before, during, and after each event. Most sessions began with a discussion of the proposed major initiative. Once a course was agreed upon, a written statement of purpose was sometimes drafted. Then, as in the Birmingham planning meeting, goals were set and a specific detailed plan of action was created—one that centered around the achievement of those goals.

This entire planning process was paramount to Martin

Luther King, Jr.'s, leadership style. He constantly advocated the need for planning and goal-setting. He gave deep consideration to the reasoning behind such planning. And then he explained his thoughts to those he wished to participate in the process. Here, in Martin's own words, are seven key points to remember:

1. *A wise leader plans before taking action.*
   "We have to put the horse before the cart."

2. *Goals and a detailed plan facilitate the process of change.*
   "What is needed is a strategy for change, a tactical program that will bring the Negro into the mainstream of American life as quickly as possible."

3. *Plans must be set in place to counteract the opposition.*
   "When evil men plot, good men must plan. When evil men burn and bomb, good men must build and bind."

4. *A detailed plan is needed to channel the masses and keep them headed in the same direction.*
   "We need a chart. We need a compass. Indeed, we need some North Star to guide us into a future shrouded with impenetrable uncertainties."

5. *Goals unify people.*
   "[People are united despite] differences of age and social status. [They are] all united around one objective. This is a powerful force which no society may wisely ignore."

6. *Goals motivate people.*
   "In any movement, you have to have some simple demand around which you galvanize forces."

7. *Goals stimulate action.*
   "Progress whets the appetite for greater progress, and the

nearer you get to the goal, often, the more determined you are to get there. . . . [There is a] glowing excitement to reach creative goals."

Martin's specific philosophy around setting goals centered on several basic and fundamental notions:

- "Goals must be clearly stated."
- "The simplest approach will prove to be the most effective."
- "[Don't] aim too low."
- "Find something that is so possible, so achievable, so pure, so simple . . . so basic to life that even the [extremists] can't disagree with it all that much."

Keeping these points in mind, Martin worked with his team to set lofty, sweeping goals for the movement around which people could unite. Those who participated in the movement, for example, were going "to end poverty, to extirpate prejudice, to free a tormented conscience, to make a tomorrow of justice, fair play and creativity." They were going to "create a beloved community," with the goal of basic integration because it is "morally and legally right." "Let us make our intentions crystal clear," said Martin. "We must and we will be free. We want freedom now. We do not want freedom fed to us in teaspoons over another 150 years. Under God, we were born free. Misguided men robbed us of our freedom. We want it back."

Such grandiose goals do not change with time—no matter how long the organization lasts or the movement goes on. On the other hand, Martin also worked with his team to set more specific objectives which were designed to mobilize action. These types of goals do, in fact, change with time. Such things as new ideas, learning from past mistakes, achievement of prior goals, and new obstacles to overcome necessitate a constant reevaluation of short-term objectives. When the civil rights movement entered new phases, strategies changed and, therefore, so did specific goals that accompanied those strategies.

During the early years of 1955–1957, main objectives included securing basic human rights and the right to vote. "We must gain the ballot," preached Martin at the time. "So long as I do not firmly and irrevocably possess the right to vote I do not possess myself. I cannot make up my mind—it is made up for me." In 1960, there was a goal to desegregate all public eating facilities in the major southern cities. In 1963, the goal was focused on awakening the moral spirit of the nation so that Congress would feel the will of the people to act on civil rights legislation. In 1965, during the Selma movement, goals not only focused on the *right* to vote, but also abolishing "voting restrictions, the poll tax, and police brutality." In 1966, in Chicago, there was a major focus on school and housing integration. And, in 1967, Martin stressed that "our emphasis must be two-fold: We must create full employment or we must create incomes."

Not one to simply offer goals to members of the organization, Martin King also stressed action in attaining those objectives. "Achievement of these goals," he noted, "will be difficult and require . . . discipline, understanding, organization, and sacrifice. . . . We must seek to develop a constructive action program to solve them." He also pointed out that "long years of experience" taught him that specific goals could be achieved when "four things occur": 1) nonviolent demonstrators go into the streets to exercise their constitutional rights; 2) racists resist by unleashing violence against them; 3) Americans of conscience in the name of decency demand federal intervention and legislation; 4) the administration, under intense pressure, initiates measures of immediate intervention and remedial legislation.

Establishing goals and gaining their acceptance from members of the organization are both indispensable and crucial tools for effective leadership. The best leaders work with their team to set goals—and then they strive to communicate them to the masses. Recall the definition of leadership: *Leaders act . . . for certain shared goals that represent the values—the wants and needs, the aspirations and expectations—. . . of the people they represent.* Having such a specific purpose serves to facilitate action and decisiveness. Once common objectives are established, a leader can look at nearly any issue and state: "Since it's in keeping with our goal, it is an easy decision to make"; or, conversely, a leader may say: "It's not tied to one of our goals. Let's not do it." Either way, having solid goals and objectives allows any issue to be placed in perspective— which, in turn, makes decision-making easier. Moreover, with a clear plan of action, the process of change is made easier because the natural fear that accompanies any change is eliminated. People focus not on the change but rather on working toward achieving their mission.

Essentially, a detailed plan of action, accompanied by specific goals, serves to mobilize people toward the future. It provides much-needed context and purpose for members of the organization. It helps unify people, motivate them, focus their talent and energy. Proper planning also helps a person— or an organization—*achieve* things.

So it was that Martin Luther King, Jr., and a handful of staff members entered Birmingham, Alabama, to change the course of American history—armed only with a set of goals, a detailed plan of action, and a determination to succeed.

The campaign officially began on April 3, 1963, with the implementation of a full-fledged economic boycott coupled with a few days of carefully timed and coordinated lunch counter sit-ins at five downtown stores. "Being prepared for a long struggle," Martin later explained, "we felt it best to begin modestly, with a limited number of arrests each day. By rationing our energies in this manner, we would help toward the buildup and drama of a growing campaign."

Steadily, the demonstrations grew more pronounced with

each passing day. On April 6, a small group of protesters were arrested and hauled off in paddy wagons after a peaceful march to city hall. There were also a series of sit-ins at the public library and kneel-ins at carefully selected white churches. Then, when the effects of the Easter economic boycott began to be felt, business leaders began to complain to city officials. In response, an injunction was obtained on April 10 ordering the cessation of all demonstrations until the arguments could be heard in court.

Martin then assembled his team to consider the injunction. After several hours of discussion in Room 30 of the Gaston Motel, the group decided to disobey the court order. It marked the first time that the movement would strategically and intentionally defy the courts—but it would not be the last. Martin then stunned the opposition by holding a press conference to announce the decision. "[It is] obvious to us," he said, "that the courts of Alabama [have] misused the judicial process in order to perpetuate injustice and segregation." The group had also decided to hold a march on Good Friday, April 12, "because of its symbolic significance." At that time, Martin said, he and Ralph Abernathy would "present our bodies as personal witnesses in this crusade." Later, at that night's mass meeting, he vowed to the cheering crowd that "Injunction or no injunction, we're going to march. Here in Birmingham, we have reached the point of no return. Now they will know that an injunction can't stop us."

But shortly after that statement was made, a crisis developed that had the potential to halt the entire Birmingham movement. Word arrived from Harry Belafonte in New York that bail bond funds were depleted. And with dozens of demonstrators languishing in jail, renewed pressure was placed on Martin to hit the campaign fund-raising trail. At another hastily called meeting of the staff at the Gaston Motel, Martin was advised by his team that he should not go to jail, that money needed to be raised, and that he was the only one who could do it.

Then came a defining moment in the life of Martin Luther King, Jr., and the American civil rights movement. Without speaking, he stood up and went back to his own bedroom to be alone for a few minutes. Upon his return, he was no longer dressed in his black suit, but instead was wearing a pair of blue jeans and a work shirt. "I don't know what will happen," he told the members of his team. "I don't know where the money will come from. But I'm going to jail."

On Good Friday, April 12, Martin, Ralph Abernathy, and a large group of demonstrators began their march on downtown Birmingham. Within five blocks, they were met by Police Commissioner Bull Connor and a large contingent of his officers. The protesters were informed they were under arrest for violating the recent court injunction and then were promptly loaded into paddy wagons. Upon arrival at the Birmingham jail, everyone was locked up together except Martin, who was put by himself in a dark cell without a mattress, blanket, or pillow. He was not allowed to make any phone calls and his lawyers, who were blocked by Connor, were not allowed in to see him.

Wyatt Walker, incensed at the way Martin was being treated, sent a telegram to President Kennedy urging him to intercede. A few days later, after a series of phone calls between movement leaders and representatives of the federal government, President Kennedy called Coretta personally and assured her that her husband was safe and would be calling her from the jail shortly. Within a half hour, Martin was given a pillow and mattress by his jailers and then escorted to a telephone where a call was placed to his wife.

After reassuring Coretta that he was okay, and hearing from her that the president had intervened in his behalf, Martin's spirits began to pick up. He was soon taken back to his cell and given a copy of the *Birmingham News* to read up on the local news. In addition to several accounts of recent events, the paper contained a statement issued by eight white clergymen who voiced objections to the demonstrations.

While commending the police and condemning King, they urged the African-American community to cease demonstrations and work through the courts instead. These were all objections and criticisms Martin had heard before but, generally, he had little time to sit down and compose responses. However, being in solitary confinement with nothing else to do, he started writing a reply to the white clergymen in the margins of the newspaper.

"While confined here in the Birmingham city jail, I came across your recent statement calling our present activities 'unwise and untimely,' " he began. "I would like to answer your statement in what I hope will be patient and reasonable terms. . . ."

Martin then stated in some detail that his team "did not move irresponsibly into direct action," and he described the technique as "a type of constructive nonviolent tension that is necessary for growth. You may well ask," he said, " 'Why direct action? Why sit-ins, marches, etc.? Isn't negotiation a better path?' You are exactly right in your call for negotiation. . . . Direct action seeks to create such a crisis and establish such creative tension that a community that has constantly refused to negotiate is forced to confront the issue. . . . So the purpose of direct action," Martin concluded, "is to create a situation so crisis-packed that it will inevitably open the door to negotiation."

Toward the end of the letter, Martin also appealed to the conscience of the white clergymen. "I had hoped," he lectured them, "that the white moderate would understand that law and order exist for the purpose of establishing justice, and that when they fail to do this they become dangerously structured dams that block the flow of social progress. I had hoped that the white moderate would understand that the present tension of the South is merely a necessary phase of the transition from an obnoxious negative peace, where the Negro passively accepted his unjust plight, to a substance-filled positive peace, where all men will respect the dignity and worth of human personality."

And he went on to say: "Oppressed people cannot remain oppressed forever. The urge for freedom will eventually come. . . . In spite of my shattered dreams of the past, I came to Birmingham with the hope that the white religious leadership of this community would see the justice of our cause, and with deep moral concern, serve as the channel through which our just grievances would get to the power structure. I had hoped that each of you would understand. But again I have been disappointed."

Martin concluded his statement with a couple of paragraphs commending the clergymen, and this eloquent statement of optimism: "I have no despair about the future. I have no fear about the outcome of our struggle in Birmingham, even if our motives are presently misunderstood. We will reach the goal of freedom in Birmingham because the goal of America is freedom. Abused and scorned though we may be, our destiny is tied up with the destiny of America."

First published in a small pamphlet, more than a million copies of Martin King's *Letter from Birmingham Jail* were quickly distributed across the nation. As such, it became a key communication expressing the goals and philosophy of the American civil rights movement. More than that, however, its basis in the goodness of man—along with its eloquence—served to inspire and motivate many people to the cause.

His imprisonment, however, had slowed the Birmingham demonstrations to a crawl. People had gone eleven days without their leaders and no one was taking any action on their own initiative. Then, on April 22, Martin, Ralph, and the other protesters were tried and convicted of violating the injunction banning all protests. The judge sentenced them to five days in jail and a $50 fine. By this time, however, Harry Belafonte had raised enough bond money to bail out the movement's leaders. And Martin, realizing that he needed to rejuvenate the movement, paid the bond and instructed his lawyers to appeal the conviction.

The first thing Martin did upon his release was call his team together to regroup. During that conference, they decided to "pick up the action because the press is leaving" by strategically setting out to recruit more troops. There was only one problem, however. Nearly all the local adults who were willing to participate were already in jail. As Wyatt Walker remembered, "We had scraped the bottom of the barrel of adults who could go." The team then debated the idea of recruiting high school students to help "fill the jails." In the end, a consensus was reached to move forward on that plan. So the direct action team went out to Birmingham's black high schools, talked to students, and circulated leaflets. While Martin was hesitant about the strategy, Ralph Abernathy later called the decision to bring the children into the protests "an act of wisdom, divinely inspired."

On May 2, the time set for the children to march, a principal at one high school locked the gates in an attempt to prevent the students from leaving. But hundreds of young people scaled the fences and headed toward the 16th Street Baptist Church where the protest was to begin. In addition, many hundreds of younger, grade-school-aged children showed up to participate.

Three waves of the youngsters were sent out in a coordinated effort led by Andrew Young and James Bevel. They were met by Bull Connor, who, this time, had not only an army of officers, but police dogs, fire hoses, and an armored tank. As the first group of children were led to the paddy wagons, they began singing "Ain't Gonna Let Nobody Turn Us Around" and "We Shall Overcome."

But the second and third waves had a different fate. As the group moved toward the policemen, they were shouting, "We want freedom. We want freedom." Connor, whose patience finally had run out, simply said: "Let 'em have it." With that command, firemen turned on hoses with pressure so high it actually stripped the bark off trees. Adults and high school students were smashed against buildings and washed down the streets. Children were viciously attacked and bitten by the unleashed German shepherd police dogs. Some adults became so enraged that they began to throw bricks and bottles—a breach of the nonviolent covenant. When that happened, the police surged forward with billy clubs in hand and beat, kicked, and mauled everyone in sight. The crowd finally broke and rushed back to the church. "Look at those niggers run," Bull Connor bellowed.

The arrogant segregationist police chief, however, had made a fatal mistake. He had unleashed his power on innocent victims in front of national news cameras. The next day, the media had a field day—splashing pictures of police dogs biting children, hoses knocking down teenagers, and officers brutally beating adults. There was no lack of participants in Birmingham after those photos appeared. Even President Kennedy said the images made him "sick."

The SCLC's conscious and skillful manipulation of the mass media had worked, as the eyes of the nation were now focused on Birmingham. As the press followed the next several days of marches, they reported every detail, including the fact that, at the height of the demonstrations, nearly three thousand people had been arrested—and that Connor had no place to put them. According to Martin, it was "the first time in the civil rights movement that we were able to put into effect the Gandhian principle of 'Fill up the jails.'"

On May 5, another defining moment in the modern era of nonviolent direct action occurred. As more than one thousand people headed toward the Birmingham jail on a prayer pilgrimage, they halted upon encountering Bull Connor's men. Martin, who was coordinating events on a walkie-talkie, watched the leaders in the front of the crowd kneel and pray. When they rose to move forward, Connor ordered his men to turn on the hoses. But the firemen just stood there, some with tears in their eyes. "Dammit!" yelled Connor. "Turn on the hoses!" As the demonstrators marched slowly forward, the ranks of firemen and policemen parted and allowed the young people to proceed. "It was one of the most fantastic events of the Birmingham story," Martin recalled. "I saw there, for the first time, the pride and the power of nonviolence."

With the world's media focused on Birmingham; with Connor's forces no longer willing to fight back; with the economic boycott now taking a significant toll on business; and with the jails filled—Birmingham's officials finally decided to contact black leaders and open negotiations. Accordingly, Martin, Andrew Young, and Wyatt Walker met secretly with white leaders at a private residence to begin hammering out a settlement.

Martin, after opening with a lofty statement, told those at the table that he had called a one-day moratorium on demonstrations, and then turned his side of the dialogue over to Andrew and Wyatt—who were more skilled at detailed negotiations. Walker played the hard-liner as he presented four basic demands: 1) all store facilities to be immediately desegregated; 2) new nondiscriminatory hiring practices to be instituted; 3) all charges to be dropped against protesters; and 4) creation of a biracial committee to monitor progress and develop new programs. When the entrenched leaders hemmed and hawed and then proposed a ninety-day cooling-off period, Wyatt ranted and raved while Andrew tried to reason by quoting the law. Both men were playing their roles well. They had done it a few times before.

After several hours, consensus was reached on three of the four points, but they could not agree on what to do with bonding and legal fees for the several thousand jailed demonstrators. With neither side willing to budge, Wyatt threatened to resume demonstrations, but Andrew and Martin searched for another answer. It was clear that the movement did not have the price of the bonds, nor could Belafonte raise the more than $150,000 needed. It was at this point that Martin's alliance-building paid a great dividend. The Kennedy administration took action and got the United Auto Workers and the Maritime Workers unions to guarantee the bonds.

On May 10, then, the "Birmingham Truce Agreement" was announced. It essentially gave the movement everything they wanted with a transition interval and a phase-in period ranging from two to three months. Martin King then issued a statement complimenting the white leaders as "men of good will" and hailing the personal courage of Fred Shuttlesworth, who had been seriously injured during the demonstrations. In a dramatic and courageous show of support, President Kennedy subsequently gave a national television address praising the settlement and pledging that he would not allow the agreement to be breached.

The success at Birmingham proved to be a turning point in the American civil rights movement. For Martin, it was dramatic affirmation that the technique of nonviolent direct action could work. More profound, however, was the impact it had on the rest of the nation. By the end of the summer, more than nine hundred cities across the country—North, South, East, and West—had ignited in a series of nonviolent protests. The largest such demonstration occurred in Washington, D.C., on August 28, 1963. By 1:00 P.M. that day, more than 200,000 people had assembled between the Lincoln Memorial and the Washington Monument to hear a series of speakers demand freedom and civil liberties from their national government. Martin culminated the historic occasion with his most famous oration—the eloquent and inspiring "I Have a Dream" speech.

One of the most significant facts of the historic March on Washington was that one quarter of the people gathered together were white—marking their first large-scale participation in the civil rights movement. They had been moved by the events of Birmingham—and so had the rest of the nation. That summer, President Kennedy proposed to Congress the most comprehensive, far-reaching civil rights legislation ever conceived. By the fall, schools across the South were integrating without even the slightest hint of violence.

The goal Martin's team had set prior to Birmingham—to "awaken the moral conscience of America" and produce federal legislation that would force desegregation everywhere—had been achieved. But the price was high.

Immediately after the announcement of the Birmingham Agreement, bombs exploded at the home of Martin's brother and at Room 30 of the Gaston Motel. Even though no one was harmed in the blasts, angry African-Americans rioted in the streets of downtown Birmingham—causing Martin to rush to the site and plead for peace and nonviolence. At the University of Alabama in Tuscaloosa, Governor George Wallace blocked the door of the administration building when Deputy Attorney General Nicholas Katzenbach attempted to enroll two black students under federal court order. Only when President Kennedy federalized the Alabama National Guard did Wallace leave.

In Jackson, Mississippi, NAACP field secretary Medgar Evers was shot and killed in the driveway of his home by a white segregationist. This first assassination of a black civil rights leader set off race riots as far away as Harlem. Martin and a host of prominent African-Americans journeyed to Jackson to attend Evers's funeral. And in Birmingham on September 15, less than a week after school desegregation began, a large bomb exploded at the 16th Street Baptist Church while Sunday school was in session. Four girls, all fourteen years old, were killed and twenty other children were injured.

Again riots broke out in the streets. And again, Martin rushed to the scene to preach nonviolence, to console the bereaved, and to personally walk through the bombed-out wreckage of the church. He stayed and gave a eulogy at the funeral for the girls, but never got over the impact of the deaths. "I shall never forget the grief and bitterness I felt on that terrible September morning when a bomb blew out the lives of those four little, innocent girls sitting in their Sunday-school class," he would later write. "I can remember thinking that if men were this bestial, was it all worth it? Was there any hope? Was there any way out?"

Meanwhile, the United States Supreme Court, in a split decision, upheld the convictions of King, Abernathy, and the other civil rights leaders for violating the Birmingham court injunction against demonstrating. As a result, Martin was sent back to jail to serve his five-day sentence.

---

"What is needed is a strategy for change, a tactical program that will bring the Negro into the mainstream of American life as quickly as possible."

Martin Luther King, Jr., 1967

---

"When evil men plot, good men must plan. When evil men burn and bomb, good men must build and bind."

Martin Luther King, Jr.

# MARTIN LUTHER KING, JR., ON LEADERSHIP

★ Create a noble mission around which everyone can rally.
★ Set a precise timetable for action.
★ Conduct a whirlwind campaign of meetings to mobilize every key person and group behind your movement.
★ Put the horse before the cart.
★ Clearly state your goals and remember that the simplest approach will prove to be the most effective.
★ In setting your goals, don't aim too low—but set something that is achievable.
★ Sweeping grandiose goals do not change with time. On the other hand, specific and detailed goals must change as circumstances change.
★ Be prepared for a long struggle. Begin modestly.
★ When you have the time, respond to unjust criticism.
★ Remember that if people go too long without a leader, little if any action will be taken.
★ Upon conclusion of a settlement, go out of your way to praise all sides.
★ Action is not in itself a virtue; its goals and its forms determine its value.
★ The best way to solve any problem is to remove the cause.
★ Organize your strength in terms of economic and political power.

> "Ultimately, a genuine leader is not a searcher for consensus, but a molder of consensus. I would rather be a man of conviction than a man of conformity."
>
> Martin Luther King, Jr.,
> March 31, 1968

> "There comes a time when one must take the position that it is neither safe nor politic nor popular, but he must do it because his conscience tells him it is right."
>
> Martin Luther King, Jr.,
> March 31, 1968

> "I want to think it over."
>
> Martin Luther King, Jr.,
> standard response
> when asked to make a
> snap decision

# 9 / Be Decisive

Emotions were running high when the SCLC staff gathered together the evening after a joint funeral for the four girls killed in the bombing of Birmingham's 16th Street Baptist Church. Martin had delivered an eloquent eulogy that afternoon where he said, in part: "These children—unoffending; innocent and beautiful—were the victims of one of the most vicious, heinous crimes ever perpetrated against humanity." At the same time, though, he cautioned against taking any vengeful actions: "In spite of the darkness of this hour we must not despair," he said. "We must not become bitter; nor must we harbor the desire to retaliate with violence."

Still, a few individuals proposed an extreme response to the tragedy that included, among other things: recruitment, formation, and drilling of a real nonviolent army; development of a revolutionary flag and insignia; an assault on Alabama's capital city of Montgomery; cutting off communications from the state capitol building; protesters lying down on railroad tracks, airport runways, and bus driveways; refusing to pay taxes; petitioning the federal government not to recognize the government of Alabama; forcing removal of George Wallace as governor; and then full-scale revolution.

The proposal was far too radical for Martin to accept, especially since it was advocating a series of extremely violent confrontations—which was clearly against his own personal philosophy and the organization's policy of nonviolence. Martin's reflex response was to blurt out: "Oh, now wait. Let's think about this." He is also reported to have laughed at the suggestion that people throw themselves in front of buses and trains. But, then again, he realized that such a fanatical suggestion was based on the emotion of the moment. After all, four children had been murdered and twenty others injured in a crime that clearly inflamed everyone's emotions. It was only natural to think about retaliating with some sort of equal response. Martin and other members of the staff did not explicitly say no to the proposal, but their reply that it would have to be carefully and more fully explored left little doubt that such an extreme plan would not be seriously considered.

Still, there was a need to reevaluate and reconsider overall strategy. So, over the next few months, several two- or three-day retreats were convened to discuss future direction for both the SCLC and the movement as a whole. Martin asked the leadership to consider whether the organization should expand from merely a coalition of member affiliates to a more formal national membership association similar to the NAACP. He also wanted not only to focus on the financial condition of the organization through increased fund-raising efforts, but to make a concentrated effort to increase general office efficiency. International attention from Birmingham had greatly increased exposure of the SCLC. And while that publicity did not solve the funding problem, the current staff was nowhere near equipped to handle the onslaught of mail that now poured into Atlanta from all over the world.

Even more important, though, was the need to consider a broad strategy in the wake of the victory in Birmingham and the remarkable success of the March on Washington. It was clear that Martin did not want the organization to rest on its laurels. He preferred to keep the momentum going. So he posed a few serious questions to his executive leadership team. What should be the direction of the movement? Where should the SCLC go now?

It was while these questions were being debated that Martin received a call for help from Dr. Robert Hayling, a dentist in St. Augustine, Florida. Under his leadership, African-Americans had been working for years to make some progress in the area of civil rights. But it had been an uphill and violent battle.

St. Augustine was the oldest European-founded city in the United States and was laying plans for a grand celebration of its four hundredth anniversary. It was also a city deeply entrenched in the practice of segregation, having been a former center for slave marketing. In fact, it still had a downtown area called the Old Slave Market. Vigilantes also roamed the streets on horseback whenever there were marches and demonstrations, harassing those who participated. For his efforts in fighting segregation and discrimination, Hayling had been kidnapped by the Klan, savagely beaten, and nearly killed. His home had also been bombed and sprayed with gunfire that injured his wife and children.

A meeting was subsequently called to discuss Hayling's request that the SCLC get involved in St. Augustine. After some discussion, it was agreed to move forward in a prudent manner. Hayling was contacted and advised that his group would be allowed to be designated as an SCLC affiliate and Martin agreed to dispatch to the site Hosea Williams, Andrew Young, and some other members of the direct action team.

Once there, Williams held mass meetings, worked with the locals to help them better understand nonviolent techniques, and helped them institute a selective buying campaign and sit-ins at lunch counters. Young, meanwhile, led a small group of men, women, and children on a protest march to the down-town Old Slave Market where they were confronted by an angry mob. When he tried to talk to the white leaders, Young was punched in the face, hit over the back of his head with a club, and knocked unconscious. A brave demonstrator rushed in and dragged him back to the group before he was beaten to death. Upon regaining consciousness, Young got back to the head of the line and led the group forward again—this time through a street lined on both sides with angry, scream-ing white men wielding chains and lead pipes. The march re-sulted in several photographers and newsmen being pummeled mercilessly. Young was again hit over the head, but he kept the small group moving forward until, finally, they all knelt and prayed for a few minutes. Then the protesters re-turned cautiously and quietly to the Shiloh Baptist Church.

Just as he had done in Birmingham, Martin came down to St. Augustine to meet with local people and speak extensively at meetings around town. He also saw to it that the move-ment's demands were presented to the white majority's city and business leadership. Essentially, all they were asking for were three things: 1) desegregation of public facilities; 2) hir-ing of black policemen and firemen; and 3) creation of a bira-cial committee to plan for further desegregation. City leaders, however, refused to even consider the requests. Instead, they filed a court injunction prohibiting any further marches and demonstrations. But a federal judge ruled in favor of the movement and allowed the protests to continue.

When the time was appropriate, Martin, who had been

actively speaking around the country to raise funds, returned to St. Augustine and accompanied a group of demonstrators to a motel that had been targeted because its management refused to serve blacks. Once there, seven of the protesters jumped into the outdoor swimming pool and refused to get out. It was one of the first swim-ins of the civil rights movement. The motel manager became so angry that in retaliation he poured acid and other pool chemicals into the water. But the protesters left only when police officers jumped in to physically remove them.

When Martin then led a group of protesters into the courtyard, they were surrounded by a swarm of sneering white segregationists yelling racial epithets. Hosea Williams remembered being scared to death and wanting to "get the hell out of here." But Martin simply said, "I'm not going to run, Hosea." Another protester recalled being terribly frightened that the group was going to be attacked and beaten. "But King was so calm," Williams recalled. "His eyes—I don't know how to describe eyes like that. You could just look at them and think, well, if he can do it, somehow nothing will happen to me." With that, Martin quietly led the demonstrators out of the courtyard and away from the potentially disastrous situation.

He also decided to lead one of the many nighttime marches the local movement was sponsoring. At an afternoon mass meeting, Martin exhorted the crowd to "march tonight as you've never marched before." And he informed everyone that he was going to jail with them in hopes of forcing the opposition to the negotiating table. "Just hearing him speak gave you the courage to go on," said one member of the audience.

That evening, Martin and a group of demonstrators marched into a restaurant with segregated services. When asked to leave by the owner, Martin not only refused, he spent fifteen minutes engaged in conversation with the man trying to make him see the error of his discriminatory policies. After the police arrived, the demonstrators were arrested and taken to jail. As he was being pushed and manhandled to his cell, Martin passed by several other jailed protesters. A woman reached out to shake his hand and, in response, Martin said: "Hello, sister. I've been in fifteen jails, but this is the first time that I have been treated like a hog." He was then placed in solitary confinement.

While Martin was imprisoned, outside in the streets a white mob assaulted four hundred demonstrators as the police stood idly by. After the protesters broke ranks and ran back to the Shiloh Baptist Church, one adviser suggested that, to protest the increased violence, Martin initiate a hunger strike. But he declined and instead posted bail in order to continue his nationwide fund-raising efforts.

After two full months of continuous demonstrations, things were not going well in St. Augustine. There was still no movement on the part of city leaders, who categorically refused to negotiate. In the meantime, the protests were becoming more and more violent—leading Martin to comment that "we have never worked in [a city] as lawless as this." Moreover, the governor of Florida, Farris Bryant, banned the movement's marches in direct defiance of the federal court order. If the protesters wanted to march, then, they would clearly be beaten and arrested by state authorities—because President Lyndon Johnson, who had recently assumed office after the assassination of John F. Kennedy, refused to send in federal marshals or offer any other assistance.

It was apparent that a decision needed to be made on whether to continue with a massive effort in St. Augustine. In addition, the 1964 Civil Rights Bill was being considered in Congress and, upon passage, would grant all the rights that were being sought in St. Augustine. Would continued efforts help or harm the chances of the bill's passage? Would additional demonstrations be effective in bringing the opposition to the negotiating table? Should the protests be continued if the 1964 Civil Rights Bill was passed by Congress and signed by President Johnson? What should they do?

Whatever the decision was going to be regarding St. Augustine, one thing was certain: Martin King would take the time necessary to devise the proper course of action. That's because, throughout his tenure as leader of the civil rights movement, he was cautious and methodical when it came to deciding big issues. "I live with one deep concern," he once said. "Am I making the right decisions? Sometimes, I am uncertain." Because of that uneasiness, whenever he was asked to make a snap decision, he would invariably reply that he wanted to think it over. One contemporary recalled that Martin preferred to mull over the issue and take what seemed to be an inordinately long period of time to make up his mind. But when he finally announced his decision, he usually "came down on the right side, although it may have taken him a while to get there."

Such deliberateness led him to be criticized regarding the manner in which he made decisions. But it was the same criticism experienced by other great leaders, such as George Washington and Abraham Lincoln, both of whom were taken to task for employing essentially the same decision-making process that Martin King used.

Like Washington and Lincoln, whenever he had a critical decision to make, King usually called together his team, or a close group of counselors. He even formally created what the SCLC termed a research committee, which provided him with advice on a regularly scheduled basis. The group consisted of ten people with diverse skills and abilities. In addition to three members of the SCLC staff, there was a lawyer, a historian, a labor leader, and several businessmen. "I consulted with my lawyers and trusted advisors," he once said about a particularly difficult decision. "Information came in. . . . I reflected. . . . I gave thoughtful consideration. . . . Taking all of this into consideration, I [made my decision]."

It was clear that Martin was willing to make the tough decisions that accompanied his role as a top leader. For him, both major and minor decisions were important because he realized that if they were not made, action would essentially come to a grinding halt. But in order to make the best use of his time, Martin usually delegated to others the smaller, day-to-day decisions that keep an organization running. For instance, during the Montgomery bus boycott, he established an executive committee comprised of all officers of the Montgomery Improvement Association and all its committee heads and then charged them with making decisions on "all minor matters of policy."

When it came to arriving at major decisions, however, he would invariably assemble the research committee, the SCLC staff, or other key people in a room with him to seek out a variety of opinions and then try to arrive at a consensus course of action. One member of the SCLC staff remarked that Martin "had a remarkable facility for sitting through long, contentious meetings and then summarizing what everybody had said." "One of his greatnesses," said another, "was his ability to master, to orchestrate a group of individuals that probably pretty much approached egomania." Andrew Young recalled that Martin would ask "somebody to express as radical a view as possible and somebody to express as conservative a view as possible. . . . He figured the wider variety of opinions you got, the better chance you had of extracting the truth."

In practice, Martin Luther King, Jr., employed a classic decision-making process that included the following four steps:

## 1. Obtain Key Information and Understand All the Facts Involved

Martin frequently went into the field to forage for information himself, or he sent trusted advisers to the field, or he got on the phone and called people who could supply him with answers. All this was part of Martin's desire to get at a basic set of facts—which were not always found on paper. "The tendency of many readers is to accept the printed word of the press as final truth," he wrote. "[But] even our authentic channels of information do not give us objective and unbiased truth. . . . Few people . . . discern the true from the false, the fact from the fiction. Our minds are constantly being invaded by legions of half-truths, prejudices and false facts."

## 2. Consider a Variety of Possible Solutions and the Consequences of Each

Martin then took the time to examine and think about the information that had been gathered. "[There is] need for a tough mind," he said, "characterized by incisive thinking, realistic appraisal, and decisive judgment. The tough-minded person always examines the facts before he reaches conclusions. . . . The tough mind is sharp and penetrating, breaking through the crust of legends and myths and sifting the true from the false."

After examining all the data, Martin and his team would then ponder a variety of options. For example, when considering whether to hold mass demonstrations in just one place at a time or many places simultaneously, the group compiled a list of advantages for both scenarios. The pros of being in one city included: 1) attracts more people to action; 2) more thorough media coverage; 3) prevention of brutality; 4) maintain discipline; 5) more dramatic to have five or six thousand people in jail in one city than scattered in others. The pros of being in many places included: 1) more communities were involved; 2) splits forces; 3) keeps state officials off balance; 4) more leaders developed. From this type of evaluation, it was determined that the SCLC would reap more benefits if it concentrated its major efforts in one city at a time.

Many leaders won't take the time required to arrive at a well-thought-through decision. But Martin viewed it as something of a duty to members of his organization. And clearly, he viewed it as hard work. "Rarely do we find men who willingly engage in hard solid thinking," he said. "There is an almost universal quest for easy answers and half-baked solutions. Nothing pains some people more than having to think."

## 3. Be Certain That Potential Action Is Consistent with Administrative and Personal Policy Objectives

If a vision or mission has been set, if specific long- and short-term goals have been agreed upon, then it's incumbent upon the leader to review each potential action step to make certain that it is in concert with the organization's plans. In this sense, having previously arrived at goals actually fosters decision-making. In the final analysis, a determination to move ahead is easier to make if it clearly falls in line with previous goals. If it is at odds with those goals or is inconsistent with an agreed-upon vision, then the decision is just as easily made to not move forward.

In addition, it is incumbent upon the leader to review the potential action in accordance with the wishes and desires of the members of the organization. The opinions of the vast majority of the people should receive overwhelming weight in making the final decision. "People of good will, who are the vast majority," said Martin, "have the challenge to be open and honest, and to turn a deaf ear to the shrill cries of the irresponsible few on the lunatic fringe."

In this regard, Martin's personal determination and commitment to the cause helped him make key decisions. "I don't believe that anyone could seriously accuse me of not being totally committed to the breakdown of segregation," he once said in an interview. That sentiment clearly guided Martin in his deliberations.

## 4. Effectively Communicate the Decision and Then Implement It

Once the decision is made, it becomes essential to communicate it to the people—not only the decision itself, but the key information gathered and the reasoning that led to the final conclusion. Martin accomplished this final step through press conferences, magazine articles, newsletters, and personal communication—whether through speeches at mass meetings and small gatherings or via private conversations.

In addition, he solicited and expected feedback from people who might have more information to offer or different opinions to express. And should additional pertinent information surface, or should a better way be found, Martin always reserved the right to remain flexible in changing decisions. It was that flexibility, that willingness to change and do the right thing, that became a trademark of his leadership style.

Throughout this four-step decision-making process, Martin did not search for a consensus so much as he tried to shape one. "I don't determine what is right and wrong by taking a Gallup poll of the majority opinion," he once stated. "Ultimately, a genuine leader is not a searcher for consensus, but a molder of consensus. I would rather be a man of conviction than a man of conformity." It follows, then, that Martin's ability to be decisive emanated from his innate courage, self-confidence, and sense of right and wrong. "There comes a time," he said, "when one must take the position that it is neither safe nor politic nor popular, but he must do it because his conscience tells him it is right."

Martin's decisions seemed always to be based on integrity, values, and what was best for the organization as a whole. "I decide on the basis of conscience," he'd explain. "We are always seeking to do the right thing," he'd say. But he also realized that sometimes the line between what was right and what needed to be done was not always a solid, well-marked one. A case in point was the decision he and the SCLC made to defy a judge's injunction not to continue mass demonstrations in the Birmingham campaign. The moral issues surrounding that hard decision had to be well thought through—and they were. "A just law is a law that squares with a moral law," Martin observed. "It is a law that squares with that which is right, so that any law that uplifts human personality is a just law. . . . Any law that degrades the human personality is an unjust law."

It was with this sound reasoning that Martin decided to disobey various court orders. As far as he was concerned, such rulings were unjust. Therefore, the crucial and risky decision to disobey such an edict was justified on moral and ethical grounds. "The individual who disobeys the law," he wrote, "whose conscience tells him it is unjust and who is willing to accept the penalty by staying in jail until that law is altered, is expressing at the moment the very highest respect for law."

From time to time effective decision-making requires taking an unusually tough stance. What happens, for instance, when conventional methods of persuasion are not effective? In order to achieve goals, then, it might become necessary to decide on a more coercive form of action. And in the final analysis, if force has to be used to gain progress, then force has to be used. As a true leader Martin always attempted first to persuade the recalcitrant majority. But when that failed, he was willing to take more drastic steps. "I must frankly say an element of coercion is necessary," he remarked in one interview. "I think [man's] capacity for goodness makes persuasion a very powerful influence, but [his] inclination toward evil makes coercion a necessity. I believe in moral nonviolent coercion," he said at another time, "and never violent or physical, immoral coercion."

Martin King's penchant for involving others in the decision-making process revolved around another observation he had made about human nature—into the basic needs of every human being. He not only felt that people in the organization had the right to participate in their future direction—but that such involvement was a kind of innate liberty that one must possess to feel equal. "The absence of freedom is the imposition of restraint on my deliberations as to what I shall do, where I shall live, or the kind of task I shall pursue," he said in a speech in 1965. "I am robbed of the basic quality of manness. When I cannot choose . . . it means in fact that someone or some system has already made these decisions for me, and I am reduced to an animal. . . . I cannot adequately assume responsibility as a person because I have been made the party to a decision in which I played no part in making."

While Martin actually made these comments in regard to the larger issue of African-American oppression by the white majority, he clearly applied the same general theory on a smaller scale—and, again, his reasoning for doing so was sound. If African-Americans as a group felt oppressed because they were not involved in controlling their own destiny in society, then surely every human being, every individual would feel the same way if decisions were made *for* them by leaders in *their own* organizations. In other words, people simply want to have a say in decisions that affect their lives. They want to be included, to at least know what's going on, to be heard. Such a desire is not a matter of personal power, but rather is more a matter of self-worth.

It often takes more courage and self-confidence to work with people—to convince and persuade them—than it does to dictate or simply issue orders. Certainly, more time is involved in being a leader than in being a dictator. At the same time, though, decisions must be made in a timely manner to keep the organization functioning. Great leaders know that decisiveness is the hallmark of someone who is committed to achieving the organization's overall vision and goals. A final decision stops debate or, as Martin noted: "Decision means cutting off alternatives." Therefore, a leader's ability to decide is also an important tool—perhaps the most important tool—in wielding the power of a leader, which Martin King defined as "the ability to achieve purpose."

Consider for a moment what an organization is like without effective decision-making: nothing happens and opportunities are lost. People wander about aimlessly, aggressive individuals become frustrated, and lethargic people are not motivated. But in an organization with decisive leadership, the atmosphere is dynamic and vibrant. People move with a spring in their step and purpose in their direction. Opportunity seeks out the organization, and the well-focused group—one backed by solid vision and well-thought-out goals—almost always succeeds.

Martin King also understood that executive decision-making is not a string of individual orders. Rather, it is more of a continuous, uninterrupted process that is similar to the beating of a heart that sends blood throughout a body. Without it there is no life.

Therefore, when events stalled and reached a stalemate in St. Augustine, Florida, during the summer of 1964, Martin knew that a decision had to be made—if for no other reason than to keep the heartbeat of the movement pulsating. So he quickly began consulting with members of his research committee to discuss the issue.

The facts were that the campaign was not going well, that the Klan would ignite significant violence should any more night marches occur, and that the civil rights bill pending in Congress would probably grant all the rights they were seeking in St. Augustine anyway. The group next narrowed their options by determining to either stay in the city and continue the demonstrations or pull out. The second option was not inconsistent with a pattern they had followed in Albany a few years before—but it would preclude them from receiving a victory like they had won in Birmingham. Martin pressed to leave. "I want out of St. Augustine," he said. "But I must come out with honor." A consensus decision was then reached to pull out if, and only if, a formal committee could be set up to work on future means of ending segregated practices in the city.

Intermediaries were then dispatched to inform local white leadership of the proposal. With some prodding by Florida's governor, a senator, and some other key individuals in the federal government, St. Augustine officials agreed to the deal. Governor Bryant then publicly announced the establishment of a biracial committee for the express purpose of opening negotiations. Martin responded in a press conference that such a development was "a significant first step" and, in a show of good faith, suspended all marches and demonstrations "for a period of two weeks." Then he and the SCLC field representatives went back to Atlanta.

Critics termed the entire ending a face-saving maneuver—which it was. Clearly, the SCLC's entrance into St. Augustine was more akin to the lack of preparation associated with the Albany campaign than it was with the well-thought-through Birmingham operation. But while St. Augustine did not culminate in a clear-cut victory, neither did it result in a terrible defeat. Additionally, national publicity surrounding the violence in St. Augustine helped the 1964 Civil Rights Bill pass through Congress. And Martin was present at the White House ceremony just a few days later when, on July 2, President Johnson signed the bill into law.

Such a potentially great stride forward in the civil rights movement, however, was once again met with white retaliation and black violence. In the small town of Philadelphia, Mississippi, three civil rights workers (two white and one black) were abducted and brutally murdered by white segregationists. The three young men had volunteered from other parts of the country to come down to Mississippi and help register black voters prior to November's presidential election. Their bodies were eventually found buried in an earthen dam after a massive manhunt that included hundreds of FBI agents, sailors of the navy, and other local and federal authorities.

But the violence was not only limited to the South this time. By mid-July, riots had broken out in Harlem and Newark after a black youth was gunned down by a white policeman. Similar uprisings also occurred in the slums of Jersey City, Chicago, and Philadelphia. Martin, at the request of New York City's mayor, flew up to Harlem to try and reestablish order. Once there, he walked through the rubble of the riot zones and, when he pleaded for everyone to abide by the doctrine of nonviolence, he was jeered and stoned by local African-Americans.

But Martin kept right on preaching his message. He also turned to the local city government and lectured them on the unnecessary use of force and tried to make them understand that much of the problem they were experiencing was of their own making. "America will be faced with the ever-present threat of violence, rioting and senseless crime," he said, "as long as Negroes by the hundreds of thousands are packed into malodorous, rat-plagued ghettoes, as long as Negroes are smothered by poverty in the midst of an affluent society; like exiles in their own land."

Just a few months later, in stark contrast to the criticism and violence directed his way in his own country, Martin Luther King, Jr., was informed that, at the age of thirty-five, he was to become the youngest person ever awarded the Nobel Peace Prize. It seems that all the publicity from the Birmingham campaign and the March on Washington in 1963 had focused world attention on his role in the American civil rights movement. Now the cause, he believed, would surely receive the attention and focus it truly deserved.

So, with Coretta and his parents in the entourage, Martin flew to Oslo, Norway, where he personally accepted the award on behalf of "twenty-two million Negroes of the United States of America [who] are engaged in a creative battle to end the long night of racial injustice." And everyone knew that he meant exactly what he said when he announced that the entire $54,000 prize would be donated to the civil rights movement. Martin did not keep even one penny for himself or his family.

Upon his return to the United States, he again stopped in the riot-torn areas of Harlem before heading home. While there, he was asked what plans he had now that he was a Nobel laureate. "For the past several days I have been on the mountaintop," he told those gathered to hear him speak. "[But] my brothers and sisters down in Mississippi and Alabama can't register to vote. I've got to go back. There are those who need hope.

"I wish I could just stay on the mountain," he said, "but I must go back to the valley."

---

"Rarely do we find men who willingly engage in hard, solid thinking. There is an almost universal quest for easy answers and half-baked solutions. Nothing pains some people more than having to think."

Martin Luther King, Jr.,
1963

---

"People of good will, who are the vast majority, have the challenge to be open and honest, and to turn a deaf ear to the shrill cries of the irresponsible few on the lunatic fringe."

Martin Luther King, Jr.,
January 1965

# MARTIN LUTHER KING, JR., ON LEADERSHIP

★ When there is a need to reevaluate and reconsider, hold several retreats to discuss future direction.

★ Create a committee that provides you with advice on a regularly scheduled basis.

★ Delegate to others the small, day-to-day decisions that keep an organization running.

★ When considering major decisions, assemble trusted advisers together and confer with them.

★ Remember that the wider range of opinions you hear, the better chance you have of extracting the truth.

★ When making a decision, understand the facts, consider various solutions and their consequences, make sure that the decision is consistent with your objectives, and effectively communicate and implement it.

★ Remember that nothing pains some people more than having to think.

★ Having previously determined goals fosters decision-making.

★ You have the responsibility to turn a deaf ear to the shrill cries of the irresponsible few on the lunatic fringe.

★ Man's capacity for goodness makes persuasion a very powerful influence, but his inclination toward evil sometimes makes coercion a necessity.

★ Remember that people want to be included in decisions that affect their future. This is not a matter of personal power, but one of self-worth.

★ Power is the ability to achieve purpose.

★ A strong person must be militant as well as moderate; a realist as well as an idealist.

★ As a leader, you must move past indecision to action.

# PART III

# WINNING WITH PEOPLE

*"We are always seeking to do the right thing."*

MARTIN LUTHER KING, JR.,
APRIL 26, 1956

"We are not asking, we are demanding the ballot. . . . If you don't do something about it, we will have no alternative but to engage in broader and more drastic forms of civil disobedience in order to bring the attention of the nation to this whole issue in Selma, Alabama."

> Martin Luther King, Jr.,
> January 2, 1965

"No work is insignificant. If a man is called a street sweeper, he should sweep streets even as Michelangelo painted, or Beethoven composed music, or Shakespeare wrote poetry. He should sweep streets so well that all the host of heaven and earth will pause to say, 'Here lived a great street sweeper who did his job well.'"

> Martin Luther King, Jr.,
> December 1956

"We must demonstrate, teach and preach, until the very foundations of our nation are shaken."

> Martin Luther King, Jr.,
> February 25, 1967

# *10 / Teach and Preach*

Even as Martin King was receiving the Nobel Prize for Peace in Norway, his leadership of the American civil rights movement was being challenged at home. Things were just moving too slow for the younger, more impatient members of the Student Nonviolent Coordinating Committee, who were expanding their operations in the deep South without waiting for the SCLC's permission. And in New York, a fiery young religious leader named Malcolm X was preaching a more militant approach in his direction of the Black Muslims. In his most modest reproaches, he had simply disagreed with the nonviolent method of change. However, at his most extreme, Malcolm had labeled Martin an "Uncle Tom" and accused him of "selling out to the white devil."

Such criticism was due, in part, to the slow implementation and limitations of new, hard-won laws. The Civil Rights Bill of 1964, for example, definitely increased the federal government's power to ban discrimination in public places, but it did little toward allowing African-Americans the right to participate in the political process—as they were not permitted to be delegates in either the Democratic or Republican party's southern state conventions. Nor did the bill do much to enforce an African-American's right to vote. As a matter of fact, in most southern states, blacks were still denied the unencumbered freedom to even register to vote.

SNCC's national chairman, John Lewis, had moved to Selma, Alabama, to supervise the organization's activities toward not only integrating public facilities after passage of the Civil Rights Act but to secure blacks the right to vote. In the preceding few years, SNCC had also launched a series of nonviolent workshops (which they had learned how to do from the SCLC) to prepare the masses for a larger campaign. Then, in 1964, they organized a bus boycott after a pregnant woman was killed while trying to get off a bus. The driver had not given her the time to disembark and she was dragged along the street.

As in other deep South towns, though, resistance to change was high among the entrenched white establishment. Selma, a town of thirty thousand—50 percent of whom were African-American—had been a prosperous slave market along the banks of the Alabama River prior to the Civil War. As such, there was very little willingness to grant blacks anything, let alone the right to vote. Registrar offices, for instance, were usually open only a few hours a week and, during those appointed times, state employees showed up late and left early. Unfair literacy tests were also required even though local people regularly demonstrated against such prejudicial practices.

In December 1964, several months after an Alabama judge issued a ban on demonstrations and meetings, African-Americans became hesitant about congregating. As a result, SNCC began to lose crucial momentum. It was at this point that Amelia Boynton, a well-known local businesswoman and civil rights activist, approached Martin and the Southern Christian Leadership Conference about getting involved in Selma. There was no better place than Selma to begin an Alabama voter registration campaign, she told the group.

Tending to agree, the SCLC's executive leadership team, while mindful of potential friction with SNCC, decided to move forward and get involved in the Selma struggle. First, however, they initiated three days of testing to determine compliance to the newly passed civil rights legislation. Their findings revealed that most of Alabama, including Montgomery and Birmingham, had desegregated public facilities fairly well. However, violations were widespread in Selma. As a result, the SCLC determined to begin there with a much larger, statewide campaign aimed at voter registration. This new endeavor included plans to distribute a pamphlet entitled *Project for Alabama: Political Freedom Movement;* initiation of direct action techniques; mass demonstrations and mass arrests; a staged event to get Martin King arrested; a communication from jail similar to the *Letter from Birmingham Jail.* The only hitch was that Martin and his team wanted the effort to be a joint initiative with SNCC leaders. After all, they had been there first and done a lot of the groundwork. It would also be a good way to ease tensions and resolve any lingering disputes.

So Martin journeyed to Selma to confer with John Lewis and other SNCC leaders and to speak at the campaign's kick-off mass meeting on January 2, 1965. Much to everyone's relief, local police did not enforce the state judge's ban. When Martin was introduced, the seven hundred people gathered in the Brown Chapel AME Church gave him an enthusiastic standing ovation. "Today marks the beginning of a determined, organized, mobilized campaign to get the right to vote everywhere in Alabama," he told the crowd. "We are not asking, we are demanding the ballot," he went on to say. "It's time for us to say to these men that if you don't do something about it, we will have no alternative but to engage in broader and more drastic forms of civil disobedience in order to bring the attention of the nation to this whole issue in Selma, Alabama."

Afterward, he met at Mrs. Boynton's house with SCLC and SNCC field leaders to ease tensions between the two groups and to work out more detailed plans. Activities to be coordinated included recruitment of volunteers; holding of initial meetings in local churches; field training; door-to-door canvassing of neighborhoods to register people to vote; and more testing to see if local establishments (such as restaurants, hotels, and other businesses) were adhering to the new Civil Rights Bill. And, in a further effort to decrease friction and increase teamwork, the two groups (SCLC and SNCC) held almost daily meetings over the course of the next two weeks.

C. T. Vivian and James Bevel of the SCLC staff were assigned to be on the ground in Selma. They not only led discussions with local demonstrators—continually preaching the nonviolent message of the movement—they also guided groups in direct action against the establishment. Bevel, for instance, led a group to the courthouse in an effort to register to vote—and was summarily jabbed and beaten with a billy club by Sheriff Jim Clark. When Bevel did not back down, the entire group was arrested and carted off to jail. While there, Bevel took sick, developed a fever, and was chained to a bed in the infirmary. C. T. Vivian, meanwhile, on the steps of the courthouse compared Sheriff Clark to Adolf Hitler where-

upon Clark punched Vivian in the face and knocked him to
the ground in front of rolling cameras. Said a defiant Vivian
immediately afterward to the sheriff: "We're willing to be
beaten for democracy."

Direct action began to pick up within a few weeks as Martin and John Lewis led several hundred Alabamans to the
Selma courthouse to register to vote. Prevented from entering the courthouse, the group stood outside on the sidewalk
for several hours without anyone being arrested before they
went on to test a few business establishments. The very next
day, Sheriff Clark had a violent confrontation with Amelia
Boynton when she did not step from a voter registration line
next to the courthouse into a nearby alley. Completely losing
his cool, Clark grabbed Mrs. Boynton by the scruff of the
neck and roughly pushed her about twenty yards into a waiting patrol car. Unknown to the sheriff, however, a television
cameraman across the street captured the incident—and it was
subsequently shown on the evening news.

Two days later, more than a hundred Selma teachers
marched on the courthouse in protest of Mrs. Boynton's arrest and treatment—all the while knowing full well that they
might be fired from their jobs. The group was turned away by
the sheriff, who poked them with his billy club and refused to
let them continue into the courthouse. In frustration, they finally headed over to the Brown Chapel Church and held a
mass meeting. This was a significant event in the Selma movement because teachers, along with preachers, were part of the
natural leadership of the community. After the teachers
showed the way, everybody in Selma was willing to march—
including the children they taught.

A few weeks later (on February 1), in a well-coordinated
event, Martin was arrested along with 150 other demonstrators as they marched from Brown Chapel to downtown
Selma. Taken to the city jail on the charge of parading without a permit, Martin refused to accept bail. "I must confess,"
he said as he was carted off, "this is a deliberate attempt to

dramatize conditions in this city, state, and community." Martin and Ralph Abernathy were placed in a cell together where, for the first two days, they fasted, prayed, meditated, and sang hymns. They also held meetings with SCLC staff and lawyers. At one point, Martin gave Andrew Young (now the SCLC's executive director) a note that recommended, among other things, that he engage in some activity every day, consider a night march, post bond for essential staff members, and try to attract some big-name celebrities to town.

Martin also penned a brief "Letter from a Selma Jail" that was widely publicized, and was published in the *New York Times* as an open letter to anyone who might be willing to help the movement. "This is Selma, Alabama," he wrote. "There are more Negroes in jail with me than there are on the voting rolls. This is the U.S.A. in 1965. We are in jail simply because we cannot tolerate these conditions for ourselves or our nation. . . ." He concluded the letter by asking for financial contributions to the SCLC. "We need the help of all decent Americans," wrote Martin.

After remaining incarcerated for five days, the two SCLC leaders finally accepted bail. Before they left, though, more than three thousand people had been arrested and stuffed in the jails in and around Selma. Press coverage of the campaign attracted sympathy from all over the nation. Even Malcolm X, the fiery militant activist from New York, paid a brief visit to express his support to SNCC and the SCLC. When Andrew Young tried to get Malcolm in to see Martin, they were turned away by authorities. But to a packed audience in Brown Chapel, Malcolm X stated: "If the white people realize what the alternative is, perhaps they will be more willing to hear Dr. King."

It wasn't long thereafter that reactions by white segregationists to black demonstrations became more intense. Just prior to the first night march in Selma on February 18, for instance, camera lenses were sprayed with black paint so that they could not record the violence. As the large crowd approached the sheriff's men, a major confrontation ensued. Hosea Williams, along with many others, was shocked with an electric cattle prod. Newsman Richard Valeriani was hit in the back of the head with an ax handle. And a young man named Jimmy Lee Jackson was shot at point-blank range and killed by an Alabama state trooper while trying to protect his mother. His death sent shock waves, not only through Selma, but throughout the nation. Speaking at the funeral, Martin expressed the sentiment of an outraged public: "He was killed by every lawless sheriff, by the irresponsibility of every politician who has fed his constituency the stale bread of hatred and the spoiled meat of racism," he said. "He was murdered by the timidity of the federal government. . . ."

In response to Jackson's death, the SCLC proposed a long march from Selma to Montgomery—a distance of some fifty-four miles. It would take five or six days—long enough to bring the issue to the attention of the nation. "I can't promise you that it won't get you killed," Martin told a crowd gathered in the church a few days before the march. "But we must stand up for what is right."

Governor George Wallace tried to stop the event by issuing an executive ban. But the demonstrators were determined to move forward. So, on Sunday, March 7, six hundred people set out from Brown Chapel. Martin King, however, was not among them. The other members of his team advised him not to march because they fully expected some major violence. Reluctantly, he went back to Atlanta to preach to his Ebenezer Baptist congregation. In Martin's absence, Hosea Williams of the SCLC and John Lewis of SNCC led the group out of Selma. Curiously, though, there were no policemen in sight along the city streets. While crossing over the Edmund Pettus Bridge headed out of town, however, Alabama state troopers met the marchers. Some officers were riding horses. Others were carrying billy clubs and dressed in riot gear. All were acting under orders from Governor Wallace to stop the marchers.

"This is an unlawful assembly," said the sheriff to the front-line leaders. "You are ordered to disperse and go back to your church or your homes." When the demonstrators stood their ground, the police formed a wedge and moved forward swinging their clubs. Mounted officers galloped into the throng of demonstrators as white onlookers cheered. As they converged on the people, police fired tear gas into the crowd. Women were battered and men were beaten mercilessly. After several minutes of bloody confrontation during which the nonviolent philosophy was somehow maintained by the demonstrators, everyone turned back toward the church, which essentially became a makeshift hospital. By some accounts, seventy to eighty people had suffered broken ribs, head injuries, broken teeth, and broken wrists, among other injuries. It was a day that would forever be remembered in the civil rights movement as "Bloody Sunday."

For the first two or three hours back at the church, hatred and anger quickly turned to talk of violent retaliation. Many of the demonstrators wanted to go home and get their guns, but Andrew Young, Hosea Williams, and other SCLC-trained staffers talked them down. "What kinds of guns do you have and how are they going to hold up against the automatic rifles and 10-gauge shotguns that the police have got?" they asked. "There are at least 200 shotguns out there with buckshot. Did you ever see what buckshot does to a deer?" Andrew Young later explained that he attempted to make the people think about the specifics of violence—"and then they realized how suicidal and nonsensical it was."

Young and the other SCLC staffers were essentially educating and coaching the people in the church about the dangers of violence and the potential long-term rewards of the movement's nonviolent philosophy. It was significant that, in Selma, they were doing so *on site*—in a potentially disastrous situation. But they had also done it many times before in more formal settings. Why? Because nonviolent direct action was not a technique that came to people naturally. It had to

be taught. Just like the people in the Selma church on Bloody
Sunday, their emotions and natural inclinations turned toward
violent retaliation. But once they thought through the potential repercussions—guided by those who had already been
trained—smarter and cooler heads began to prevail.

It was with this deep, intuitive understanding of human nature—of how people thought and reacted—that Martin
strategically laid out plans in the civil rights movement to educate and coach the masses. He started simply enough in
1956 (toward the end of the Montgomery bus boycott) by
holding a week-long conference entitled "Institution for
Nonviolence and Social Change." A more formal education
process increased gradually and, shortly after the SCLC was
formed, Martin created a "Leadership Training Committee"
that screened and provided intensive instruction for participants in the movement.

One of the first such programs took place in April 1959
when Martin convened a training conference at Shaw University in Raleigh, North Carolina, for the purpose of educating
students taking part in mass demonstrations. With the SCLC
funding the program, several hundred young people gathered
to participate in workshops on nonviolence and direct action
techniques. The idea, said Martin, was to have these things
"in our minds over and over again." In the workshops, people were taught to tolerate, as Martin said, "the harsh language and physical abuse of police," "to be cursed and not to
reply," and "to be beaten and not hit back." He also later
pointed out that "courses where we go through the experience of being roughed up . . . proved very helpful in preparing those who are engaged in demonstrations."

Eventually, the SCLC set up a more formal leadership
training program at a facility in Dorchester, Georgia, designed, as Martin said, to create "noncommissioned officers of
the civil rights movement." Volunteers from across the country came to learn, not only direct action nonviolent techniques, but also to be trained in specific missions such as

conducting voter registration drives like the ones in Selma. Many of the workshops were funded by corporate sponsors. The Ford Foundation, for example, contributed $230,000 in one payment to help kick off the Dorchester facility. And it was people like Andrew Young, Jim and Diane Bevel, James Lawson, and Dorothy Cotton who went through the early training sessions and then became teachers in future sessions. Some people who went through the programs could not pass the strict requirements. Others progressed with flying colors and returned to their local communities to teach others.

Part of the reason for such intensive training was to develop new leaders from the organization's existing ranks—those who could take over when the current leaders were long gone. The struggle, Martin realized, was not going to be won in his lifetime. "We shall have to create leaders who embody virtues we can respect, who have moral and ethical principles we can applaud," he would tell his associates. "Those of you who read and think . . . must assume the leadership responsibility for educating our brothers and sisters."

In general, the more formalized SCLC education centers served to train future leaders from a centralized campus-like facility. But there were also a multitude and a variety of on-site training venues that were designed specifically to mobilize and involve local citizens. Hundreds of people would show up to attend nonviolent workshops and mass meetings, which were a standard part of virtually every campaign conducted by the SCLC during the civil rights movement. In Birmingham, for example, adults, along with children as young as seven years old, took part in the workshops. Martin, who had personally conducted several of those sessions, commented that none of the children were permitted "to engage in any of the demonstrations before going through this kind of teaching session."

Martin's focus on education and training was paramount in his overall leadership philosophy. "Education gives us not only knowledge, which is power, but wisdom, which is control," he wrote in an article early in his career. "[It] gives one not only power of concentration, but worthy objectives upon which to concentrate. . . . To save man from the morass of propaganda is one of the chief aims of education—to discern the true from the false, the real from the unreal, and the facts from the fiction. . . . If an individual can't think critically, he really isn't educated. Intelligence is not enough," said Martin King. "Intelligence plus character—that is the goal of true education."

From his study of African-American history, Martin also realized the impact education had had on overall progress. "At emancipation only five percent of the Negroes were literate," he wrote in 1960. "Today more than ninety-five percent are literate." He also noted that for the first time significant numbers of African-Americans were completing college. This, in turn, had led to "the gradual improvement of his economic status."

So Martin strategically set about using every avenue he could think of for the daunting task of educating the masses—which, of course, was no easy endeavor. "It is a backbreaking task," Martin admitted, "to arouse, to organize, and to educate tens of thousands for disciplined, sustained action." He enlisted the help of the church, which he believed could do "a great deal to remove the fears and the half-truths that are disseminated." He also pointed out that "even the law itself is a form of education. The words of the Supreme Court, of Congress, and of the Constitution are eloquent instructors." And, of course, he made strategic use of the national media to inform and educate. By raising awareness in a public forum, Martin was able, in essence, to educate the entire nation. Accordingly, he and the other leaders of the SCLC strategically choreographed campaigns to have their maximum impact on the public's psyche. He noted, for example, that many "early demonstrations [were] more geared toward educational purposes—to educate the nation on the nature of the problem and the crucial aspects of it."

Knowing that they were the future of the movement, Martin particularly focused on the education and coaching of young people. "We in this generation must stimulate our children to learn and acquire higher levels of skill and technique . . ." he would advocate, "to become more efficient, to achieve with increasing facility the legitimate goals of [their] lives. . . . We must make it clear to our young people that this is an age in which they will be forced to compete with people of all races and nationalities." In a sermon on Mother's Day, 1956, Martin entreated women in the congregation to prepare their children with "a sense of dignity, of self-respect," and an "awareness that they must acquire excellence in everything they do. . . . We must constantly stimulate our youth to rise above the stagnant level of mediocrity and seek to achieve excellence in their various fields of endeavor."

Martin also preached personal responsibility, professional pride, and being the best that a person could be no matter what the situation. "We must seek to do our life's work so well that nobody could do it better . . ." he said. "No work is insignificant. If a man is called a street sweeper, he should sweep streets even as Michelangelo painted, or Beethoven composed music, or Shakespeare wrote poetry. He should sweep streets so well that all the host of heaven and earth will pause to say, 'Here lived a great street sweeper who did his job well.'"

"In the final analysis," said Martin on another occasion, "if first-class citizenship is to become a reality for the Negro, he must assume the primary responsibility for making it so. . . . A productive and happy life is not something that you find; it is something that you make. . . . [And] like life, racial understanding is not something that we find but something that we must create."

For the particular situation in which his organization was engaged, for the grand goal that they were attempting to achieve—which was freedom and equality for African-Americans everywhere—education of the masses was more than just a fundamental leadership principle, it was an absolute necessity. "Historical victories have been won by violence," Martin pointed out. "But the Negro revolution is seeking integration, not independence. . . . Here in America, we've got to live together. We've got to find a way to reconcile ourselves to living in a community, one group with the other. To be successful, the struggle must be waged with resolute efforts that are kept strictly within the framework of our democratic society. This means reaching, educating and moving large enough groups of people of both races to stir the conscience of the nation." Therefore, said Martin, "we must demonstrate, teach and preach, until the very foundations of our nation are shaken."

Martin King committed himself totally to this principle. It was a commitment that would last through the darkest days of the civil rights movement—right up to the last days of his life. "If nonviolent protest fails this summer," he had written in an article that was published two weeks after his death, "I will continue to preach it and teach it."

On Bloody Sunday national television networks broke into regularly scheduled programming and flashed across the country the violent and bloody scenes from Selma's Edmund Pettus Bridge. Almost immediately, the public's wrath came down on local government and the state of Alabama. A defiant George Wallace, however, responded by banning night marches and labeling the SCLC staff "professional agitators with pro-Communist affiliations."

The SCLC's response was to send out a call to people of good will asking them not only to show up in Selma but to deluge the federal government with telegrams asking for intervention. Then Martin released a statement, which said, in part: "In the vicious maltreatment of defenseless citizens of Selma, where old women and young children were gassed and clubbed at random, we have witnessed an eruption of the disease of racism which seeks to destroy all America."

As people from all over the nation, led by hundreds of white clergymen and nuns, began converging on Selma, the

SCLC laid plans for another Selma-to-Montgomery march to commence on Tuesday. Martin King then gathered the entire SCLC executive team together for support and counsel. It was clear that a decision had to be made as to whether or not to march. Everyone agreed that it was Martin's decision alone to make. While he consulted with both his staff and leaders in the SNCC, the pressure not to march became intense. A court order banning the march was issued by a federal judge and President Johnson lobbied King to alter his plans. When Assistant Attorney General John Doar visited Selma to personally express the president's wishes, Martin recalled the conversation: "He very strongly urged us not to march. I listened attentively. I explained why I felt it was necessary to seek a confrontation with injustice on Highway 80. I asked them to try to understand that I would rather die on the highway in Alabama than make a butchery of my conscience." And Martin later wrote that "[I] held on to my decision despite the fact that many people were concerned about breaking the court injunction issued by one of the strongest and best judges in the South."

On Tuesday, March 9, more than two thousand marchers gathered together outside Brown Chapel to begin the march to Montgomery. Martin led the group in prayer. "We have no alternative but to keep moving with determination," he said. "We've gone too far now to turn back. We cannot afford to stop because Alabama and our nation [have] a date with destiny."

Then the huge throng set out toward the Edmund Pettus Bridge—only this time there were both white and black demonstrators—and they were comprised of politicians, labor and church leaders, entertainers, and people who had been beaten just two days earlier on Bloody Sunday. Martin was strategically positioned at the head of the column, along with Ralph Abernathy and other SCLC and SNCC leaders. When the crowd reached the bridge, they were again met by sheriff's deputies, mounted police, and state troopers who shouted orders to cease and desist. The marchers then knelt and prayed. Martin got down on his knees with the others while Abernathy offered a lengthy prayer. But then, seemingly in a direct reversal of his earlier statement about not turning back, Martin rose, turned around, and led the people back to the church.

Many of the marchers expressed disappointment in the turnaround, but Martin—who had hesitated at the last moment and tacitly agreed with federal and state officials not to force another confrontation on the bridge that day—had his reasons. He did not want a recurrence of the awful violence that had happened just a few days earlier. Nor did he want to overtly disobey the federal court order at a moment when he felt there was a good chance to have it overturned. But he went through with what was essentially a symbolic gesture because, as he stated a few days later, "I did it to give them an outlet. I felt that if I had not done it, the pent-up emotions, the inner tensions . . . would have exploded into retaliatory violence."

Over the next ten days there ensued a great deal of maneuvering, lobbying, and position-taking. Sheriff Clark set up barricades around the church to intimidate any potential protesters from marching. The SCLC argued its case in front of federal judge Frank M. Johnson, Jr. George Wallace met for two hours with President Johnson. And Martin King met separately with the president for more than an hour.

After these meetings, Lyndon Johnson addressed the U.S. Congress and proposed a comprehensive voting rights bill aimed at protecting African-Americans' right to vote. "All of us must overcome the crippling legacy of bigotry and injustice," he said. "And we shall overcome." Johnson's use of the slogan of the civil rights movement gave African-Americans a big boost in morale while, at the same time, disheartening the white opposition in Alabama.

But after the president's remarks, riots erupted in Montgomery between defiant whites and determined blacks. After being informed of the violence, Martin immediately drove to the scene to try and calm the situation. While in the streets preaching nonviolence, he was told by Andrew Young of the federal court's ruling (which had just been handed down) on the Selma-to-Montgomery march ban. "Let me give you this segment which I think will come as an expression of deep joy to all of us," he told the crowd. "Judge Johnson has just ruled that we have a legal and constitutional right to march from Selma to Montgomery." That ended the violence in Montgomery—and Martin returned to Selma to lay plans for the full-scale fifty-four-mile march.

Back came the marchers from all over the nation. President Johnson federalized the Alabama National Guard for protection. And on March 21, 3,200 people of all ages and races assembled at the Brown Chapel AME Church to begin their journey to Montgomery. Again, Martin addressed the crowd before they set out. "We are tired now," he said. "We've waited a long time for freedom. Now is the time to make real the promises of democracy. Now is the time to transform Alabama, the heart of Dixie, to join with the heart for brotherhood of peace and good will. Now is the time to make justice a reality for all of God's children."

People then began their journey—marching arm in arm, singing freedom songs, carrying sleeping bags and other provisions. This time, as they crossed the Edmund Pettus Bridge, there were no police officers there to stop or beat them—only those to protect them. The marchers covered seven miles that first day. On one of the rest breaks, Martin pulled two little girls on his lap. He told them it was wonderful to have them there and asked them why they were marching. "So we can be free; so other people can be free; and so troopers can't hit no one," one of the girls replied. "All right," said Martin with a big smile.

As the march progressed, the number of marchers grew steadily. Five days later, more than 25,000 people marched into Montgomery, Alabama. They marched past Dexter Avenue Baptist Church—Martin's first parish. They marched right up to the state capitol building. And Martin spoke on those same steps where Jefferson Davis had taken the oath as president of the Confederacy a little over a hundred years earlier. "I stand before you this afternoon with the conviction that segregation is on its deathbed in Alabama," he told the crowd, "and the only thing uncertain about it is how costly these segregationists and Wallace will make the funeral. . . .

> We have walked on meandering highways and rested our bodies on rocky byways. Some of our faces are burned from the outpourings of the sweltering sun. Some have literally slept in the mud. We have been drenched by the rains. . . . Our bodies are tired, and our feet are somewhat sore, but today as I stand before you and think back over that great march, I can say as Sister Pollard said, a seventy-year-old Negro woman who lived in this community during the bus boycott and one day she was asked while walking if she wanted a ride and when she answered, "No," the person said, "Well, aren't you tired?" And with her ungrammatical profundity, she said, "My feets is tired, but my soul is rested." And in a real sense this afternoon, we can say that our feet are tired, but our souls are rested.

"We must come to see that the end we seek is a society at peace with itself, a society that can live with its conscience," concluded Martin. "That will be a day not of the white man, not of the black man. That will be the day of man as man."

In the days and months that followed, Martin King's stirring oratory gave way to the realization that the Selma campaign had, indeed, significantly moved the needle of progress in the right direction. For the first time, huge numbers of white people were supporting the mission of the movement. That, in and of itself, was a monumental achievement. But even more significant was the fact that the United States Congress, that summer, passed the Voting Rights Act of 1965—which Lyndon Johnson signed into law on August 6.

But, once again, there was a price that had to be paid by those who had pressed for change and progress. Two white ministers were clubbed in the streets of Selma and one of them, Reverend James Reed, died as a result of his injuries. A white housewife named Viola Liuzzo was killed by members of the Klan as she transported marchers back to Selma. Malcolm X was murdered in New York City. And the Watts area of Los Angeles exploded into massive rioting.

The violence directed personally at Martin was also intense. While attempting to register at Selma's all-white Albert Hotel, for instance, he was attacked by a young white segregationist who landed two harsh blows to King's right temple. Martin, however, stood his ground and refused to fight back. The attacker was subsequently arrested and Martin not only became the first African-American to occupy a room at the old Albert Hotel, he went on to speak at that night's mass meeting. In addition, during the Selma-to-Montgomery march, the SCLC got wind of a plot to assassinate King. But when they informed him of the supposed attempt, he blew it off and refused to leave.

The personal pressure on Martin, however, was beginning to take its toll. Just prior to, and during parts of the Selma campaign, poor health and an overwhelming feeling of depression resulted in his being confined to bed for several days at a time. Friends and family expressed serious concern for his well-being and urged him to delegate more and take additional time to rest.

One night, while back in Atlanta, Martin left the house without telling anyone where he was going. He had been concerned about a pending strike against a local factory's discriminatory practices because many of the company's employees were members of his congregation at Ebenezer Baptist. Martin's mother, who had been extremely worried about her son's recent depression, had been keeping a close eye on him. When he left without warning, she feared the worst and called an old friend of Martin's, Howard Baugh, who was the highest ranking African-American police officer in Atlanta. Also alarmed at Martin's unusual behavior, Baugh jumped in his car and began cruising the streets in search of his old childhood friend. Remembering the ongoing strike, on a hunch he drove by the factory around midnight. It was there that he found Martin—standing by himself outside the entrance. He was waiting for the shift to change so that he could encourage and give hope to the workers.

---

"We shall have to create leaders who embody virtues we can respect, who have moral and ethical principles we can applaud with an enthusiasm that enables us to rally support for them based on confidence and trust. We will have to demand high standards and give consistent, loyal support to those who merit it."

Martin Luther King, Jr.,
June 11, 1967

---

"Intelligence plus character—that is the goal of true education."

Martin Luther King, Jr.,
1947

# MARTIN LUTHER KING, JR., ON LEADERSHIP

★ When there is friction between two important groups in your organization, create a joint initiative involving both and hold daily meetings to beef up communication and increase teamwork.

★ When a powerful adversary is creating an unethical and immoral situation, make a deliberate attempt to dramatize the conditions.

★ Set up a formal leadership training program in your organization.

★ You have to create leaders who embody virtues you can respect, who have moral and ethical principles you can applaud.

★ Remember that education gives you not only knowledge, which is power, but wisdom, which is control.

★ Intelligence plus character is the goal of true education.

★ Don't forget that the law itself is a form of education.

★ By raising awareness in a public forum, you are able to educate the entire organization.

★ Remember that no work is insignificant.

★ A productive and happy life is not something that you find; it is something that you make.

★ You have no alternative but to keep moving with determination.

★ When necessary, provide people with an outlet to release pent-up emotions and inner tensions.

★ Ultimately, the thing that keeps the true fires of your organization burning is the existence of people of good will.

"I met these boys and heard their stories in discussions we had on some long, cold nights last winter at the slum apartment I rent in the West Side ghetto of Chicago. I was shocked at the venom they poured out against the world. At times I shared their despair and felt a hopelessness that these young Americans could ever embrace the concept of nonviolence as the effective and powerful instrument of social reform."

Martin Luther King, Jr.,
1967

"Not long ago, I toured in eight communities of the state of Mississippi. And I have carried with me ever since a visual image of the penniless and the unlettered, and of the expressions on their faces—of deep and courageous determination to cast off the imprint of the past and become free people."

Martin Luther King, Jr.,
January 1965

"I don't march because I like it. I march because I must, and because I'm a man."

Martin Luther King, Jr.,
August 1966

# 11 / March with the People

Early in the civil rights movement, while still living in Montgomery, Martin flew to the Atlanta airport to meet with several high-ranking officials of other civil rights organizations. Just before they were about to begin their discussions, a porter who was sweeping the floor pulled Martin aside and engaged him in a conversation. After waiting for fifteen minutes, one of the executives complained to another that he hadn't traveled "a thousand miles to sit and wait while [King] talked to a porter." The other shot back: "Well, when the day comes that he stops having time to talk to a porter—on that day I will not have the time to come one mile to see him."

Later in the movement, while living in Atlanta, Martin was running half an hour late for a critical meeting at his Ebenezer Baptist parish. As he walked through the church entrance with an SCLC adviser, he encountered the janitor sweeping up. "How's your wife?" asked Martin.

"Well, she ain't doing too well. Her back's still bothering her," came the reply.

"Really? It didn't get any better from the medicine?"

Recalling the incident, the SCLC adviser remembered thinking that there were three hundred people sitting in the church waiting for Martin—and he was taking the time to inquire about the janitor's wife. "I was so impressed," he remembered.

Here were two completely different reactions to essentially the same situation. The high-ranking executive was annoyed while waiting for Martin to finish speaking to a floor sweeper because he didn't want his time wasted. But another administrator, with less of a lofty title, was glad to wait. In fact, he was inspired. So who was the better leader—the impatient executive, the inspired administrator, or Martin Luther King, Jr.?

Of interest to note is that these two incidents, virtually identical in nature, occurred nearly nine years apart—indicating that this type of behavior was something that Dr. King repeated on a regular basis. As a matter of fact, he never wavered in his desire to listen to virtually anyone who wished to speak with him. That's one reason, as many of his staffers later noted, that he always ran late. "It would literally take him an hour to walk one and a half blocks," recalled one. "If you wanted to talk to him, he was going to take time to talk to you. That's just the way he was, that was his nature."

This part of Martin's nature showed itself early when, as a young man, he took jobs that did not necessarily challenge his intellectual abilities. He worked, for instance, as a harvester in the tobacco fields of the South. He had a job on the truck-loading dock of a mattress firm; and another unloading freight from trains. In recalling these jobs in later years, Martin told Coretta that he had wanted to "learn the plight [of the underprivileged] and to feel their feelings." And he certainly experienced their problems firsthand as he ended up quitting one job because his manager called him a "nigger," and another when he noticed that blacks were paid substantially less than whites for performing the same work.

Clearly, Martin cared about people and had a genuine interest in everyone he met. But more than that, circulating among the people was an integral part of his leadership style. Speaking to regular folks every day kept him in touch with what was really going on. It helped him learn how people felt; about their current situation; what their hopes and aspirations were.

It follows, then, that when Martin became the acknowledged leader of the American civil rights movement he was always on the go. As a matter of fact, between 1956 and 1968, Martin visited every major American city and many smaller ones as well. He also traveled extensively abroad—to Europe, Africa, Central America, and the Far East—not only making formal speeches to raise money for the SCLC, but to watch, observe, and listen. He then would report back to his audiences what he saw. To one group, he commented on the miserable conditions in which most people of color lived around the world. "Like a monstrous octopus, poverty spreads its nagging, prehensile tentacles into hamlets and villages all over our world," he explained. "They are ill-housed, they are ill-nourished, they are shabbily clad. I have seen it in Latin America; I have seen it in Africa; I have seen this poverty in Asia."

As much as he enjoyed traveling to other nations, as much as he knew the importance of traveling through America to raise much-needed funds, Martin was also constantly worried that "being away from the scene of action so often" would hurt the momentum of the movement. He often felt guilty for not being right there, on the ground, in the middle of things—all the time. Recall, for instance, that Martin was not there for Selma's Bloody Sunday—having taken the advice of his team to stay away due to expected violence. It was a decision for which Martin would never forgive himself. "I shall never forget my agony of conscience," he later wrote, "for not being there when I heard of the dastardly acts perpetrated against nonviolent demonstrators that Sunday."

In general, though, Martin's absence from the scene of action was the exception rather than the rule. Usually, he rode to the sound of the guns. Recall, for example, that when the 16th Street Baptist Church was bombed in 1963, he immediately went to Birmingham and walked through the bombed-out rubble. When violence broke out in Harlem in late 1964, he flew to New York to tour the riot sites and speak with the people. He did the same thing when riots occurred in the Watts area of Los Angeles during the summer of 1965. When Montgomery exploded in violence in the wake of Selma's Bloody Sunday, he headed straight for the streets of Montgomery where he sought to calm others and preach nonviolence. And he was on the ground during the major campaigns in Montgomery, Albany, Atlanta, Birmingham, St. Augustine, Selma, and others that occurred later.

Moreover, Martin would not simply come into a city, talk the high talk, and then leave town. He would usually make a concerted effort to get out and speak with those everyday people who were most affected by whatever was taking place at the moment. For example, when emotions outran reason in Albany and Birmingham—leading to violent retaliation against white police officers—Martin circulated through the beer joints and the pool halls of both cities. In 1962 in Albany, he created quite a stir by walking into one establishment, grabbing a cue stick, and walking up to a group of young people: "I hate to hold up your pool game," he said as he took off his jacket and loosened his tie. Others laughed as Martin took a few errant shots and then said: "I used to be a pool shark . . . but my skills have atrophied." Then he stopped and addressed the crowd with a serious tone. "We are in the midst of a great movement and we are soliciting the support of all the citizens of Albany," he said. "In order that we can continue on a Christian basis with love and nonviolence, I wanted to talk to you all and urge you to be nonviolent, not to throw bottles. I know if you do this, we are destined to win."

Reflecting on the importance of his sojourns to these pool halls, Martin recalled in 1967 that he had "walked among the desperate, rejected and angry young men" and explained to them that "Molotov cocktails and rifles would not solve their problems"—and that he had "tried to offer them my deepest compassion while maintaining my conviction that social change comes most meaningfully through nonviolent action."

Martin's philosophy of getting out and meeting with as many people as he possibly could was put into concrete action through what were labeled the SCLC's "People-to-People" tours. For three summers in the mid-1960s, Martin and members of the organization's "Freedom Corps" hit the ground in Virginia, Alabama, and Mississippi with the express purpose of recruiting volunteers and registering voters. But in visiting dozens of small towns and rural communities in countless counties, by getting out and interacting with thousands of people, Martin became increasingly amazed at the stories he heard—and was profoundly affected by them. "I never realized how many unknown heroes there were in the Freedom struggle of the Negro in the South until I began our People-to-People tours," he wrote in one of his weekly newspaper columns.

"I have just returned from a tour of Mississippi . . . and nothing has inspired me so much for some time," he wrote in another column. "We walked the streets, preached on front porches, at mass meetings or in the pool halls. . . . I have carried with me ever since a visual image of the penniless and the unlettered, and of the expressions on their faces." And wherever Martin went, to whomever he spoke, he told stories of the people he encountered. He spoke of hearing about "little black children of Grenada, Mississippi, beaten by grown men as they walked to school" and of "farm workers risking their lives and livelihood to march out of the cotton fields and vote for freedom and democracy."

"I was in Marks, Mississippi, the other day," he said in one speech. "I tell you I saw hundreds of little black boys and black girls walking the streets with no shoes to wear. . . . I saw mothers and fathers who said to me not only were they unemployed, they didn't get any kind of income—no old-age pension, no welfare check, nor anything. I said, 'How do you live?' And they said, 'Well, we go around to the neighbors and ask them for a little something. When the berry season comes, we pick berries; when the rabbit season comes, we hunt and catch a few rabbits, and that's about it. . . .'" When the parents told Martin that sometimes they could get nothing to eat, even for their children—Martin remembered that he "literally found myself crying."

About a year after Martin wore blisters on his feet walking in the Selma-to-Montgomery march, he got another chance to walk even farther. This time, though, it would be through some of those same counties in Mississippi where he had encountered the shoeless, poverty-stricken children.

On June 5, 1966, James Meredith, who had received his degree from the University of Mississippi, began what he called a "March Against Fear" in Memphis. Starting out alone, his intention was to walk two hundred miles through Mississippi in order to demonstrate to African-Americans that they could, in fact, overcome the fear associated with registering to vote. But on the second day out of Memphis, Meredith was shot in the back by a white segregationist with a shotgun loaded with buckshot.

Martin was in an SCLC staff meeting when he initially received word that Meredith had been killed. Another report, however, followed shortly and said that he had suffered only superficial wounds but was unable to go forward. Almost immediately, Martin and several members of the staff flew to Meredith's bedside in a Memphis hospital. They were quickly joined by the militant Stokely Carmichael, who had replaced John Lewis as the head of SNCC, and CORE's new leader, Floyd McKissick. Outraged at the unprovoked attack on Meredith, the SCLC, CORE, and SNCC decided to assume responsibility for continuing the March Against Fear. Roy Wilkins of the NAACP and Whitney Young of the National Urban League also joined the procession.

The group picked up the march just outside the small community of Hernando, Mississippi, on the very spot where Meredith had been shot. Their trek began with King, Carmichael, and McKissick walking in the middle of Highway 51 locked arm in arm. State police, however, arrived and began shoving them over to the shoulder. "Get off the pavement," yelled the officers.

"We walked from Selma to Montgomery in the middle of the road," protested Martin.

"You had a permit to do that," came the stern reply. "Get off the pavement."

When one officer shoved Stokely Carmichael after he stepped back on the pavement, Carmichael tried to lunge at the policeman—only to find that Martin had locked his arm so tightly within his own that he couldn't move. And so the marchers continued along the shoulder of the road—resolving that it was better to march there than not at all.

The number of marchers swelled quickly as many Mississippians filtered in along the way. In Grenada, 1,300 local citizens joined the marchers, who, in turn, escorted them to the courthouse so they could register to vote. Things were going fairly smoothly until they arrived in the town of Greenwood, where government officials announced they would not allow the marchers to camp on public property. And when Carmichael and a few others tried to set up a tent at a local school, they were immediately arrested. Released on bail, Carmichael spoke at a rally that evening on private church property where he defiantly started chanting, "We want black power. We want black power." And in response, the crowd repeated back the same words: "We want black power. We want black power."

In Philadelphia, Mississippi, the marchers attended an outside service on the second anniversary of the kidnapping and murder of the three volunteer workers Goodman, Chaney, and Schwerner. On the steps of the county courthouse, Martin was met by Deputy Sheriff Cecil Ray Price—who refused to let him go any further. Martin then stopped and led the several hundred marchers in a short prayer service. During his remarks, however, hundreds more angry white citizens yelled at and heckled the demonstrators. Sensing violence might erupt at any moment, Martin decided to end his remarks. "I believe in my heart," he said finally, "that the murderers [of the three young men] are somewhere around me at this moment."

"You're damn right," muttered Cecil Price over Martin's left shoulder. "They're behind you right now."

A stunned and shaken Martin then led the group back to the sanctuary of the local church where they had camped for the night.

A few days later, in Canton, the marchers were attacked by police officers who wielded billy clubs and fired tear gas. Stokely Carmichael and Floyd McKissick were enraged and their instincts impelled them to fight back. But Martin remained calm in the face of all the violence. "There's no point in fighting back," he said. "Don't do it. . . . Nobody leave. Nobody fight back. We're going to stand our ground." But the onslaught of police was just too much—and the marchers broke ranks and ran, once again, back to a local church.

The Meredith March Against Fear finally concluded with a rally in Jackson, the capital of Mississippi. Over ten thousand people showed up to hear Martin and the other civil rights leaders speak. In general, though, the march accomplished little—and some even felt it was a blunder for Martin to have participated. While the event had renewed publicity for the movement in the South (through coverage by the media)—it had also been fraught with divisiveness and bickering among leaders of the various civil rights organizations. It was becoming apparent that a new, more militant faction was emerging in the African-American ranks. Led by Stokely Carmichael, more and more people were beginning to listen to the Black Power approach to change rather than to Martin King's nonviolent strategy. As a matter of fact, Carmichael and McKissick both openly advocated that the practice of nonviolence had outlived its usefulness. Clearly, the black community across the nation was becoming polarized. And violence was threatening to erupt almost everywhere.

With the increasing contentiousness between various factions in the movement, Martin, although somewhat discouraged, renewed his determination to get out and interact with people on a local basis as often as possible. Why was it, then—at such a critical time—that Martin Luther King, Jr., wished to step up his interaction with people rather than withdraw? Why did Martin march?

He may have developed the idea, in part, from his detailed study of Mohandas K. Gandhi. Not only did Martin learn that Gandhi was able to evoke tremendous emotional responses from the people by the simple yet profound act of symbolic civil disobedience—he was well aware that Gandhi had achieved amazing results in his famous Salt March of 1930.

At the age of sixty-one, Gandhi started out with a small group of followers that grew in size as they traveled from Ahmadabad to the sea. He walked 240 miles in twenty-four days, resting frequently, but never riding. At each rest stop, he patiently explained his mission to the crowds that gathered and invited them to come along. People of all ages joined him until they numbered in the hundreds of thousands—strung out in a line that stretched for nearly two miles. When they reached the Indian Ocean, Gandhi waded into the water and picked up a handful of salt—which technically made him a criminal because mining salt was against the law. The Great Salt March eventually led to a revolution in India that ultimately resulted in India's independence.

The idea of a mass march, however, was only a technique central to the more encompassing principle in leadership that leaders must maintain a high degree of contact with the people they represent. Martin's constant interaction with others fit a pattern similar to that of other well-known leaders of the past.

During the six years of the American Revolution, for instance, General George Washington literally spent every waking and sleeping moment in the field with his troops. Abraham Lincoln made daily walks to the War Department during the Civil War. He also toured the capital on horseback and visited the troops and battlefields in neighboring Maryland, Virginia, and Pennsylvania. Lincoln's top general, Ulysses S. Grant, resolved that he would not rent "a house at the capital and direct the war effort from an armchair in Washington." Franklin Roosevelt, because he was confined to a wheelchair, brought others to the White House and kept a crowded schedule of meetings and interviews. Frequently his wife, Eleanor, would travel in the president's place—proudly noting that she was "her husband's legs." And Harry Truman was famous not only for his "whistle-stop" campaign, but also for regular evening walks.

All these leaders attempted to maintain as little distance as possible between themselves and the people they represented. By circulating widely, they were able to provide members of their organization with a chance to have a say in how things were done. By being on site, so to speak, they were also able to show respect and admiration for the efforts of others, which, in turn, enhanced their own credibility.

In corporate America, the very same strategy was dubbed MBWA (Managing by Wandering Around) by Tom Peters and Robert H. Waterman in their book *In Search of Excellence*. The concept has also been referred to as "roving leadership," "being in touch," or "getting out of the ivory tower." Whatever the label, it is simply the process of stepping out and interacting with people, of establishing personal human contact.

Peters and Nancy Austin, in *A Passion for Excellence*, defined this technique as "the technology of the obvious." "It is being in touch, with customers, suppliers, your people. It facilitates innovation, and makes possible the teaching of values to every member of an organization. Listening, facilitating, and teaching and reinforcing values. What is this except leadership? Thus, MBWA is the technology of leadership. Leading is primarily paying attention. The masters of the use of attention are also not only master users of symbols, of drama, but master storytellers and myth builders."

For all they knew, Peters and Austin could have been describing not only the very methods employed by Martin King, but King himself: master user of symbols, and drama, and master storyteller and myth builder. As a matter of fact, one of the reasons Martin marched was to create drama—and a sense of urgency. Marching, he said in 1966, was "part of a program to dramatize an evil, to mobilize the forces of good will, and to generate pressure and power for change." "I'm still convinced," he said on another occasion, "that there is nothing more powerful to dramatize a social evil than the tramp, tramp of marching feet."

Generally, Martin marched to keep himself from being stuck in "a ring of isolation and alienation"; to be "buoyed with the inspiration of another moment"; to commend others for "the beauty and dignity and the courage" in which they acted in any given situation; and because he felt that it was part of his responsibility. "The path is clear to me," he said. "I've got to march. I've got so many people depending on me. I've got to march."

When Martin marched with the masses, people perceived, rightfully so, that he was part of the crowd; he was one of the people, not a monarch housed in an ivory tower. It also helped facilitate his strategy of alliance-building and development of strong personal relationships. And it was symbolic of his action and achievement as a leader. Martin not only realized the importance of the symbolism, he played upon it to make sure the masses understood. "We are on the move now," he said at the end of the Selma march. "Like an idea whose time has come, not even marching of mighty armies can halt us. We're moving to the land of freedom."

Achieving results is directly proportional to a leader's willingness and ability to interact with people. In other words, the more frequent the human contact, the more results that will be achieved. It's merely common sense that leaders cannot be effective unless they have the consent of those who would follow them. Generally, there are five benefits why leaders should employ the strategy of seeking frequent human contact:

## 1. Obtain Key Information

The best leaders realize that obtaining accurate and timely data is important in formulating new ideas as well as creating a vision for the future. They also personally seek and require access to reliable, up-to-date information unfiltered by newspapers, television, or polls. Broad contact provides leaders the firsthand knowledge needed to make informed, accurate, and timely decisions without having to rely solely on the word of others.

## 2. Keep People Informed

Frequent human contact with others also allows the leader to keep people informed about what's going on, what's being presented, what's being achieved on behalf of the entire organization. The adage "knowledge is power" is never more appropriate than in the relationship between leaders and the people they represent.

## 3. Obtain Feedback

Dialogue with others allows leaders to receive feedback on both personal performance and ideas they have presented. This not only keeps the leader on track with the desires of the people, but also aids in the refinement and improvement of new initiatives. Moreover, it fulfills the basic human need for personal growth and the comfort that comes with knowledge that one's actions are appreciated. Being open and receptive to new ideas—as well as criticism—is an important trait for a leader to possess.

## 4. Facilitate Learning

Daily personal contact with people accelerates a leader's learning curve. It allows the leader to acquire new skills and knowledge from a variety of sources on a wide range of subjects. Doing so ties back to the innate trait possessed by effective leaders involving a capacity and desire for continuous learning. Mingling and holding meaningful conversations with a variety of knowledgeable people is the single best way for a leader to learn while on the job.

## 5. Understand What People Think and Feel

If leaders regularly seek personal contact with the people, they will know exactly what others think and how they feel; what their hopes and dreams are. Therein lies the most fundamental of all leadership principles, which ties back to the definition of leadership: *Leaders act for the wants and needs, the aspirations and expectations—* . . . *of the people they represent.*

In order to maintain their position out in front, and to remain effective, leaders must also often follow the direction of others. In short, they must lead by being led. A comment made in a 1963 article indicates that Martin King clearly understood this principle. "Gandhi's oft-quoted statement is so applicable today," he wrote. "There go my people, I must catch them, for I am their leader."

Having made such an observation, it's not surprising, then, that Martin took very seriously a request he received in September 1965 from Reverend Al Raby, chairman of Chicago's Coordinating Council of Community Organization (CCCO), an alliance of seventy-five local civil rights groups. Through boycotts and mass demonstrations, CCCO had been active in fighting public school segregation in the city, but had not been making a great deal of progress. Essentially Raby asked Martin to bring the SCLC to Chicago and lead a massive campaign similar to what had been done in Birmingham and Selma. "We came South to help you in Selma," Raby reminded Martin. "Now we need you here."

Martin quickly gathered the SCLC staff for a pow-wow in Atlanta to consider Raby's request. During a rather lengthy and heated debate, the group considered Chicago's complex politics, the increased costs of conducting a campaign in the North, and the emotions of African-Americans in Chicago where, as compared to southern cities, they seemed to be more angry than afraid.

Going to Chicago, then, not only might result in major violence, it would definitely mark a significant shift in emphasis from the South to the North. Several staffers did not want to do it, but Martin intervened: "Well, it seems to me we've got to begin dealing with the North sometime," he said. "We can't just concern ourselves with the South if we call ourselves a national movement."

Once Martin made his feelings known, the group began making plans to begin a People-to-People campaign in key northern and Mid-Atlantic cities. Several cities, including Washington, D.C., New York, Cleveland, and Philadelphia, were explored in great detail. But it would be Chicago where the new campaign would start.

In early January 1966, Martin arrived in Chicago to lead a series of joint meetings with the SCLC and CCCO. The Reverend Jesse Jackson, a Chicago native and leading civil rights activist, was appointed a member of the SCLC staff to coordinate activity with the CCCO. From that point on, the SCLC and the CCCO acted as a coalition when it came to any event or decision involving the Chicago campaign.

After several days of meetings, a press conference was called where Martin announced that the Chicago movement was going to focus on three main objectives regarding the situation in the city's ghettos. First, they were going to educate people about slum conditions. Second, they planned to organize slum dwellers into a union. And third, they hoped to create a nonviolent army comprised primarily of slum tenants to demonstrate the poor conditions in which they lived. "The purpose of the slum," he noted, "is to confine those who have no power and perpetuate their powerlessness. . . . The slum is little more than a domestic colony which leaves its inhabitants dominated politically, exploited economically, [and] segregated and humiliated at every turn."

After the announcement of the SCLC's plan to get involved in Chicago, Martin not only stayed in town, he moved into a dilapidated two-bedroom apartment in the Lawndale ghetto—complete with broken refrigerator, frayed wallpaper, and faulty heaters. With freezing cold temperatures outside, he and other staff members sometimes had to wear overcoats inside the building just to keep warm. "You can't really get close to the poor without living and being here with them," Martin explained to several newsmen who followed him into the tenement.

Martin, Andrew Young, and the SCLC maintained the apartment for nearly a year. Later that first summer, Coretta brought the children there for a short while so they could spend time with their father. In looking back on the experience, Martin reflected that "it was only a few days before we became aware of the difference in [the children's] behavior. Their little tempers often flared; they sometimes reverted to almost infantile behavior. And as the riot raged around them outside, I realized that the crowded flat in which we lived was about to produce an emotional explosion in my own family. . . . And I understood anew the emotional pressures which make the ghetto an emotional pressure cooker."

The day after moving into the Lawndale apartment, Martin and other members of the staff embarked on their first "walking tour" of the local neighborhood. They dropped by police headquarters to assure the chief that they would keep the police informed of his plans. They ate at a local café. They also met several members of a youth gang who agreed to show the group around. Even though the temperature hovered near zero, when word got around that Martin Luther King was walking the streets, many people came out to meet him and shake his hand. And despite the cold, Martin took the time to greet everyone with a smile and a kind word.

Over the next several months, the SCLC-CCCO coalition organized block meetings that pulled together tenants of various apartment buildings. In one building near Martin's apartment, conditions were so deplorable that he and the staffers simply took over. They collected rent money from the occupants and began to remedy many conditions that had long been neglected—such as repairing faulty heating, picking up trash, and exterminating rats. When the building's landlord protested, Martin essentially ignored him. And by the time a court order was secured to stop the action, most of the repairs had already been made. When asked how he could break the law so blatantly, Martin simply replied: "The moral question is far more important than the legal one."

In order to dramatize the slum situation, the SCLC staff held press conferences in the middle of the tenements so that cameras could show the degradation to the outside world. In addition, they staged a "Chicago Freedom Festival" that successfully raised $80,000 for the SCLC-CCCO alliance. And, at the urging of Jesse Jackson, a local chapter of the SCLC's "Operation Breadbasket" program was created. Research was done and statistics were gathered—and from that information discriminatory businesses in black neighborhoods were boycotted. Within a year, Operation Breadbasket had created nearly one thousand new jobs for African-Americans.

The SCLC team also invited members of local gangs to visit Martin in his apartment. The leaders of such gangs as the Vice Lords, Cobras, and Roman Saints accepted the invitation. So over the first few months of the campaign, Martin spent many hours listening to the young men speak about how they lived and what they thought about major issues that confronted them. "I met those boys," recalled Martin in a later speech, "and heard their stories in discussions we had on some long, cold nights last winter at the slum apartment I rent in the West Side ghetto of Chicago. I was shocked at the venom they poured out against the world. At times I shared their despair and felt a hopelessness that these young Americans could ever embrace the concept of nonviolence as the effective and powerful instrument of social reform."

Many of the gangs were known to have committed violent crimes. Martin nevertheless spoke about nonviolence and tried to convince them that they should try his method. The gang members listened with respect—perhaps because they were somewhat in awe of him. "You mean to tell me I'm sitting here with the cat who's been up there talking to Presidents?" said one gang leader. "He's been up there eating filet mignon steaks, and now he's sitting here eating barbecue just like me." Overall, it was estimated that several hundred gang members agreed to participate in the SCLC-CCCO demonstrations and to at least give the nonviolent method a chance.

By July 1966—having spent time on the ground getting to know people, organizing and counseling a "nonviolent army" of tenement dwellers, and raising sufficient funds—the SCLC-CCCO alliance was ready to begin serious demonstrations. One of the first things they did was to plan a rally at Soldier

Field—where the Chicago Bears professional football team played its games. For the event, which they called "Freedom Sunday," thirty thousand people showed up to hear addresses by Chicago's Archbishop John Cody, CORE's Floyd McKissick, and SNCC's Stokely Carmichael. Martin spoke last. "Freedom is never voluntarily granted by the oppressor; it must be demanded by the oppressed," he said to the crowd. "We must say to [Chicago] Mayor [Richard] Daley: 'If you do not respond to our demands, our votes will decide [who will be] the next mayor of Chicago. We will fill up the jails here in order to end the slums. . . .' "

At the conclusion of the rally, Martin led a march to city hall where he taped to the front door a list of the movement's demands. Martin got the idea for this dramatic gesture from his namesake, Martin Luther, the sixteenth-century German monk who began the Protestant Reformation by nailing ninety-five theses on the door of the Catholic church in Wittenberg. Martin called the list of demands his "Ninety-six Theses." In part, they included such things as desegregation of public schools, an end to all housing discrimination, new legislation to protect tenement dwellers, ending discriminatory real estate practices, and creation of a civilian review board for the Chicago police.

The following day, a meeting was held with Mayor Daley to discuss the long list of demands. The discussion quickly turned hostile and antagonistic as Daley refused to acknowledge any of the requests and Rev. Al Raby threatened immediate direct action. Martin took a more conciliatory and peaceful tone during the conference. Afterward, however, when it became abundantly clear that the city's leadership had no intention of taking any concrete steps toward progress, he committed the movement to begin mass demonstrations, sit-ins, and economic boycotts.

The very next afternoon, on July 12, violence broke out in one of the West Side ghettos as police rushed in to shut off fire hydrants that people had turned on in order to cool off in the 100 degree heat. When fistfights broke out among residents and officers, one gang member threw a Molotov cocktail at a police car, setting it on fire. Six people were subsequently arrested and hauled off to jail. Martin rushed to the police station and secured the release of the arrested youths—whom he quickly took to a hastily arranged mass meeting. Hoping to avoid further violence, he asked the hundreds of people gathered there to remain true to the nonviolent philosophy. But the crowd essentially shouted him down until they finally walked out of the church.

Not willing to give up, Martin next called a meeting of 150 clergymen and begged them to get involved, to go on walking tours through the riot zones, and to plead for peace in the tenements. But shortly after that gathering, even worse violence broke out—this time in Martin's area of Lawndale. In response to the uproar, hundreds of police officers in riot gear marched through the streets in a wedge-shaped formation. When that happened, local residents hurled bricks and bottles at them from the windows of apartment buildings. White-owned stores were fire-bombed, more bricks were thrown into store and car windows, and gunfire broke out between policemen and snipers perched in the high-rise tenements.

Upon receiving word that their adopted neighborhood had essentially turned into a war zone, Martin, Andrew Young, and entertainer Dick Gregory immediately jumped in a car and headed to Lawndale. Once there, they worked block by block trying to quell the young rioters—urging them to calm down, to turn away from violence, to go home. The three men stayed until nearly four in the morning when people finally began to disperse.

Shortly thereafter, Mayor Daley made several concessions at Martin's urging. Portable swimming pools were brought into local neighborhoods, sprinkler attachments were affixed to fire hydrants, and a citizens committee was created to work with the police department. Over the next few weeks, things calmed down significantly. But there was still a great deal of tension in the city. White segregationists were now poised to attack—and blacks weren't sure what the next step would be. It was Martin who provided that answer by announcing that the time had come to create enough tension to force Mayor Daley and other city authorities to the bargaining table.

Accordingly, on August 5, Martin led six hundred people out to Marquette Park for a march through an all-white middle-class community. Nearly one thousand Chicago police officers also showed up to escort the marchers and, hopefully, prevent any violence. Just before they set out, Martin spoke to the gathered throng. "We aren't gonna march with any Molotov cocktails," he told them. "That isn't our movement. We aren't gonna march with any weapons. That isn't our movement. We aren't gonna march with bricks and bottles. We're gonna march with something much more powerful than all of that. We're gonna march with the force of our souls. . . . We're gonna move out with the weapons of courage. We're gonna put on the breastplate of righteousness and the whole armor of God. And we're gonna *march!*"

Thousands of white onlookers lined the streets of the marchers' route. As the procession began, the angry white crowd waved Confederate flags, flashed Nazi swastikas, and shouted racial epithets: "Nigger go home!" "Martin Luther Coon!" "Kill the niggers!" "Hate! Hate! Hate!" they screamed over and over and over again. Then the white crowd began to overturn automobiles, set them on fire—and throw rocks, bricks, and bottles at the demonstrators. Police and marchers alike were pelted. "You nigger-loving sons of bitches," the mob yelled at the officers.

Someone flung a knife at Martin but it narrowly missed. He wasn't so lucky, though, when a brick was hurled his way—striking him in the head just above the right ear and knocking him to the ground. He was immediately surrounded by people hoping to help. But after taking a moment to recover on one knee, Martin stood up and shrugged it off. "I've been hit so many times I'm immune to it," he said. "We can't stop the march."

And the march did continue—although dozens of people were injured by the time it was all over. Martin, while seriously alarmed at the attacks of the hate-filled mobs, was also proud of the fact that no one fought back. The marchers had remained true to the nonviolent creed.

But over the next few days, it seemed as though all of white Chicago turned its anger toward Martin Luther King, Jr. Politicians, the press, and members of the clergy attacked him. He was to blame for all the violence. He was the agitator, they charged. End the marching now, they demanded.

Martin quickly responded to all the criticism at a mass rally. "You want us to stop marching?" he asked. "[Then] make justice a reality. . . . I'm tired of marching for something that should have been mine at birth," he went on to say. "If you want a moratorium on demonstrations, put a moratorium on injustice. . . . I don't march because I like it. I march because I must, and because I'm a man."

----

"Will we continue to march to the drum beat of conformity and respectability, or will we, listening to the beat of a more distant drum, move to its echoing sounds? Will we march only to the music of time, or will we, risking criticism and abuse, march to the soul-saving music of eternity?"

Martin Luther King, Jr.,
September 26, 1966

----

"I'm still convinced that there is nothing more powerful to dramatize a social evil than the tramp, tramp of marching feet."

Martin Luther King, Jr.,
August 9, 1966

----

"I saw with my own eyes."

Martin Luther King, Jr.,
January 1965

# MARTIN LUTHER KING, JR., ON LEADERSHIP

- ★ Take as much time to speak with a floor sweeper as you would a corporate executive.
- ★ If people want to speak with you, take the time to listen. Greet them with a smile and a kind word.
- ★ Put yourself in situations that will enable you to learn the plight and feel the feelings of the people you represent.
- ★ Go to where the action is taking place. Ride to the sound of the guns.
- ★ Don't ride into town, talk the high talk, and then leave. Go down in the trenches and talk to the people.
- ★ Implement people-to-people campaigns and walking tours. Find the heroes in your own organization—and tell their stories.
- ★ Remain calm in the face of violence and adversity.
- ★ There is nothing more powerful to dramatize a social evil than the tramp, tramp of marching feet.
- ★ Achieving results is directly proportional to your willingness and ability to interact with people.
- ★ Remember the words of Gandhi: "There go my people, I must catch them, for I am their leader." In other words, lead by being led.
- ★ Spend time living with the people you represent. Doing so will allow you to understand anew their emotional pressures.
- ★ Remember that a moral question is far more important than a legal one.
- ★ Freedom is never voluntarily granted by the oppressor, it must be demanded by the oppressed.

"We've got to have a crisis to bargain with. To take a moderate approach, hoping to get white help, doesn't work. They nail you to the cross, and it saps the enthusiasm of the followers. You've got to have a crisis."

Martin Luther King, Jr.,
January 3, 1964

"We read in the scripture, 'Come, let us sit down and reason together.'"

Martin Luther King, Jr.,
August 26, 1966

"We must now measure our words by our deeds, and it will be heard. . . . But if these agreements aren't carried out, Chicago hasn't *seen* a demonstration."

Martin Luther King, Jr.,
August 26, 1966

# 12 / Negotiate and Compromise

When the SCLC and CCCO formally combined their alliance into the Chicago Freedom Movement, Martin King went before the press and told reporters: "Our primary objective will be to bring about the unconditional surrender of forces dedicated to the creation and maintenance of slums." Through mass demonstrations, boycotts, sit-ins, and negotiation, it was the movement's intention, he said, to force the city of Chicago to "find imaginative programs to overcome the problem." "We will fill up the jails here in order to end the slums," Martin had said at the Soldier Field rally.

Unfortunately, even with such a grand alliance of social and political organizations, all was not rosy in the African-American community. There were, in fact, some heated opponents—although minor in number—to the strategy that Martin was following. The Reverend Joseph H. Jackson (a long-standing leader in Chicago's African-American community), for example, stated that the SCLC's tactics were "not that far removed from open crime." He further contended that Chicago's white city leadership were true friends of the African-American community and were doing all they could. Martin, who realized that Jackson was from the old guard and had previously criticized nonviolent direct action techniques, essentially ignored the criticism. "I don't think Dr. Jackson speaks for one percent of the Negroes in this country," he replied.

Exacerbating the movement's problem was the fact that Mayor Richard Daley, a shrewd and calculating politician, had adeptly started out by embracing Martin's role in Chicago and then subtly working behind the scenes to discredit him. Daley even attended a meeting with Martin and forty-five black ministers in hopes of swaying their opinions. At that gathering, the mayor was bold enough to suggest that King return to Georgia. But only a small minority of those present supported that proposal and it soon became apparent to Daley that he would have to deal with Martin King one way or another because he enjoyed the support of the vast majority of African-Americans in Chicago. To top it all off, Archbishop John Cody switched his support away from the Chicago Freedom Movement by urging a halt to ongoing demonstrations and granting concessions in any future negotiating process.

But Martin refused to waver in his persistence and determination and, as the movement in Chicago progressed, political pressure mounted on Mayor Daley to negotiate. Violence in the city—some of the worst in the nation's history—was drawing increased media attention. And the boycotts and protests were also hurting the economy, tourism, and the image of Chicago.

Reluctantly, then, Daley agreed to open a dialogue with Martin in hopes of arriving at a solution that, in his mind, would result in the end of demonstrations. In August 1966, after the violence-plagued march from Marquette Park, a summit meeting was convened at Palmer House between Mayor Daley and city officials and Martin King and movement leaders (including Al Raby, Andrew Young, James Bevel, and Jesse Jackson). In all, a total of seventy-nine representatives from all Chicago's key social and political alliances participated in the negotiating conference.

In his opening statement, Martin thanked the mayor for convening an honest dialogue about conditions in the city. Then he turned the podium over to Al Raby, who read the movement's specific proposals regarding open housing. In all, there were nine demands that included such things as tough enforcement of Chicago's fair housing ordinance; withdrawal of the Chicago Real Estate Commission's opposition to existing ordinances and to fair-housing legislation being considered in the Illinois legislature; high-rise public projects would no longer be confined to existing slum areas; an end to racial discrimination in housing referrals and placements; and a pledge from the Real Estate Commission to end all practices based on racial segregation. Another movement demand included complete racial integration of public schools in the Chicago area.

Demands such as these required a significant sacrifice on the part of the recalcitrant white majority of Chicago—more so than requirements that had been insisted upon by the movement in southern cities. Integration of public facilities and putting an end to discriminatory hiring practices required relatively little sacrifice from southern leaders. However, housing and school integration would necessitate the leaders of this northern city to redistribute tax dollars from white to black students while, at the same time, allow African-Americans (synonymous with slum conditions and crime) the right to move into prosperous all-white neighborhoods. These very real effects were no doubt the reasons that violence had been so intense against black marchers in the white Chicago neighborhoods.

In response to Raby's reading of the proposals, one business leader stated that they could not end discrimination because "we are not the creators, we are the mirror." Martin, however, quickly responded with a request that the issue be viewed in terms of ethics and morality rather than only a strict interpretation of the law. "All over the South I heard the same thing . . . from restaurant owners and hotel owners," he responded. "They said they were just the agents, that they were just responding to the people's unwillingness to eat with Negroes in the same restaurant or stay with Negroes in the same hotel. . . . I must appeal to the decency of the people on the Chicago Real Estate Board. You are confronted with a moral issue. . . . The real estate industry has not only reflected discriminatory attitudes, it has played a significant part in creating them. In fact, in California the real estate people spent five million dollars to kill the open occupancy law there. . . . I appeal to the rightness of our position and to your decency."

After a three-hour break and additional prolonged discussion, city and business leaders essentially agreed to all the movement's demands if the Chicago Freedom Movement would immediately halt all demonstrations. Andrew Young then suggested that the only additional thing needed was a specific plan of implementation over the next month or two. But the opposition expressed reluctance at committing in any detail, preferring, rather, to agree philosophically to the movement's demands in return for a moratorium on demonstrations. Al Raby, however, categorically refused to end the protests until some action steps were concretely set forth.

When Mayor Daley then stated that he needed some evidence to show the Chicago City Council that movement leaders were going to stop the marches before the legislation could be passed, Raby exploded in anger. "If I come before the Mayor of Chicago some day, I hope I can come before the Mayor of Chicago with what is just and that he will implement it because it is right rather than trading it politically for a moratorium."

It was at this point, just when the negotiating session looked like it was going to fail miserably, that Martin spoke up after a long silence. "This has been a constructive and creative beginning," he said. "This represents progress and a sign of change. . . . I hope we are here to discuss how to make Chicago a great open city and not how to end marches. Now, gentlemen, you know we don't have much. We don't have much money. We don't have much education, and we don't have political power. We have only our bodies and you are asking us to give up the one thing that we have when you say, 'Don't march.'

"We're not trying to overthrow you; we're trying to get in. We're trying to make justice a reality. We want peace, but peace in the presence of justice. . . . Our marching feet have brought us a long way, and if we hadn't marched I don't think we'd be here today.

"We appreciate the meeting," Martin concluded. "We don't want to end the dialogue. We don't see enough to stop the marches, but we are going with love and nonviolence. This is a great city and it can be a greater city."

The calming influence of Martin's oratory thoroughly changed the mood of the meeting—from angry and tense to soothing and conciliatory. Seizing the opportunity, Andrew Young proposed forming a working committee to hash out the details of the agreement in principle. The independent mediator immediately agreed to the idea. "The purpose of the subcommittee," he said, "[will be] to come back with proposals designed to provide an open city." He also determined that the group's first meeting would be held in about nine days. Reactions from the extreme elements on both sides were negative at this compromise step. On the city of Chicago side, people were upset that the demonstrations had not been halted; on the side of the movement, that the proposals had not been acted upon.

During the nine-day interim period, Mayor Daley requested and received a local court order limiting the scope of any future demonstrations. Those limitations included no nighttime marches; no more than one march per day; twenty-four-hour advance notice in writing of any planned demonstration; and no more than five hundred participants.

At first, Martin reacted angrily at the Mayor's tactic. "I deem it a very bad act of faith on the part of the city in view of the fact we're negotiating," he told the press. "This just stands in the way of everything we're trying to do." After conferring with his team, however, Martin agreed that negotiations should continue and that any new marches should conform to the court injunction. The next Sunday, Martin personally led a march through the city's South Deering area. The movement also held two other demonstrations that same day in Chicago Heights and Evergreen Park—areas that were outside the Chicago city limits and therefore not affected by the court order.

Movement leaders then decided to put their own pressure on the negotiators by threatening to hold a march in the suburb of Cicero where white supremacist Nazis were known to be planning a counterattack against demonstrators. In response, Cook County Sheriff Richard Ogilvie, who anticipated significant violence, begged movement officials to call off the Cicero march. When they refused, Illinois Governor Otto Kerner stated that the National Guard would be called upon to preserve peace at the march. Predictably local and national media then focused heavily on the anticipated confrontation among nonviolent demonstrators, members of the American Nazi Party, and the Illinois National Guard. The threat of the Cicero march was intended by King to force the committee to take some concrete action. He clearly understood, recalled Andrew Young, "that a march in Cicero was more effective as a threat than as a reality."

It was under this cloud that the subcommittee held several emotion-packed meetings where they finally hammered out a settlement. In essence, all the movement's demands were agreed to—and there was a major commitment by the Chicago Real Estate Commission to implement a fair and open housing policy along with establishment of a system to deal with complaints. The "Summit Agreement," as it would come to be known, also called for the creation of the "Leadership Council for Metropolitan Open Housing." This group, which was created as a direct result of Andrew Young's insistence on a plan of implementation, would be comprised of the major leaders in the city and was designed specifically to execute the agreement in terms of real, concrete action.

Just before the larger committee was to reconvene, Martin called his team together for a discussion of the agreement in total. Most members favored acceptance of the terms. A minority faction, however, did not. Martin listened patiently to both sides. But before he could announce his decision, it was time to proceed to the scheduled meeting of the larger group.

At that meeting, after the agreement was read aloud, Mayor Daley called for a vote to approve the proposal. Martin, however, interrupted and (reflecting on the previous discussion with his team) pointed out that there were still a few questions that remained to be resolved. "First," he said, "we are much concerned about the [court] injunction we face. We feel that injunction is unjust and unconstitutional. . . . We want to know if the city will withdraw the injunction." Martin looked straight at Mayor Daley when he said: "I hope we are operating here by the law of life which is that reconciliation is always possible. But I think I've got to say that if that injunction stands, somewhere along the way we are going to have to break it.

"Second," he went on to say, "we are very concerned still

about implementation. We want to know if the continuing body that will be established to hammer out the specifics will be an action body or whether it will be just a forum. We want to know how soon it will be underway. . . .”

After some additional discussion, city leaders assured Martin that the new implementation committee would be established within a week and that it would be set up as an action group. In addition, a compromise was worked out that would involve a separate negotiation through the new action committee to resolve the issue of the court injunction. Martin and his team agreed to these proposals and, subsequently, a vote taken was unanimous in favor of adopting the plan.

After Mayor Daley and the mediator made a few closing remarks and thanked the participants, Martin rose to speak. “I want to express my appreciation for everybody's work and the appreciation of the Chicago Freedom Movement,” he said graciously. “I want to thank the subcommittee. We read in the scripture, ‘Come, let us sit down and reason together,’ and everyone here has met that spiritual mandate. . . .

“But I want to reiterate again that we must make this agreement work. Our people's hopes have been shattered too many times, and an additional disillusionment will only spell catastrophe. Our summers of riots have been caused by our winters of delay. . . . We must now measure our words by our deeds, and it will be heard. This agreement [is] a victory for justice and not a victory over the Chicago Real Estate Board or the city of Chicago. I am as grateful to Mayor Daley as to anyone else here for his work. I think now we can go on to make Chicago a beautiful city, a city of brotherhood.”

After the meeting adjourned, Martin stepped outside and related the terms of the agreement to the press. He called the Summit Agreement “the most significant program ever conceived to make open housing a reality in the metropolitan area.” He also announced that the planned Cicero march would not take place. “But if these agreements aren't carried out,” he warned, “Chicago hasn't *seen* a demonstration.”

The compromise Summit Agreement, however, was not well received by all members of the African-American community. Martin was denounced by members of CORE and SNCC for compromising too easily, for giving in too quickly, for giving up too much. Some even publicly stated that the final Summit Agreement was a "sell-out" by Martin. And then, to make matters worse, two hundred members of both organizations went ahead and staged a march through Cicero anyway. At that demonstration, more than two thousand members of the Illinois National Guard were barely able to hold back thousands of incensed whites and thereby prevent any major violence from occurring.

Martin, however, took it all in stride. He realized that a compromise is always less than people want or seek—sometimes less than they deserve. But compromise and negotiation both are essential elements to the leadership process because they create attainment of goals and, hence, allow for the realization of substantial achievement. While compromises are almost never popular—and often equated with "kissing your sister"—the best leaders know that negotiation, by its very definition, demands compromise on both sides.

As a matter of fact, creative compromise has always been a part of American political leadership—starting with the United States Constitution. There would have been no Constitution had not the founding fathers agreed to work together in 1787. And before the Civil War, the Missouri Compromise was established in 1820 to maintain a balance between slave and non-slave-holding states. Compromise has often been utilized in more modern political dealings. One of the most famous instances occurred in 1962 when President Kennedy avoided nuclear war during the Cuban Missile Crisis. Kennedy compromised with Russian Premier Nikita Khrushchev when he agreed to remove American nuclear weapons from Turkey in exchange for removal of those in Cuba. This action embodied Kennedy's comment that "Compromise need not mean cowardice."

Moreover, many of the world's greatest leaders were known for their ability to compromise. In addition to his nonviolent stands, Gandhi was perhaps best known for his desire to search for common ground. He achieved much for India by utilizing a strategy that included self-improvement for all parties involved in a dispute, a peaceful settlement of differences, and a compromise solution so that everyone could save face.

Take, for instance, how Gandhi produced a win-win situation for both India and his followers in a labor dispute which was frequently called "The Event" because it catapulted him to national prominence. Because business was good, inflation was soaring, and taxes were high, textile workers in Ahmadabad went on strike for higher wages. When Gandhi could not get the attention of the mill owners, he staged a fast—which was the first time such a strategy had been used in a public forum. Ultimately, he managed to forge a deal that both workers and mill owners viewed with satisfaction.

Gandhi set that example in 1918, and three quarters of a century later experts continue to stress the need for compromise in leadership. There is, for example, a noticeable trend with members of the baby-boom generation that reflects achievement through consensus and compromise—as articulated in Stephen Covey's premise of the Win/Win situation. "Win/Win is not a technique," he wrote in *The Seven Habits of Highly Effective People*, "it's a total philosophy of human interaction." Covey further explained: "Win/Win is a frame of mind and heart that constantly seeks mutual benefit in all human interactions. [It] means that agreements or solutions are mutually beneficial, mutually satisfying. With a Win/Win solution, all parties feel good about the decision and feel committed to the action plan. Win/Win sees life as a cooperative, not a competitive arena. . . . It's based on the [idea] that there is plenty for everybody, that one person's success is not achieved at the expense or exclusion of the success of others."

In addition to creating a situation where everybody wins,

skilled compromise can be a leader's key to success—especially in changing times when attempting to break new ground. Because people are resistant to change, compromise is often the only practical tool that allows a leader to make any progress at all. Along with helping leaders to achieve their goals, compromise can be used as a vehicle to help persuade people to take action. Since the definition of leadership omits the use of coercive power, leadership is, in effect, the antithesis of dictatorship. Yet, compromise is never used by dictators to exert control over followers. Rather, it is the tool of a true leader—one who attempts to move followers through persuasion and inspiration.

In the final analysis, leaders have virtually no real power over the people they represent. Followers will rally around almost any leader when there is a war or some other major crisis but, in a peacetime situation, leaders do not enjoy that luxury. In the postmodern political era, with instantaneous news and communications, that fact becomes even more recognizable. The art of compromise, then, is no longer an option—it is a necessity. Leaders are increasingly faced with well-informed lobbyists and special-interest groups who make it nearly impossible to garner sweeping change in one fell swoop. Such a trend may also explain why some late-twentieth-century observers have noted that women seem to be enjoying more success in leadership. Deborah Tannen, for instance, in her book *You Just Don't Understand,* noted that most men perceive compromise as a weakness, but that a woman's natural inclination is to "preserve harmony by compromise."

Clearly, Martin Luther King, throughout the entire civil rights movement, displayed this more feminine tendency to find a middle course. He constantly sought negotiation in order to achieve progress *and* preserve harmony. "We began with a compromise when we didn't ask for complete integration," he noted of his strategy during the Montgomery bus boycott. "We will always be willing to talk and seek fair compromise," he said in 1962. "The key word is respect," he advocated in Chicago. "We must have patience," he advised in 1967.

Through bargains driven and compromises struck, Martin constantly preached dialogue and negotiation—wherever he went. In Chicago, for instance, the movement employed an army of local ministers to direct hundreds of small, separate negotiations all over Chicago. These preachers, led in large part by Jesse Jackson, looked into discriminatory hiring practices of individual white-owned businesses that had a large African-American clientele. Martin later pointed out that such negotiation sessions were educational, as well as productive. "They seek to arouse an awareness of the problems . . . and point out the immorality of companies that make profits."

The ability to compromise was both an attribute and a virtue that made Martin Luther King, Jr., a good leader. He enjoyed an innate talent that provided him with the capacity to recognize and bring to light areas of common ground between opposing points of view. Moreover, he followed a ten-step sequence in the process of negotiation and compromise that was developed and refined over the course of the civil rights movement. In its simplest and most general terms, here is that sequence:

## 1. Seek Dialogue to Discuss Concerns

Martin's first step in the Birmingham campaign (as it was in Selma, St. Augustine, Chicago, and other places) was to go to the city and announce his goals and plans. He stated that unless the demands were met within two weeks, serious demonstrations would start. Of this crucial first step, Martin noted: "It is absolutely essential to establish a documented moral record that relief was sought via negotiations. Then and only then does it seem that such a drastic program of civil disobedience should be launched."

## 2. Create a Crisis

It was clear to everyone involved in the movement that creating a crisis through marches and demonstrations was what got them to the bargaining table in almost every campaign they conducted. "We've got to have a crisis to bargain with," noted Martin. "To take a moderate approach, hoping to get white help, doesn't work. They nail you to the cross, and it saps the enthusiasm of the followers."

"We set out to precipitate a crisis situation that must open the door to negotiation," he said of this step in the process. "I am not afraid of the words 'crisis' and 'tension.' Innate in all life, and all growth, is tension. Only in death is there an absence of tension. To cure injustices, you must expose them before the light of human conscience and the bar of public opinion, regardless of whatever tensions that exposure generates. Injustices must be brought out into the open where they cannot be evaded."

## 3. Set Out Demands and Conditions

"Throughout the [Birmingham] campaign," Martin noted, "we had been seeking to establish some dialogue with the city leaders in an effort to negotiate on four major issues: 1) Desegregation of lunch counters, rest rooms, fitting rooms and drinking fountains in department stores; 2) Upgrading and hiring of Negroes on a nondiscriminatory basis throughout the business and industrial community of Birmingham; 3) Dropping of all charges against jailed demonstrators; and 4) Creation of a biracial committee to work out a timetable for desegregation in other areas of Birmingham life."

Setting out demands and conditions early in the negotiating process lets everyone know exactly what it is that the leader is trying to accomplish. The opposition cannot say they didn't know what the issues were—and supporters will not be kept in the dark about what their leaders are trying to do.

## 4. Stay Firm and Keep Up the Pressure

Once demands are set forth, it's important that the opposing side realize that a leader will remain firm and not easily bend to pressure. "We will have to learn to refuse crumbs from the big-city machines," Martin advised others, "and steadfastly demand a fair share of the loaf." He also believed it important to keep people on both sides of the issue informed. "You can't just communicate with the ghetto dweller and at the same time not frighten many whites to death," he said. "My role perhaps is to interpret to the white world. There must be somebody to communicate to two worlds."

And during the negotiating process, Martin preached that demonstrations and pressure be kept up to facilitate action. In Birmingham, for instance, he advocated putting "pressure on the merchants to carry out all aspects of the agreement. We must press the city council and mayor to make immediate good faith steps to restore a sense of hope and protection in the Negro community." He also utilized the services of two assistants to the U.S. attorney general, "to help open channels of communication between our leadership and the top people in the economic power structure."

## 5. Meet and Regroup with Your Team

In every campaign he conducted during the civil rights movement, Martin frequently called his team together at key junctures. He not only kept his team informed, but doing so allowed him to make better decisions as the negotiation process progressed. Recall, for instance, that Martin's first reaction when Chicago Mayor Richard Daley went behind his back to get a court order limiting marches was to chastise the mayor and react in a negative manner. However, after meeting with his team and thinking the matter through more thoroughly, Martin altered his opinion and decided to comply with the terms of the injunction. The team had made Martin, the ultimate decision-maker, realize that his first reaction was not the best course of action. In fact, it could have derailed the entire negotiating process. At that moment, it was better for the movement to comply with the injunction. Martin's actions not only resulted in a better decision, but a show of good faith.

## 6. Be Prepared to Intensify Pressure if Demands Are Not Met

In 1963, Martin issued the Birmingham Manifesto warning that demonstrations would continue until all movement demands were agreed upon. And when negotiations broke down, major demonstrations intensified. When businessmen went out for lunch and stepped outside on the streets of Birmingham, they encountered several thousand protesters staging sit-ins and singing freedom songs. "These businessmen," wrote Martin, "suddenly realized that the movement could not be stopped." It was at that point that they went back to the bargaining table. And Martin pointed out that "one of the men who had been in the most determined opposition cleared his throat and said: 'You know, I've been thinking this thing through. We ought to be able to work something out.' "

"Don't be too soft," Martin wrote Andrew Young from the Selma jail. "We have the offensive. In a crisis we must have a sense of drama."

## 7. Insist on a Plan of Implementation and Create a Committee to Assure Follow-through

In Birmingham (as in Montgomery, Chicago, and Selma) a biracial committee was established to improve communications and to implement the final accord. As a result, within the first week, department store fitting rooms were desegregated. Within the first month, all "white only" signs were removed from stores and public facilities. And within two months, all lunch counters were desegregated. The Birmingham Accord further provided for the establishment of an ongoing committee to implement and monitor future programs.

Martin believed the formation of a committee to ensure follow-through was absolutely essential. Words on paper are just that—words. It takes people with a mission to implement true, meaningful change. Recall what Martin said near the end of the Chicago summit: "We must now measure our words by our deeds."

## 8. Show Good Faith, Use Discretion, and Allow the Opposition a Graceful Way Out

When asked in Birmingham to suspend demonstrations while negotiations were in progress, Martin agreed to a one-day moratorium. He essentially did the same thing in Chicago when he did not fight the court injunction secured by Mayor Daley. Of this decision, Martin noted: "Because we are engaged in negotiations now with the city, with labor and industry and other forces of power and good will in the community, we decided that we would abide by this [court injunction] until we have our negotiating session next Friday."

Most people, once they've won the battle of negotiation, will remain hard-nosed and not allow the opposition to save face. But there's no use rubbing people's noses in the dirt once the battle has been won. To do so only makes leaders look bad and may very well harm any future negotiations in which they may become involved. As Martin once noted: "Humanity is waiting for something other than a blind imitation of the past."

## 9. Praise the Other Side

After Birmingham's accord, Martin praised the white negotiators as "men of good will." After the Chicago Summit Agreement, he said that he was "as grateful to Mayor Daley as to anyone else here for his work. I think now we can go on to make Chicago a beautiful city, a city of brotherhood."

Martin made these kinds of statements even though he was attacked during the negotiation process. He was verbally abused, politically stabbed in the back, and physically harmed during a march. Why did he do it? Why, in the end, did he praise the other side?

Martin didn't do it just because he was a good and kind person. He did it because he wanted to ensure further progress. He wanted the opposition to feel as good about what they had agreed to as was humanly possible. In so doing, Martin was hoping to turn words into action—to guarantee cooperation and reconciliation in carrying forth the final agreements.

## 10. Stick to the Agreement

After the Birmingham Accord was announced, many people believed Martin had sold them out. So he went before the people and urged compliance. "If this contract is broken," he said, "it will be a disaster and a disgrace. If anyone breaks this contract, let it be the white man."

Breaking an agreement in any form simply gives the opposition an excuse to do the same. If leaders wish to ensure progress, then they must maintain their commitments. Accordingly, Martin not only suspended the Cicero march in Chicago, he halted all demonstrations in Birmingham after the final agreement was reached.

Reactions to what had happened in Chicago in 1966 were some of the strongest and most widespread in the entire American civil rights movement. During that summer, unusually violent riots broke out in the slums of forty cities. Particularly affected were such northern metropolitan areas as Newark, Cleveland, and Dayton. Most analysts attributed the outbreaks to the violence in Chicago—which was broadcast on television across the country.

Personally, Martin also had suffered from the Chicago campaign. He had been directly attacked by Mayor Daley, one of the most powerful politicians in the United States at the time. And he had been chastised by Archbishop Cody, the most powerful member of the clergy in America at the time. Moreover, the rioting hurt the SCLC's mission and Martin's stance on nonviolence. Whites felt he was to blame for what all blacks did. And more and more African-Americans seemed to be turning away from the SCLC—and toward leaders of the Black Power movement.

And yet, Martin Luther King, although worried, remained strikingly determined and tenacious. For instance, after the final Chicago Summit Agreement was announced, Martin accepted an invitation to give a "victory speech" at a Baptist church in Chicago's West Side ghetto. "Some people tried to frighten me," he told his audience. "They said nonviolence couldn't work in the North. They said you can't fight city hall; you better go back down South. But if you look at what happened here, it tells you nonviolence can work."

And then he tried to help people understand that change was not going to happen overnight—even though they deserved better conditions *right now.* "Let's face the fact," he said. "Most of us are going to be living in the ghetto five, ten years from now. . . . Morally, we ought to have what we say in the slogan, Freedom Now. But it all doesn't come now. That's a sad fact of life you have to live with."

Those words—made in the wake of victory—reflected the very essence of negotiation and compromise. You can't have everything you want right now. But *you can* get *something* right now if you compromise during the negotiation process. If you don't compromise, however, you get nothing.

To put it in perspective, a great leader is always looking toward making progress in the long term. And compromise solutions are steps in the right direction.

---

"The key word is 'respect.' "

Martin Luther King, Jr.,
August 9, 1966

---

"We must have patience."

Martin Luther King, Jr.,
1967

---

"We will always be willing to talk and seek fair compromise."

Martin Luther King, Jr.,
July 19, 1962

# MARTIN LUTHER KING, JR., ON LEADERSHIP

★ Appeal to the sense of morality and decency of the people on the other side of the negotiating table.

★ When it looks like talks are going to fail miserably, speak up and reassure the opposition that you appreciate their efforts and do not want to end the dialogue.

★ Remember that sometimes the threat of action is more effective than the real thing.

★ Operate by the law of life that reconciliation is always possible.

★ Always be willing to talk and seek fair compromise.

★ Establish a documented moral record that relief was sought via negotiation.

★ A moderate approach doesn't work. The opposition nails you to the wall and it saps the enthusiasm of followers.

★ Do not be afraid of the words "crisis" and "tension." They are innate in all life and all growth.

★ Injustices must be brought out into the open where they cannot be evaded.

★ Your role as a leader is to communicate to two worlds.

★ Measure people's words by their deeds.

★ Remember that humanity is waiting for something other than a blind imitation of the past.

★ Compromise solutions are steps in the right direction.

★ There must be more than a statement to the larger society—there must be a force that interrupts its functioning at some key point.

"The softminded man always fears change. He feels security in the status quo, and he has an almost morbid fear of the new. For him, the greatest pain is the pain of a new idea."

> Martin Luther King, Jr.,
> 1963

"There is something within human nature that can be changed, and this stands at the top of . . . the philosophy of nonviolence."

> Martin Luther King, Jr.,
> December 16, 1961

"The essence of man is found in freedom."

> Martin Luther King, Jr.,
> 1967

# 13 / Understand Human Nature

From the moment the civil rights movement began in 1955 to the moment it ended in 1968, there was great resistance to the new ideas being proposed that, if implemented, would change the social norm. There was resistance against the Montgomery bus boycott, resistance against desegregation of public facilities, resistance against integration of schools, and so on. Martin and other leaders of the movement clearly realized that some resistance was to be expected. They knew that, in general people love the idea of change, but naturally resist even the smallest alterations in their daily routine.

But events turned into a crisis when, as Martin pointed

out, "the emerging new order, based on the principle of democratic equalitarianism, came face to face with the old order, based on the principles of paternalism and subordination." The white South, he said, was trying to "perpetuate a system of human values that came into being under a feudalistic plantation system which cannot survive in a day of growing urbanization and industrial expansion."

The tremendous obstruction and violent fighting put up by white segregationists all through the South—and then in northern cities such as Chicago—frightened many African-Americans and alarmed the moderate white majority across the nation. But Martin sought to quell their fears and relate the movement's events to the natural human tendency to resist change. "Let nobody fool you," he said, "all the loud noises we hear today in terms of nullification and interposition are nothing but the death groans of a dying system. The old order is passing away, the new order is coming into being. . . ."

Martin also astutely pointed out that in the emergence of any new order "we must be willing to confront the onslaught and the recalcitrance of the old order." Most experienced leaders understand that derision, slander, and violence are natural by-products of implementing change on a massive scale. Abraham Lincoln knew it. He once said: "The pioneers in any movement are not generally the best people to carry that movement to a successful issue. They often have to meet such hard opposition, and get so battered and bespattered, that afterward, when people find they have to accept reform, they will accept it more easily from others." Woodrow Wilson knew it. "If you want to make enemies," he said, "try to change something." And, of course, Martin King knew it when he described the recurring pattern of violence that occurred after each successful SCLC campaign as "the inevitable counterrevolution that succeeds every period of progress."

Martin also frequently pointed out to his audiences that he was the target of the old order's attacks as much as anybody else, but that history showed such occurrences to be natural results of being at the forefront of meaningful change. "The guardians of the status quo lash out with denunciation against the person or organization that they consider most responsible for the emergence of the new order," he said. "Often this denunciation rises to major proportions. In the transition from slavery to restricted emancipation, Abraham Lincoln was assassinated. In the present transition from segregation to desegregation, the Supreme Court is castigated and the NAACP is maligned and subjected to extralegal reprisals."

In recalling the events of the Montgomery bus boycott, Martin documented five specific methods employed by the "old guards who would rather die than surrender" to halt the progress of the movement:

1. They tried to negotiate us into a compromise. When that didn't work . . .
2. They tried to divide the leadership. They tried to conquer by dividing and they spread false rumors throughout the community about the leaders. Then they attempted to establish petty jealousy among the leaders. After that didn't work . . .
3. They moved to a "get tough" policy.
4. Then came actual physical violence.
5. Then came the method of mass indictment.

In some ways, leadership is a perilous business because most people will resist change—and sometimes they will take their opposition to the most extreme ends. Initially, when a new idea is proposed, many members of an organization will respond by saying things like "Leave things the way they are"; "Hey, we don't want you stirring things up"; "If it ain't broke, don't fix it"; or the old standby, "We've been doing it this way for thirty years and I don't see any need to change now."

Martin Luther King, Jr., was confronted with more than

only the recalcitrance of the white majority. There was also obstinance, jealousy, and competition from people within the ranks of the African-American community. The old guard leadership did not approve of such direct action techniques as boycotts, sit-ins, and mass demonstrations. They had never had to resort to them before and thought the tactics too confrontational, too likely to precipitate violent reactions from whites.

On the other end of the spectrum, however, younger blacks passionately approved of such tactics. As a matter of fact, their youthful tendency to be less patient and more inclined to lash out violently eventually led to the militant Black Power movement, which came about partly in response to the white majority's unwillingness to make changes. Martin explained the violent and bitter reactions of young blacks by noting: "When there is rocklike intransigence or sophisticated manipulation that mocks the empty-handed petitioner, rage replaces reason." He also pointed out that "Disappointment produces despair and despair produces bitterness, and the one thing certain about bitterness is its blindness. Bitterness has not the capacity to make the distinction between one and all. When some members of the dominant group, particularly those in power, are racist in attitude and practice, bitterness accuses the whole group."

As resistance by whites to racial change increased, the ranks of the militant black faction swelled—and Black Power leaders became increasingly more militant. Stokely Carmichael advocated that blacks should "kill the Honkies." His successor as chairman of SNCC, H. Rap Brown, encouraged African-Americans to "get their guns" and start a civil war.

Martin very quickly realized that these calls for violence were not only exactly the opposite of what he had been preaching for years, but they posed a direct challenge to his leadership of the American civil rights movement as a whole. At first, his response to the threat was cautious. While agreeing with the need to "appreciate our great heritage" and to "be proud of our race," Martin also "pleaded with the group to abandon the Black Power slogan" because of what he called "the harmful connotation of the words." He felt that the slogan conveyed "hostile connotations," fostered divisiveness, and that "we are not interested in furthering any divisions in the civil rights movement." Racial separatism was a misguided path as far as Martin was concerned. It created internal divisiveness that led to hostility. "Whenever Pharaoh wanted to keep the slaves in slavery," he reminded his audiences, "he kept them fighting among themselves."

Divisiveness among people over proposed changes is, indeed, a phenomenon older than the Egyptian pyramids. Those who do not want to change will fight those who do—for no rational reason whatsoever. "Men are not easily moved from their mental ruts or purged of their prejudiced and irrational feelings," Martin once noted. "The softminded man always fears change," he said. "He feels security in the status quo, and he has an almost morbid fear of the new. For him, the greatest pain is the pain of a new idea."

Clearly, Martin King understood that it is a fundamental human tendency for people to resist nearly any form of change if they have not been prepared in advance for the transformation. Effective leadership, in part, requires understanding this fact among other important aspects of human nature.

In essence, change is what leadership is all about. Leaders are change-makers, they are masters of change. By helping followers achieve goals, they lead people to where they've never been before. Leaders blaze new trails. They plow new ground. They sail uncharted waters. Leaders are out in front.

How, then, do the best leaders institute a new order, new methods, or even a new idea?

The first step in the change process centers around raising awareness. The earlier people are forewarned of the proposed change, the better. The next step is, quite simply, to involve others in planning the proposed transformation—whatever it might be. Involving people in the planning process tends to alleviate the anxiety associated with massive change—thereby giving people a higher level of security. Personal involvement also leads to a higher education of the changes involved, which, in turn, essentially eliminates fear. Such education is often the best change agent available to a leader because it binds people together and instills a sense of pride and responsibility.

In general, effective leaders first make the case for change by *persuading* people to become committed to the new endeavor. Then, through teamwork, members of the organization become immersed in formulating specific goals and recommendations. The leader next works with others to achieve those objectives. Furthermore, leaders continually reassure members of the organization that the changes made were necessary and will pay off in the long run. Lastly, when things go well, strong leaders will give other people credit for making it all happen; conversely, they'll accept full responsibility if things go awry.

This was precisely the process used by Martin Luther King, Jr., during the civil rights movement. The central idea was to introduce change gradually and allow people to become comfortable with the suggested idea. When beginning any new campaign, Martin and other SCLC leaders first went into the city, as they did in Birmingham or Chicago, and let people know what their intentions were. Then they went around to the local churches and made speeches. Often they walked the streets to recruit volunteers and persuade people that nonviolent resistance was the best way to achieve change. And, of course, they worked endlessly with the local African-American leadership to solicit input into the planning of details—and to help understand the culture and politics of the town.

Martin also stressed the need for a wide array of initiatives designed to be implemented over a long period of time. The lesson to be learned is that people can only take so much change at any one time and that they have to get used to the idea of changing before they actually modify their behavior. So leaders should think in the long term and extend their plans for change over a broad timeline. Of this philosophy, Jesse Jackson noted that during the Chicago movement, "Dr. King said it would take from three to five years for a sustained nonviolent movement to begin to change the thing." And Andrew Young wrote: "Martin used to say that America was a ten-day nation. The first ten days, no matter what we did it was wrong, and we were told we shouldn't be doing it at all. The second ten days, the opposition would admit there was a problem, but say that we were going about a solution in the wrong way. The third ten days, they would try to take the problem away from us, saying, 'We were going to do something about this anyway, and if you hadn't interfered we could have solved it sooner.' Getting to the third phase is the goal of a transformational movement," concluded Young. "You *want* people to internalize and claim the changes as their own."

Initial negative reactions to change are as natural as when people blink in reaction to something being thrown into their faces. It is exceedingly important for leaders to understand such simple points of human nature. And, at a very early age, Martin Luther King, Jr., set out on a quest to do just that— to understand the motivations, reactions, and feelings of people. In fact, he embarked on a lifelong study of human nature.

At the age of nineteen, Martin graduated from Morehouse College with a degree in sociology—the study of human social behavior. Early in his education, he became "absolutely convinced of the natural goodness of man and the natural power of human reason." But as time passed, and his youthful idealism began to temper, he became more aware of "the complexity of human motives." "The more I thought about human nature," he wrote in *Stride Toward Freedom,* "the more I saw how our tragic inclination for sin causes us to use our minds to rationalize our actions. . . . I came to recognize the complexity of man's social involvement and the glaring reality of collective evil. I came to feel that liberalism had been all too sentimental concerning human nature and that it leaned toward a false idealism."

Unethical people will, as Martin later noted, "sacrifice truth on the altars of self-interest" and they may be "more prone to follow the expedient [rather] than the ethical path." It may be true, he also said, that "morality cannot be legislated, but behavior can be regulated. The law may not change the heart, but it can restrain the heartless. It will take education and religion to change bad internal attitudes, but legislation and court orders can control the external effects of bad internal attitudes."

As Martin grew older and wiser, he continued to think deeply about human nature. He continued to delve into his own personal thoughts, emotions, and inner conflicts. And, like any good philosopher, he realized that his own feelings were probably similar, if not identical, to those of human beings everywhere. In many of his speeches, he conveyed these thoughts. "Plato, centuries ago said that the human personality is like a charioteer with two headstrong horses, each wanting to go in different directions," he said in one of his sermons. "Each of us has two selves. . . ." On the one hand, he said, because people have "a fear of what life may bring, [we often] develop inferiority complexes, a lack of self-confidence, and a sense of impending failure." On the other hand, he noted, "deep down within all of us, [we have] an instinct. It's a kind of drum major instinct—a desire to be out in front, a desire to lead the parade, a desire to be first."

Much of the racial problem in America, Martin believed, was due to this instinct. He described it as "a need that some people have to feel superior. A need that some people have to feel that they are first, and to feel that their white skin ordains them to be first." He went on to say that the "final great tragedy is the fact that when one fails to harness [the drum major instinct], he ends by trying to push others down in order to push himself up." That, in turn, Martin concluded, results in a person spreading "evil, vicious, lying gossip on people" and believing that "he's a little better than [others]."

Essentially, Martin's study of sociology, philosophy, and great writers like Plato, Aristotle, Rousseau, Locke, Niebuhr, and others led him to a better insight and understanding of the negative aspects of human nature. As a result, he came to realize that love and good will toward one's fellow human beings alone could not overcome racial oppression and achieve meaningful change. He had to do more. He somehow had to help educate others on the lessons of history that he, himself, had learned.

One of his strategies was to place the overall civil rights movement into a much broader context. "Indeed, we are engaged in a social revolution," he said, "and while it may be different from other revolutions, it is a revolution just the same. It is a movement to bring about certain basic structural changes in the architecture of society. This is certainly revolutionary."

In addition, Martin eloquently articulated the long-term impact that slavery and segregation had on African-Americans in general. "For many years, the Negro tacitly accepted segregation," he wrote. "He was the victim of stagnant passivity and deadening complacency. The system of slavery and segregation caused many Negroes to feel that perhaps they were inferior. This is the ultimate tragedy of segregation. It not only harms one physically, but it injures one spiritually. It scars the soul and distorts the personality. It inflicts the segregator with a false sense of superiority while inflicting the segregated with a false sense of inferiority."

"But there comes a time when people get tired of being trampled over by the iron feet of oppression. There comes a time when people get tired of being flung across the abyss of humiliation where they experience the bleakness of nagging despair."

"So," he concluded, "there has been a revolutionary change—a determination to achieve freedom and human dignity. . . . This determination springs from the same longing for freedom that motivates oppressed people all over the world."

On a more specific and detailed basis, Martin could also explain, through his understanding of human nature, the spontaneous action of Rosa Parks (who initiated the Montgomery bus boycott by refusing to give up her seat to a white man) by describing it as "an individual expression of a timeless longing for human dignity and freedom." "Eventually the cup of endurance runs over," he said, "and the human personality cries out, 'I can take it no longer.'"

Such a development, as far as he was concerned, should not surprise any student of history. "Oppressed people cannot remain oppressed forever. The yearning for freedom eventually manifests itself."

"Freedom," Martin would say, "is the act of deliberating, deciding and responding within our destined nature." Therefore, he concluded: "Freedom is necessary for one's selfhood, for one's intrinsic worth. . . . The essence of man is found in freedom."

In his writings, Martin suggested that the oppression during the civil rights movement created "discontent so deep, anger so ingrained, restlessness so wide" that something had "to serve as a channel through which these deep emotional feelings" could be funneled. He then described in some detail the forms of behavior in which people react to oppression.

ɪ One way people react is with acquiescence. "But acquiescence," wrote Martin in *Stride Toward Freedom*, "while often the easier way—is not the moral way." He went on to call it "the way of the coward," and say that a person "cannot win the respect of his oppressor by acquiescing," but that such behavior "merely increases the arrogance and contempt." "Acquiescence," he also said, "is proof of inferiority."

ᐯ Second, there is a natural reaction "to strike out against oppression" with "physical violence and corroding hatred." However, violence "can reap nothing but grief," he noted. "It solves no social problem; it merely creates new and more complicated ones." Martin also characterized violence as "immoral because it seeks to humiliate the opponent rather than win his understanding; it seeks to annihilate rather than to convert; it thrives on hatred rather than love; it destroys community and makes brotherhood impossible; it leaves society in a monologue rather than dialogue; [and] it creates bitterness in survivors and brutality in the destroyers."

3 The third way people could react to oppression, according to Martin, was through nonviolent resistance, which, he said, "seeks to reconcile the truths of two opposites—acquiescence and violence." This behavior was, of course, the one he preferred and preached. But it is also the least natural, in that people first have to overcome their emotions and gain courage to implement it properly.

Interestingly enough, Martin also pointed out that nonviolence not only serves as an outlet for anger among the oppressed, it has a compelling impact on the oppressors. "I think it arouses a sense of shame within them in many instances," he said. "It does something to touch the conscience and establish a sense of guilt. . . . This approach doesn't make the [oppressor] feel comfortable. I think it does the other thing. It disturbs his conscience and it disturbs this sense of contentment that he had."

In general, the ability of leaders to understand human nature is in direct proportion to their level of effectiveness. Knowing how people will react in any given situation, how they may be inspired and motivated, and how they will behave no matter what a leader does, is a critical skill for effective leadership. Quite simply, to understand human nature is to understand reality.

Specifically, there are two overarching reasons leaders must have a good understanding of human nature:

## 1. To Understand the Motives and Reactions of the People They Lead

This principle involves such simple points of human nature as a person's negative reaction at being told what to do rather than being asked his or her opinion. By understanding what makes people tick, leaders will be better prepared for the reactions they will experience from followers. Accordingly, they'll be better able to implement the changes they desire.

Those who do not understand human nature may find themselves in a similar situation to the one in which the editor of the *California Star* newspaper found himself when a rumor reached town in 1848 that gold had been discovered at Sutter's Mill. Author John McPhee related the incident in *Assembling California*:

> In an April memorandum, the editor of the *California Star* says, in large letters, "HUMBUG" to the idea that gold in any quantity lies in the Sierra. Six weeks later, the *Star* ceases publication, because there is no one left in the shop to print it. . . . [In San Francisco] ministers have abandoned their churches, teachers their students, lawyers their victims. Shops are closed. Jobs of all kinds have been left unfinished.

## 2. To Improve Themselves by Effectively Interacting with Others

Leaders must also understand human nature so that they may better understand themselves. By having an awareness of why people behave the way they do, a good leader will be able to apply that knowledge to his or her own specific performance and interactions. The most frequent result of such self-analysis causes the leader to become more compassionate and more empathic. When leaders display such tendencies toward followers, it almost always results in greater acceptance and genuine affection for the leader.

This fundamental notion, however, is certainly not a new

idea. It was clearly noted several thousand years ago in this Taoist story of ancient China:

> When Yen Ho was about to take up his duties as tutor to the heir Fo Ling, Duke of Wei, he went to Ch'u Po Yu for advice. "I have to deal," he said, "with a man of depraved and murderous disposition. . . . How is one to deal with a man of this sort?" "I am glad," said Ch'u Po Yu, "that you asked this question. . . . The first thing you must do is not to improve him, but to improve yourself."

Great leaders think deeply about human nature—about what motivates others, how people react in different situations, how their thought processes work in various situations, and about how factions and extremist points of view manifest themselves. Without effective leadership, human nature is such that people will withdraw into their own world and create their own group of dissidents. There is an unwillingness to accept new situations or to act quickly. A conservative approach is more common than a liberal one.

People are more likely to stick with the old ways, to not try new things until they're absolutely certain, absolutely convinced that they should act—and then action is taken only precipitously and tentatively. An underlying premise of leadership, therefore, is to unite separate factions and mobilize them toward a common end. Essentially, the entire process of change should be repeated at regular intervals. And leaders, as agents of change, must understand human nature if they are to move large numbers of people down the same path—toward a new destination.

Successful leaders also realize that from profound change spring new opportunities. In order to seize those opportunities, leaders cannot live on the momentum that was created by the leadership team of the past. They have to create their own legacy. They have to do something other than just continue to ride the wave. They have to lead in their own time.

That's what Martin Luther King, Jr., did—he seized the opportunities generated from change and he attempted to lead in his own time without being encumbered by the "dogmas of the quiet past." And even with his deep understanding of the negative aspects of human nature Martin remained optimistic. "There is something within human nature that can be changed," he noted, "and this stands at the top of . . . the philosophy of nonviolence." "There is within human nature an amazing potential for goodness [and] something that can respond to goodness," he also said. And, of the recalcitrant white majority, he once noted simply, "I have seen them change in the past."

Because violence is an unavoidable part of human nature—both in resisting oppression and reacting to change—an extraordinarily volatile stage was set for the American civil rights movement in the year 1967. That summer, in an effort to head off rioting, the SCLC began a massive voter-registration drive and Operation Breadbasket program in Cleveland, Ohio. Martin spent a great deal of time walking the streets of Cleveland's ghettos, mingling with unemployed African-Americans, preaching to them the benefits of nonviolence.

While the SCLC project there was proving extremely successful, the worst riots of the era broke out across the United States. Things got so bad in Detroit that federal troops and tanks were sent in to maintain order. That action prompted Martin to complain that the Johnson administration had "created the bizarre spectacle of armed forces of the United States fighting in ghetto streets while they are fighting in the jungles of [Vietnam]."

In all, more than a hundred cities erupted in uncontrollable violence—which resulted in widespread death, destruction, and despair.

But no riots occurred in Cleveland that summer.

"Deep down within all of us, [we have] an instinct. It's a kind of drum major instinct—a desire to be out front, a desire to lead the parade, a desire to be first."

Martin Luther King, Jr.,
February 4, 1968

"Morality cannot be legislated, but behavior can be regulated. The law may not change the heart, but it can restrain the heartless."

Martin Luther King, Jr.,
1959

# MARTIN LUTHER KING, JR., ON LEADERSHIP

★ In the emergence of any new order, you must be willing to confront the onslaught and recalcitrance of the old order.

★ Remember that the guardians of the status quo will lash out against the person or organization that they consider most responsible for the emergence of the new order.

★ Don't be surprised if the opposition tries to divide your leadership or spread false rumors about you.

★ Remember that disappointment may produce despair and bitterness.

★ People are not easily moved from their mental ruts or purged of their prejudiced and irrational feelings.

★ The first step in the change process is raising awareness. The second step is to involve others in the planning process.

★ Extend your plans for change over a broad timeline.

★ Remember that unethical people will sacrifice the truth on the altars of self-interest.

★ Temper your drum major instinct.

★ Freedom is necessary for a person's selfhood and intrinsic worth.

★ Remember that noncooperation with evil is as much a moral obligation as is cooperation with good.

★ Victor Hugo once said that progress is the mode of man; that when it is blocked, just as an obstacle in a river makes the water foam, so an obstacle to progress makes humanity seethe.

★ Within the best of people there is some evil, and within the worst there is some good.

★ People fail to get along with each other because they fear each other—and they fear each other because they don't know each other.

★ A movement that changes both people and institutions is a revolution.

# PART IV

# ENSURING THE FUTURE

*"As I stand here and look out upon the thousands of Negro faces, and the thousands of white faces, intermingled like the waters of a river, I see only one face—the face of the future."*

MARTIN LUTHER KING, JR.,
APRIL 18, 1959

> "We must combine the toughness of the serpent and the softness of the dove—a tough mind and a tender heart."
>
> Martin Luther King, Jr.,
> 1963

> "We as leaders lifted hope. We had to do it."
>
> Martin Luther King, Jr.,
> December 15, 1966

> "All the darkness in the world cannot obscure the light of a single candle."
>
> Martin Luther King, Jr.,
> February 16, 1960

# 14 / Preach Hope and Compassion

In November 1966, Martin Luther King, Jr., called for a gathering of the entire SCLC staff for a three-day retreat in Frogmore, South Carolina. In the wake of the turbulent Chicago campaign, he felt it was appropriate timing to get everyone together to discuss the future of the organization. At that meeting, seventy-five people from all levels of the SCLC debated and discussed events that had occurred over the previous nine years—their wins and their losses; what they did right and what they did wrong. Much discussion revolved around the rise of the more militant Black Power faction and related increased violence in the movement.

Drawing on his background in sociology and understanding

of human nature, Martin rose to speak about the contrasting elements of hope and hate. Throughout history, he said, the hope element in all revolutions was "expressed in the rising expectations for freedom and justice and human dignity on the part of those who had been caught in oppressive situations." He went on to explain how most major revolutions, even though violent in nature, originally "moved on the wave of hope—the hope that the old order could be removed and that a new order could come into being." On the other hand, he said, the hate element "came into being as an expression of the hatred and bitterness toward the perpetrators of the old order."

Martin then related this historical explanation to the current situation involving the rise of Black Power and widespread rioting across the nation. "Certainly we have had these rising expectations for freedom and justice that I just mentioned," he said, "but we transformed the hate element of the traditional revolution into positive nonviolent power, and it was precisely this hope and nonviolent power that guided the psychological turning point through all of the victories that we achieved.

"As long as the hope element was fulfilled, there was very little question of nonviolence," he continued. "But the minute hopes were blasted; the minute people realized that in spite of all of these gains their conditions were still terrible: then violence became a part of the terminology of the movement from some segments. It is in this context that we must see what is happening now."

From these insightful remarks to the members of his team, it becomes readily apparent that a major part of Martin King's leadership style was to keep hope alive among the masses. "We must accept finite disappointment, but we must never lose infinite hope," he once wrote. "Because when you lose hope you die." Just about wherever he went, that was the message he preached. "Basic in our philosophy," he would say, "is a deep faith in the future. . . . Ours is a movement based on hope."

Martin realized that hope is a sustaining element, not only

in leadership, but in life. Hope motivates and inspires. It causes people to take action. What's more, he never wavered in his intensity of preaching this message throughout all the years of the movement. During a speech in New York in 1956, for instance, he noted that "I do not come here with a message of bitterness, hate or despair. I come here with a message of love and a message of hope." In 1963, at an early church mass meeting, he stated: "In spite of my shattered dreams, I came to Birmingham with hope." After the campaign, he reasserted: "We must keep alive the great hope that Birmingham brought to Negroes all over the nation. . . ."

"We as leaders lifted hope," he said in a moment of reflection on the Chicago movement. "We had to do it." And to a large groups of church leaders in 1967, Martin asked: "Shall we say the odds are too great? Shall we tell them the struggle is too hard? Or will there be another message, of longing, of hope, of solidarity with their yearning, of commitment to their cause, whatever the cost?"

Whenever a significant positive event occurred, Martin and the other movement leaders played up the good news. Each positive court decision, for instance, served "to transform the fatigue of despair into the buoyancy of hope." And they actively encouraged all types of communications, slogans, and freedom songs in order to "add hope to our determination."

"The students have developed a theme song for their movement," Martin explained to one audience, "maybe you've heard it. It goes something like this, 'We shall overcome, deep in my heart, I do believe, we shall overcome.'" To another group, he described how the students on the Freedom Rides who knew they were going to "face hostile and jeering mobs," who knew they "would be thrown into jail," who realized they might "even face physical death," could still sing, "We shall overcome, we are not afraid."

"Then something caused me to see at that moment the real meaning of the movement," he said. "That the students had faith in the future. That the movement was based on hope."

In his speeches, Martin not only employed alliteration, but similes and metaphors in an effort to raise hopes and expectations among the people—especially when times were toughest. "Like the ever-flowing waters of a river, life has its moments of drought and its moments of flood," he'd say. "Like the ever-changing cycle of the seasons, life has the soothing warmth of the summers and the piercing chill of its winters."

He also made numerous analogies between a new day dawning and hope within the civil rights movement. "Although we stand now in the midst of the midnight of injustice," he said in Montgomery, "we are only a few steps from the daybreak of freedom and equality." In Birmingham, he stated that "no midnight long remains. The weary traveler by midnight who asks for bread is really seeking the dawn. Our eternal message of hope is that the dawn will come." And in a famous Mother's Day sermon, Martin mentioned that "Something beautiful will happen in this universe because we were able to look out into the darkness and see the pressing daybreak."

Most often, however, he would compare the extremes of despair and hope to darkness and light. Here are a few examples:

- "The sins of a dark yesterday will be redeemed in the achievements of a bright tomorrow."
- "[We] can transform dark yesterdays of hatred into bright tomorrows of love" and "see on the horizons radiant stars of hope."
- "All the darkness in the world cannot obscure the light of a single candle."
- "I believe that even amid today's mortar bursts and whining bullets, there is still hope for a brighter tomorrow."
- "Darkness cannot drive out darkness, only light can do that. Hate cannot drive out hate, only love can do that."

Martin also wove the basics of the American dream through many of his speeches. He resurrected the Declaration of Independence and dusted off the Constitution to remind everyone that "equality" was at the heart of America. "There is a basis of hope in the democratic creed," he told people. "The American people are infected with racism—that is the peril," he said. "[But] they are also infected with democratic ideals—that is the hope."

He wanted to "call our nation to a higher destiny, to a new plateau of compassion . . . to make the American dream a reality," as he said. "I do not think the tiny nation that stood in majesty at Concord and Lexington; that electrified a world with the Declaration of Independence would defame its heritage."

In an attempt to turn his inspiring words into concrete action, in August 1966 Martin appealed directly to the president, Lyndon Johnson, to "provide the poor with new hope and opportunity . . . to avoid an ever-growing despair and bitterness." In a lengthy, detailed letter, he pointed out that earlier in the year many "homeless Mississippi Delta Negroes went to the empty Greenville Air Base seeking shelter from the winter cold [but] were forcibly driven off by Federal troops." Another similar group who "have no jobs and almost no food," as Martin pointed out, "struggled through the long winter in tents because of the Federal Government's failure to respond to their pleas for housing."

Martin went on to chastise Johnson for the "callous disregard of the Federal Government for the plight of tens of thousands of other poor Mississippi Delta Negroes," whose unemployment rate hovered near 66 percent. Then he advocated "immediate mobilization of new, massive Federal, State, and private resources—human, physical, and financial." He also made a specific proposal that the Greenville Air Force Base, which contained "hundreds of buildings suitable for classrooms, workshops, and living quarters," be converted "into a huge center for providing training, housing, and supportive programs for poverty stricken citizens of the Mississippi Delta, most of whom are Negro."

This letter to President Johnson vividly demonstrated Martin King's great compassion for people. He had heard about the plight of the Mississippians living in poverty—and he simply had to try to do something about it. And not only did Martin appeal to the president, he took his message to the public.

Through many public speeches, he championed the idea that America seize the opportunity to "bridge the gulf between the haves and the have-nots," noting that "we now have the techniques and the resources to get rid of poverty." "If America is to remain a first-class nation," said Martin Luther King, Jr., "we cannot have second-class citizens."

"We must rapidly begin the shift from a 'thing-oriented' society to a 'person-oriented' society," he said. "When machines and computers, profit motives and property rights are considered more important than people, the giant triplets of racism, materialism, and militarism are incapable of being conquered."

In advocating specific proposals, he noted that "We spend far too much of our national budget establishing military bases around the world rather than bases of genuine concern and understanding. . . . It is a cruel jest to say to a bootless man that he ought to lift himself by his own bootstraps," Martin pointed out. "Ultimately, society must condemn the robber and not the robbed." But, on the other hand, he also noted that "true compassion is more than flinging a coin to a beggar."

Accordingly, he proposed that a variety of innovative initiatives be undertaken by the government, including "effective new and nondiscriminatory training programs . . . training for unemployed and underemployed Negroes for jobs at every level from nonprofessional and unskilled to technical and professional," and implacement of "the necessary resources and supply consultant staff on a continuing basis to assure that the most effective and innovative programs are initiated and maintained."

The advocating of specific initiatives to help people stemmed, in large part, from Martin's innately compassionate nature. It is clear that, from an early age, he was more caring

PREACH HOPE AND COMPASSION

than the average individual. He had often said, for instance, that he was "deeply interested in political matters and social ills," and that he wanted to play a part "in breaking down legal barriers to Negroes." As a matter of fact, he chose a profession that conformed to this particular part of his personality—and the biblical teaching that "he who is greatest among you shall be your servant."

He had told people that he heard a voice saying "Do something for others." "My call to the ministry," he wrote, "was an inner urge calling me to serve humanity."

"I am here," he said in Albany, Georgia, in 1961, "because I love America . . . [and] because there are twenty million Negroes in the United States and I love every one of them. I am concerned about every one of them. What happens to any one of them concerns all directly."

"I choose to identify with the underprivileged," he said in a speech in Chicago in 1966. "I choose to identify with the poor. I choose to give my life for the hungry. I choose to give my life for those who have been left out of the sunlight of opportunity."

"Some people are suffering," he said to his Ebenezer Baptist congregation in 1966. "Some people are hungry this morning. Some people are still living with segregation and discrimination this morning. I'm going to fight for them."

And in so many ways, Martin's actions mirrored his words. When someone was harmed in the movement, he often rushed to their side—such as when James Meredith was shot outside Memphis. Recall that, in Birmingham, he gave the eulogy for the four girls killed in the bombing of the 16th Street Baptist Church—as he did for Medgar Evers and Jimmy Lee Jackson.

Martin also took time away from his busy schedule to write hundreds of thank-you notes for people who wished him well or contributed to the cause. To two children, ages nine and twelve, he wrote: "I am deeply grateful to both of you for the very fine contribution of $3.31. It means so much to all of us here to know that there are little folks like you who are genuinely interested in the struggle for justice. Such moral support and Christian generosity from you, our friends, in this momentous struggle, are of inestimable value in the continuance of our humble efforts."

One of the most poignant examples of Martin King's compassion occurred in 1956 when he learned that a trusted adviser, Rev. U. J. Fields, had announced to the press that members of the Montgomery Improvement Association had misused money sent from all over the nation and had appropriated funds for their own personal use. When the young and emotional Rev. Fields spoke personally with Martin, he admitted that he had made it all up in a moment of anger and that he deeply regretted what he had said. Martin then asked Fields if he would be willing to tell his story at that evening's mass meeting in Montgomery's Beulah Baptist Church. When he agreed, Martin took the lead.

As people began filling the pews for the meeting, Martin positioned himself at the rostrum next to Fields—and both of them heard at least one angry member of the crowd yell: "Look at that devil sitting right next to Reverend King." Martin recorded what happened next in his book *Stride Toward Freedom*.

"I had a double task ahead," he wrote. "One was to convince the people that there had been no misappropriation of funds and that the internal structure of the MIA was still stable; the other was to persuade them to forgive Fields for his errors and to give him a hearing. I plunged immediately into the first issue."

After explaining the relevant facts, Martin turned to the second issue: "I call upon you to forgive the Reverend Fields," he said as he saw several heads shaking in refusal. "We are all aware of the weaknesses of human nature. We have all made mistakes. Now some of us are here this evening to stone one of our brothers because he has made a mistake. Let him who is without sin cast the first stone."

"I recited the parable of the prodigal son," he wrote. "Will

we be like the unforgiving elder brother, or will we, in the
spirit of Christ, follow the example of the living and forgiving
father?

"Then," said Martin, "as Fields rose to speak, instead of the
boos and catcalls he had expected he was met with respectful
silence. . . . By the time he finished the audience was deeply
moved [and] he left the platform to solid applause."

Martin King's forgiving, compassionate nature compelled
him to act for the benefit of human rights and world peace.
And clearly, that underlying purpose, coupled with his achievements in American civil rights, led to his being awarded the
Nobel Peace Prize in 1964. Not only did Martin give the entire $54,000 prize money to various organizations associated
with the movement, he then personally interpreted the award
as a "commission to work harder [for] the brotherhood of
man."

Imbued then with a sense of personal renewal, he continued
to preach the very messages that he had felt as a child, that had
propelled him into the ministry. "Let us remember that as we
struggle, we must have love, compassion and understanding
goodwill for those against whom we struggle." He advised
that people not sink to "the passionless depths of hardheartedness" because the hardhearted person "lacks the capacity for
genuine compassion; is unmoved by the pains and afflictions of
his brothers; depersonalizes life; and never sees people as people, but rather as mere objects." "We need leadership that is
calm and yet positive," he advocated. "There is no place for
misguided emotionalism. . . . We must never struggle with
falsehood, hate or malice."

Over and over again, Martin reminded people that "[We]
don't need to hate anybody" and that "the chain of hatred
must be cut" because "hate is too great a burden to bear." And
he constantly reminded everybody that "There is no easy way
to create a world where men and women can live together,
where each has his own job and house and where all children
receive as much education as their minds can absorb. If such a

world is created in our lifetime, it will be done by people of good will . . . by persons who have the courage to put an end to suffering . . . by working toward a world of brotherhood, cooperation, and peace." "I believe that unarmed truth and unconditional love will have the final word in reality," he said in his Nobel address.

In general, leaders are in the business of working with people—working with them, interacting with them, achieving results in the best interests of the majority or the group at large. People do not follow leaders who don't care about the values, the wants and needs, the hopes and aspirations of those in the organization. People do not follow leaders who don't care about children. People do not follow leaders who don't care, period.

Many of the world's greatest leaders were known for their compassionate and caring natures. During the Civil War, for example, Abraham Lincoln was famous for pardoning young soldiers who were to be shot for desertion. He appealed to the "better angels of our nature," and was certain to have let the South move easily back into the Union had he not been assassinated. Lincoln's unusual empathy for people can be traced to his having grown up in abject poverty and never having forgotten the plight of the underprivileged.

On a grand scale, Mohandas K. Gandhi, in successfully achieving India's independence, preached nonviolence and compassion toward the enemies of his people. On a smaller, more intimate level, he required the highest possible standards from his associates while, at the same time, nurturing their personal development. He told his followers that "there is a limit to the development of the intellect but none to that of the heart." At the time, the extent of Gandhi's caring nature had not been equaled by any leader in world history except for perhaps Jesus Christ. And the Indian people responded in kind.

With both genuine compassion and an empathic nature, Franklin Roosevelt bonded with American citizens during the Great Depression and World War II as no other leader had ever before done. Of great interest to presidential scholars is how this leader, who had grown up under privileged circumstances in a wealthy family, could have been so caring, so compassionate, so attuned to average people who were out of jobs, who had lost everything, who had no hope.

Clearly, such a caring nature tied to the fact that, at the age of thirty-nine, Roosevelt permanently lost the use of his legs due to the ravaging effects of polio. His subsequent rehabilitation process with other patients caused a deep and permanent change in FDR's character. Before the disease struck, Roosevelt was considered to be a typical rich politician. Afterward, however, he maintained a lifelong feeling of compassion for his fellow man.

Lincoln grew up in poverty. Roosevelt experienced a debilitating disease. And while the qualities of compassion and empathy are not limited to those leaders who experienced difficult circumstances earlier in life, it should be remembered that Martin Luther King, Jr., has always been regarded as a compassionate man of the common people. As a matter of fact, when *Time* magazine named him 1963 "Man of the Year," the cover story acknowledged that he had "an indescribable capacity for empathy that is the touchstone of leadership."

People listened to him and followed him precisely because he articulated their longings, their hopes, their aspirations, and their dreams—and because he experienced what they experienced. Martin, like so many African-Americans across America, had been refused service in a public restaurant; had received less wages than a white man for doing exactly the same job; had been called a "nigger"; had seen his young son refused admission to a school because of his race; and had stammered as he explained to his six-year-old daughter why she couldn't go to the amusement park that had been advertised on television. People identified with Martin not only because he cared, but also because he had also been, as he said, "the victim of deferred dreams, of blasted hopes."

In *Principle-Centered Leadership,* Stephen Covey pointed

out that "an attitude of empathy is enormously attractive because it keeps you open, and others feel that you are learning, that you are influenceable." It follows, then, that such an "attitude of empathy" or a "capacity to care" can translate into an important form of communication.

But Martin King did more with communication than simply let people know that he cared. He listened patiently and shared ideas. He established common ground and commiserated with people. And he echoed the core values articulated in the Declaration of Independence and the Constitution—the core values of freedom and equality with which virtually everybody agreed.

It should not be ignored, however, that, unless leaders are careful, they may experience some pitfalls while practicing such compassionate leadership. In general, it's true that the more leaders care about others, the more likely it is they are going to be liked by people in the organization. However, it does not follow that the more compassionate and caring a person is, the better leader he or she will be. Caring too much can lead to an unwillingness to make tough decisions, especially when it may mean firing someone, sending troops into battle, or other actions that may cause unpleasantness to individuals. Many managers in large corporations resist even telling a worker when they've done something wrong for fear of hurting their feelings.

If a leader is going to be successful, however, a compassionate and caring nature must be combined with a strong desire to achieve. Such a drive usually offsets any lost action that the "caring too much" syndrome may cause. Martin Luther King, Jr., had it right when he said: "We must combine the toughness of the serpent and the softness of the dove—a tough mind and a tender heart."

Martin's capacity to combine toughness and tenderness as a leader was propelled, in part, by his steady optimism. Even though he was prone to spells of depression because of the personal attacks he suffered, Martin always seemed to rebound. "During days of human travail," he said during a speech in

Chicago in 1967, "we must not permit ourselves to lapse into pessimism." Years earlier, he had described pessimism as "a chronic disease that dries up the red corpuscles of hope and slows down the powerful heartbeat of positive action."

"People are surprised to learn that I am an optimist," he wrote in an article published after his death. "They know how often I have been jailed, how frequently the days and nights have been filled with frustration and sorrow, how bitter and dangerous are my adversaries. They expect these experiences to harden me into a grim and desperate man."

It was May 10, 1967, and Martin had hastened from Atlanta to Louisville, Kentucky, to take part in local demonstrations that protested the city council's recent rejection of a nondiscriminatory fair housing law. Participating in the parade by car, Martin (riding with Ralph Abernathy and his brother, A. D. King) came upon a group of angry white segregationists who were outraged at the protests.

When the car pulled up to the corner where the group was standing, Martin rolled down the passenger window and attempted to speak with the young people. "We've got to learn to live together as brothers," he said.

One teenager yelled back that he was "not your brother"— and another spit at him.

"I love you as I love my four children," Martin responded in earnest. "You're going to grow up in a world that we're going to live together in."

Then a rock flew out of the crowd and hit Martin in the neck.

Martin was not hurt, but the car sped off quickly. He did not seem to be bothered by the incident, and he took the rock to a mass meeting that night and used it as a speech prop.

All throughout the movement, even after events such as this one—where he was stoned, slapped, and slandered—Martin Luther King, Jr., was courageous enough to say, "I am optimistic." "There is nothing to keep us from molding a recalcitrant status quo with bruised hands until we have fashioned it into a brotherhood," he remarked in 1967. And in a subsequent live interview on *Meet the Press,* Martin made one of the statements that continually set him apart from the crowd and distinguished him as a great leader: "I think we can do it," he said simply. "I think we can do it."

---

"I am here because there are twenty million Negroes in the United States and I love every one of them. I am concerned about every one of them. What happens to any one of them concerns all indirectly."

> Martin Luther King, Jr.,
> December 1961

---

"True compassion is more than flinging a coin to a beggar."

> Martin Luther King, Jr.,
> March 4, 1967

---

"People are surprised to learn that I am an optimist."

> Martin Luther King, Jr.,
> March 1968

# MARTIN LUTHER KING, JR., ON LEADERSHIP

- ★ You must accept finite disappointment, but never lose infinite hope.
- ★ When hopes are blasted, violence may set in.
- ★ Hope motivates and inspires. It causes people to take action.
- ★ When you know that people are suffering, fight for them.
- ★ Take the time to write thank-you notes to people who help you.
- ★ Remember the scripture: "Let him who is without sin cast the first stone."
- ★ Never sink to the passionless depths of hardheartedness.
- ★ Cut the chain of hatred, as it is too great a burden to bear.
- ★ Remember the words of Gandhi: "There is a limit to the development of the intellect but none to that of the heart."
- ★ Combine a tough mind with a tender heart.
- ★ Even when you are stoned, slapped, and slandered—try to remain optimistic.
- ★ The one thing that keeps the fire of revolutions burning is the ever-present flame of hope.
- ★ Remember that hope really, finally means a refusal to be stopped. It means going on anyhow.
- ★ Every crisis has not only its danger points, but its opportunities.

"The people are looking to me for leadership—and if I stand before them without strength and courage, they too will falter."

Martin Luther King, Jr.,
January 27, 1956

"There is an agonizing loneliness that characterizes the life of the pioneer."

Martin Luther King, Jr.,
March 14, 1966

"Somebody is saying stand, so I guess I'll have to stand."

Martin Luther King, Jr.,
March 25, 1968

# 15 / Have the Courage to Lead

In the spring of 1967, the vast majority of American citizens supported America's growing involvement in the Vietnam War. For the most part, news reports were favorable, major antiwar demonstrations had not yet begun, and the tragic events at Kent State University were still more than three years away.

Overall, Martin had been fairly quiet about his personal opposition to the war. In 1965 he had stated that the Vietnam War, racial injustice, and poverty were "inextricably bound together" and had urged the United States government to stop all present and future bombing. And in 1966, he stated that "Violence is as wrong in Hanoi as it is in Harlem." But that was really about as harsh as he got in his public remarks regarding the conflict in Southeast Asia—largely because he was so busy directing the SCLC's involvement in the civil rights movement. Of course, he also realized that it would be politically unwise to alienate President Johnson, who was currently supporting the movement.

However, Martin had diligently stayed up-to-date on facts related to America's involvement in Southeast Asia. He was aware that the federal government had increased its spending to the point that taxpayers were now footing a yearly $20 billion bill to support the war effort. He also knew that nearly half a million American soldiers had become involved in the conflict.

While this information concerned Martin, it wasn't until he was reading a magazine article over lunch with a friend that he seemed to have finally decided to take a much more dramatic stand. As he was flipping the pages, he came upon graphic pictures of Vietnamese children burned and killed by American napalm attacks. Deeply disturbed, he pushed his plate of food away. "Doesn't it taste any good," asked Bernard Lee, his lunch companion. "Nothing will ever taste any good for me until I do everything I can to end that war," came the terse reply.

It wasn't long thereafter that Martin appeared at Riverside Church in New York City to give his first major public policy address on the Vietnam War. It was April 4, 1967, and more than three thousand people, including a multitude of reporters, filled the pews to listen to what he had to say.

"A few years ago there was a shining moment in the struggle," he said. "It seemed as if there was real promise of hope for the poor—both black and white—through the Poverty Program. There were experiments, hopes, new beginnings. Then came the build-up in Vietnam and I watched the program broken and eviscerated as if it were some idle political plaything of a society gone mad on war, and I knew that America would never invest the necessary funds or energies in rehabilitation of its poor so long as adventures like Vietnam continued to draw men and skills and money like some demonic destructive suction tube."

The government, he said, "was sending their [poor] sons and their brothers to die in extraordinarily high proportions relative to the rest of the population." They were taking young black men "who had been crippled by our society and sending them 8,000 miles away to guarantee liberties in Southeast Asia which they had not found in Southwest Georgia or East Harlem.

"So we have been repeatedly faced with the cruel irony," he continued, "of watching Negro and white boys on TV screens as they kill and die together for a nation that has been unable to seat them together in the same schools." Then, in an unusual series of sweeping reproaches, Martin let the government have it with both barrels: "A nation that continues year after year to spend more money on military defense than on programs of social uplift is approaching spiritual death," he said. "The greatest purveyor of violence in the world today," he charged, is "my own government." He even suggested that young men who might be drafted consider the "alternative of conscientious objection."

Next, Martin listed five steps of action that the government should take: stop the bombing; declare a cease-fire; pull out of Laos and Thailand; allow North Vietnam to be present in peace negotiations; and set a date for troop withdrawal from Vietnam. He also pointed out his reasons for speaking out so forcefully at the present time. "I could not be silent in the face of such cruel manipulation of the poor," he said. Moreover, he had made the decision to "break the betrayal of my own silences and to speak from the burnings of my own heart." "Somehow this madness must cease," he concluded. "We must stop now. I speak as a child of God and brother to the suffering poor of Vietnam."

Reaction to the speech was immediate and extraordinarily hostile. He was called an extremist, a communist, and a traitor to his country. He was castigated by the media, including such exemplar publications as *Newsweek, Life,* the *New York Times,* and the *Washington Post.* Individuals who had sided with him in the past—people like Whitney Young of the National Urban League, Roy Wilkins of the NAACP, sports legend Jackie Robinson, and African-American U.S. Senator Edward Brooke—now broke ranks and criticized him. Jewish groups and civil rights groups joined in the attacks. The entire sixty-person NAACP board of directors unanimously opposed him. Even the SCLC's board asked Martin to stop making further critical remarks about the war.

Most of the internal flak Martin received was for criticizing President Johnson, who was, of course, viewed as a friend of the movement after pushing through the Civil Rights and Voting Rights acts of 1965. "We need President Johnson," fellow civil rights leaders told Martin. "Now you're attacking him and making him our enemy."

But it was too late. Johnson would no longer speak to him. And J. Edgar Hoover of the FBI, who had called Martin "the most notorious liar in the country," began attacking him surreptitiously with surveillance that included agents following him and his staff wherever they went, and tapping telephones in the home office and on the road.

Throughout the public condemnation, there were basically two reactions by Martin King that were evident to his personal friends and associates. Andrew Young noted that, at times, he was "almost reduced to tears by the criticism directed against him." On the other hand, Young also said, most of the time, "Martin was on fire with determination."

By the time he took his stand against the Vietnam War, Martin had more than a decade of experience under his belt in suffering and dealing with the vilification and abuse that comes with being a leader. As he said, he "had to stand so often amid the chilly winds of adversity, staggered by the jostling winds of persecution"—and had gone "to my bed many nights scared to death."

Before delivering his Riverside Church speech, he had thought through what might happen in terms of negative reactions. More simply put—he knew the risk he was taking because he had taken similar stands before and endured the repercussions. He had dealt with the friction between the SCLC and other civil rights organizations caused by jealousy on the part of the already-established NAACP and National Urban League. During speeches, he had been heckled and booed by Black Muslims, members of SNCC, and supporters of the Black Power movement. He had also been denounced by his own associates for moving too swiftly on the one hand and, on the other, for being too slow to make decisions.

By whites, Martin had been called just about every racial epithet imaginable, including "black son of a bitch," "nigger," "Martin Luther Coon," and a "dolled-up Uncle Tom." He had received thousands of vicious phone calls. "Some days," he wrote, "more than forty telephone calls would come in, threatening my life, the life of my family, the life of my child." During some of these calls he heard ranting, raving, and the sound of spitting into the receiver. "Nigger," said one anonymous caller, "if you aren't out of this town in three days we are gonna blow your brains out and blow up your house." He also received thousands of pieces of hate mail similar to one that read: "This isn't a threat but a promise—your head will be blown off as sure as Christ made green apples."

White segregationists in Montgomery circulated rumors that Martin was embezzling money from the MIA and that he had purchased himself and his wife brand-new cars. He was continually harassed by police. At first, they stopped his car and cited him for minor traffic violations. Such petty occurrences eventually progressed to arm-twisting and formal arrests. He was indicted on two counts of perjury for making false statements about his Alabama state income tax returns. Dozens of times, he was arrested and thrown in jail in cities throughout the South while participating in nonviolent demonstrations. Several times, he was thrown into solitary confinement, held for twenty-four hours without anyone knowing where he was, and once was, as Martin remembered it, within eight days "transferred to three different jails within the state of Georgia."

Moreover, it was clear that many people hated Martin and wanted him dead. The Ku Klux Klan not only threatened his life, one white extremist actually offered a $20,000 payoff to anyone who would kill "the big nigger." The FBI alone had documented nearly fifty assassination threats against his life.

And Martin endured an unbelievable number of personal physical attacks over the course of the civil rights movement. His home was bombed. He was spat upon. He had been beaten by police billy clubs, hit in the head by a brick, stoned in the neck, punched in the face, and stabbed in the chest. Some thought it a miracle that he had not been shot and killed for his personal stands and brave leadership. Despite all these personal attacks, he still had the courage to go on, the courage to stand up for his beliefs, the courage to lead the civil rights movement as far as he could and as long as he could.

Martin's methods of dealing with and overcoming the attacks hurled his way were, by and large, professional, courteous, and almost always free of ill will and bitterness. He handled each situation depending on the allegation and the issue. The following six strategies in dealing with criticism, which are appropriate for leaders at any level, were clearly discernible in Martin King's leadership style over an extended period of time.

## 1. Turn the Other Cheek

As a rule, Martin largely ignored the daily drumbeat of personal attacks—preferring, rather, to focus on his long-term goals and strategies. To allow oneself to be afraid "drains a man's energy and depletes his resources," he said. "I don't think you can be in public life without being called bad names. As Lincoln said, 'If I answered all the criticism, I'd have time for nothing else.'"

In reality, Martin felt he just didn't have time for it. "I have been so concerned about unity and the final victory that I have refused to fight back or even answer some of the unkind statements that [have] been said about me," he told a reporter. "The job ahead is too great, and the days are too bright to be bickering in the darkness of jealousy, deadening competition, and internal ego struggles," he wrote to baseball great Jackie Robinson.

Martin also believed in the biblical teaching that "he who lives by the sword will perish by the sword." Accordingly, he literally turned the other cheek on many occasions. While a student at Crozer, for example, a white student from North Carolina pulled out a gun and threatened to kill him. The student backed down but, in this incident, Martin refused to press any charges and the two later became friends. After his house was bombed in Montgomery in 1956, Martin addressed the crowd gathered out front and urged them "to manifest love, and to continue to carry on the struggle with the same dignity and with the same discipline" with which they had started. When he was stabbed in the chest at a book signing in Harlem, the blade lodged within a fraction of an inch from his heart. Martin remained calm even during the scuffle to subdue his assailant. "Don't do anything to her," he later said about the woman who had attacked him. "Don't prosecute her; get her healed." And when he was punched in the face while giving a speech in Birmingham, Martin made no effort to defend himself or fight back against the younger, larger white man who was assaulting him. He simply turned the other cheek and tried to engage the young Nazi in a conversation.

Part of the reason Martin didn't respond to every attack was that he was getting used to the onslaught. In Selma, for instance, when Stokely Carmichael announced that he had used King's status to manipulate public opinion, Martin demurely responded: "That's all right. I've been used before. One more time won't hurt." When hit on the head with a brick in Chicago, he stood back up and continued with his march. "I've been hit so many times I'm immune to it," he said to a friend. And when asked about a recent injunction filed against him, he responded: "I have so many injunctions, I don't even look at them anymore. I was enjoined January 15, 1929, when I was born in the United States a Negro." He also noted that "the price one has to pay in public life is that of being misquoted, misrepresented and misunderstood. I have tried to condition myself to this inevitable situation."

## 2. Remember the People You Represent and What You're Fighting For

Martin knew that he was not alone. Others were suffering; others depended on him. In Birmingham, he could not forget that he had "seen youngsters refuse to turn around from the onrush of a police dog, refuse to turn around before a pugnacious Bull Connor in command of men armed with power hoses." He remembered the people who were "attacked by tear gas," who "had snakes thrown on them," who "endured only the filthiest kind of verbal abuse," and "barrages of rocks and sticks and eggs and cherry bombs." He could not forget that young men would "leap into the air to catch with their bare hands the bricks and bottles that were sailed toward us." "This is Selma, Alabama, [where] there are more Negroes in jail with me than there are on the voting roles," he wrote from a jail cell. "Thousands of Negroes have come to see that it is ultimately more honorable to suffer in dignity than accept segregation in humiliation."

Martin also was acutely aware that people expected him to be strong, to be courageous, to take a stand. After all, he was their leader. "I feel that the confidence that the people have in me," wrote Martin, "and their readiness to follow my leadership have thrust upon me a responsibility that I must follow through with."

But it wasn't only the people that gave him sustenance. He was sustained in the knowledge that his cause was noble. "There is nothing to be afraid of if you believe and know that the cause for which you stand is right," said Martin. "You are ready to face anything and you face it with a humble smile on your face, because you know that all of eternity stands with you and the angels stand beside you and you know that you are right."

Deep in his heart, Martin believed that he was fighting for nothing less than freedom and for the principles upon which his country was founded. "Democracy demands responsibility [and] courage," he said. To a fellow preacher in a small town in Mississippi, Martin wrote: "The fear of physical death and being run out of town should not be your primary concern. Your primary concern should be a devotion to truth, justice, and freedom."

## 3. Have Faith

In Birmingham, Martin found himself in a dilemma when his advisers told him that he couldn't go to jail because he was the only one who could raise funding for the depleted coffers. If he participated in the demonstrations and went to jail, there might not be any money to bail out the thousands who were already in jail—and more volunteers would likely not get involved. On the other hand, if he did not go to jail, he would not be setting the right example nor would he be following his own conscience. After a few moments, he went into another room and changed into his work clothes. "I'm going to jail," he announced upon returning. "I don't know what will happen. I don't know where the money will come from."

It was that kind of faith, in part, that helped Martin deal

with the many obstacles that confronted him. It was a faith, not only in God, but in his own destiny—and a belief that, in the end, justice would win out. "No lie can live forever," he said in quoting Thomas Carlyle. "Truth crushed to earth will rise again," he recalled William Cullen Bryant as saying. "Man's history is a path upward, not downward," he said himself.

Because his chosen profession was that of Baptist minister, it's not surprising that an abiding faith in God also provided Martin with sustenance and a firm conviction to move forward. "Faith can give us courage to meet the uncertainties of the future," he said in one sermon. In another, he noted that it was "possible for me to falter," but that he was "profoundly secure in my knowledge that God loves us."

But there was one particular personal event he experienced during the Montgomery movement that seemed to have special significance in propelling him onward. After being awakened in the night by a threatening phone call, Martin brewed a pot of coffee and sat down at his kitchen table. He was all alone, worried, and fearful for himself and his family. "Oh, Lord," he prayed, "I'm down here trying to do what is right. But . . . I'm afraid. The people are looking to me for leadership, and if I stand before them without strength and courage, they too will falter." Then he leaned on the table with his head in his hands and, as Martin himself related it, he heard an inner voice: "Martin Luther, stand up for righteousness. Stand up for justice. Stand up for truth. And, lo, I will be with you, even unto the end of the world." Afterward, Martin said to himself: "I can stand up without fear. I can face anything."

## 4. Keep Your Sense of Humor

Martin frequently turned to humor to help relieve the strain of his responsibilities, to give him a momentary respite, and to ease tension during a difficult situation. "Well, I'll tell you," he said during the Birmingham campaign. "When I was growing up, I was dog bitten—for nothing! So I don't mind being bitten by a dog for standing up for freedom!"

Many of Martin's closest associates recalled that he had a great sense of humor and delighted in swapping preacher jokes with his close associates. He also enjoyed teasing people in a fun-loving way and was famous for his hilarious impersonations of other people. "Martin was so much fun when he relaxed," Coretta once said, "he'd just tell jokes for hours."

Even a reporter for *Time* magazine noted Martin's sense of humor. "The jetliner left Atlanta and raced through the night toward Los Angeles," he wrote. "From his window seat, the black man gazed down at the shadowed outlines of the Appalachians, then leaned back against a white pillow. . . . Suddenly, the plane sputtered in a pocket of severe turbulence. The Rev. Martin Luther King, Jr. turned a wisp of a smile to his companion and said: 'I guess that's Birmingham down below.'"

But Andrew Young noted, poignantly, that Martin "never had the time to be the fun-loving man that he really was." Mostly, Martin was deadly serious in his speeches. But every now and then, he would slip in a timely, well-told anecdote. In one sermon, for instance, he related the story of a conversation he had had with a white woman he'd met on an airplane. "She believed that we should have the right to vote, and have access to public accommodations," he recounted. "And she went on and said, 'But now, I must say, Dr. King, that I wouldn't want a Negro to marry my daughter.' And Martin responded, 'Well, I wouldn't want my daughter to marry George Wallace.'"

## 5. Turn a Negative into a Positive

During the early years of the civil rights movement, after being severely criticized by members of SNCC, Martin reflected on what he might have done wrong. Rather than lashing back at them for their personal attacks, he first listened. Later he admitted that he had made some mistakes and would try to learn from them.

Throughout his tenure as leader of the SCLC, Martin King repeatedly tried to take a negative situation and turn it into a positive one. For him, this was a refined skill firmly grounded in reality—one developed largely from an inner drive to achieve. It was as if, with each negative situation, Martin asked himself the question: "All right, this issue is not going away. How can we turn it around and make it work for us?"

"As my sufferings mounted, I soon realized that there were two ways that I could respond to my situation," he said. "Either to react with bitterness or seek to transform the suffering into a creative force. I decided to follow the latter course. Recognizing the necessity for suffering, I have tried to make of it a virtue. I have attempted to see my personal ordeals as an opportunity to transform myself. . . ."

In the book *Extraordinary Minds,* Howard Gardner called this introspective ability "framing." In leaders it is the "capacity to construe experiences in a way that is positive, in a way that allows one to draw apt lessons and, thus freshly energized, to proceed with one's life." Clearly, Martin King had the capacity to view each setback as an opportunity to learn something new or, as Gardner put it, "to reflect on it, work it over, and discern which aspects might harbor hints about how to proceed differently in the future."

Accordingly, Martin always tried to "transform the suffering into a creative force"; to funnel his anger into some sort of useful channel; to "do a little converting when I'm in jail." "No one can know the true taste of victory if he has never swallowed defeat," he said.

"You don't get to the promised land without going through the wilderness."

## 6. Fight Back When You Must

Frequently, Martin would deny charges and fight back against harsh criticism—especially if he deemed it consequential to his long-term goals. When it was charged that the SCLC was filled with communists, he responded quickly by stating, "There are as many Communists in this freedom movement as there are Eskimos in Florida." And when the FBI attacked his personal character, one of his colleagues advised him to forget it. "Don't forget it," Martin quickly shot back. "No, let's do what we can to stop it. If something like this comes out, even if it isn't true, it will damage all of us in the whole movement."

Martin especially guarded attacks on his personal character with a fierce determination. When he was indicted and tried for perjury regarding his Alabama state income tax returns, he immediately fought back. "Though I am not perfect," he said, "if I have any virtues, the one of which I am most proud is my honesty where money is concerned." And Martin vigorously denied any wrongdoing during the trial. "I have nothing to hide," he said. "I have never misappropriated any funds." The jury found him not guilty in less than an hour.

Martin Luther King fought for his reputation because he realized that leadership is entirely about character. If leaders are not trusted by the people they represent, their credibility will be lost and no one will then follow. And by definition, if those out in front do not have followers, they are not leaders.

In general, there are only two things for which leaders can legitimately be criticized: for not doing their jobs properly, and for not accepting the fact that they are going to be criticized. It is precisely because leaders are out in front—blazing new trails and producing significant change—that they will be attacked. Abraham Lincoln said it well: "The pioneers in any movement are not generally the best people to carry that movement to a successful issue. They often have to meet such hard opposition, and get so battered and bespattered, that afterward, when people find they have to accept reform, they will accept it more easily from others."

Martin King clearly understood this leadership fact of life. He frequently spoke about "the agonizing loneliness that characterizes the life of the pioneer." In his Nobel acceptance address he stated: "Those who pioneer in the struggle for peace and freedom will still face uncomfortable jail terms, painful threats of death; they will still be battered by storms of persecution, leading them to nagging feelings that they can no longer bear such a heavy burden." And he reminded people in the movement that there would be "difficult days ahead," and that "we are still in for a season of suffering." "Freedom is never free," Martin wrote. "It is always purchased with the high price of sacrifice and suffering."

Aristotle once said that "The first and most basic of the moral virtues is courage." And Winston Churchill noted: "Courage is the greatest of all human qualities because it guarantees all the others." For leaders, in particular, these words seem especially appropriate. The importance of courage cannot be underestimated because, without it, a leader has no chance to persevere, no chance to succeed, no chance to be great.

Many of the greatest leaders of the past are known to have displayed tremendous courage in the face of adversity. By mere virtue of the fact that he was elected president, for instance, Abraham Lincoln was faced with the sober realization that half the nation would rather go to war than have him as their leader. During the Great Depression, Franklin Roosevelt, a man of means, was disliked by wealthy Americans because they believed he was taking money from them while increasing the power of the federal government through his New Deal legislation. And Harry Truman was vilified for trying to enact national health care and because he had no previous experience in foreign affairs. And yet, each of these leaders (along with hundreds of others not here mentioned) continued to strive forward to achieve their vision and goals.

Perhaps the most that good leaders can do is keep moving forward. And then hope that the majority of the people they represent will recognize their contributions and, in the long run, judge them for their commitment and for their achievements rather than by what others have said about them. In the final analysis, the courage to lead means standing up for what you believe in, acting when you know you're going to be attacked for doing so, and continually trying to do the right thing. As Helen Keller once wrote: "Character cannot be developed in ease and quiet. Only through experience of trial and suffering can the soul be strengthened, vision cleared, ambition inspired, and success achieved."

Martin King defined courage as "the power of the mind to overcome fear" and "the determination not to be overwhelmed by any object." He believed that courage was "an inner resolution to go forward in spite of obstacles and frightening situations"; that "courage breeds creative self-affirmation"; and that "courage faces fear and thereby masters it." As a result, he constantly preached to people in the movement that "the forces that threaten to negate life must be challenged by courage." "We must not permit adverse winds to overwhelm us as we journey across life's Atlantic," he told the SCLC staff in 1967. "We must be sustained by engines of courage in spite of the winds. This refusal to be stopped, this courage to be, this determination to go on in spite of, is the hallmark of great movements."

It was also a hallmark of Martin Luther King, Jr.—because time and time again, he put his life on the line for his beliefs. One remarkable event that illustrated his personal courage occurred during a demonstration in Selma, Alabama, where he had been spat upon and cursed unmercifully. As his group of protesters approached the Selma courthouse, they were met by more than three hundred angry white segregationists. Fearing for Martin's safety, Andrew Young pulled up in a car and asked him to get in. "No," came the reply. "I'm going to walk." Hosea Williams recalled what happened next:

> You know that man turned around to leave, and he went dead toward that mob. He got about three or four feet away, and you could hear the breathing. They got just as quiet as a mouse. And Dr. King smiled and said, "Excuse me, please." And the line just opened up. He walked right on up through them and got on the sidewalk. The line just opened up as he went along and closed behind him. And not one of them touched him. They got so quiet, it was like they were all spellbound, I guess, that the man who they were all raving about would come and submit his body to them. They didn't touch him.

"I've decided that I'm going to do battle for my philosophy," Martin once told a friend. "You ought to believe something in life, believe that thing so fervently that you will stand up with it till the end of your days." Perhaps that's why, in the fourth week of March 1968, he said simply: "Somebody is saying stand, so I guess I'll have to stand."

What is it that gives a person such courage? Is it something innate—some deep-seated energy emanating from the soul of an individual? In Martin King's case, that certainly seems to have been true. But even the most casual analysis of his life can also discern that his desire to achieve the goals of the movement, coupled with the fact that he cared so deeply about what he was doing, outweighed any personal risk he might encounter.

"When a person lives with the fear of the consequences for his personal life, he can never do anything in terms of lifting the whole of humanity and solving many of the social problems that we confront," he told a judge just before being sentenced to jail in 1957. "It is better to shed a little blood from a blow on the head or a rock thrown by an angry mob than to have children by the thousands grow up reading at a fifth- or a sixth-grade level," he said nearly a decade later in 1966.

Despite the crushing criticism of his stance on the Vietnam War, Martin never backed down, never wavered, never re- canted his position. In fact, he actually stepped up his criti- cism. "I do plan to intensify my personal activities in taking a stand against this war," he told one newsman. "And I do that because the war is hurting us in all of our programs to end slums and to end segregation in schools and to make quality education a reality, to end the long night of poverty."

He vowed never again to be quiet. "I will not be intimi- dated. I will not be harassed," he said. "I will not be silent, and I will be heard." He had thought about the consequences of his actions ahead of time. But he was "not going to segre- gate my conscience," he said. "Wherever I see injustice, I'm going to take a stand against it whether it's in Mississippi or whether it's in Vietnam."

Moreover, on April 15, 1967, Martin attended one of the largest rallies the country had yet seen in protest of the war. At least 100,000 people participated in a march from Central Park to the United Nations. Included were such celebrities as Harry Belafonte, Pete Seeger, and Dr. Benjamin Spock. Mar- tin agreed to be one of the keynote speakers and, during his address, boldly stated that the nation was "presently moving down a dead-end road that can only lead to national disas- ter. . . . The promises of the Great Society have been shot down on the battlefields of Vietnam," he said. "The bombs in Vietnam explode at home; they destroy the hopes and possi- bilities for a decent America."

After that speech, Martin continued speaking out against the war and, as was his wont, began to take action to imple- ment his beliefs. He not only advocated "a radical reordering of our national priorities" he pushed through a resolution in the SCLC that would oppose all political candidates who supported the war in Vietnam. Then he announced that he would oppose Lyndon Johnson in the 1968 presidential race and would personally "go all out" to see that he was defeated in any reelection bid.

About this time, friends and associates began noticing that Martin seemed to be tiring; that he "was not the buoyant, energetic King one had known." More than a decade of physical and emotional strain was finally taking its toll.

Over the years, Martin had complained about "almost breaking down under the continual battering." He had even collapsed once at the podium while giving a speech in Montgomery. Other times he had worked himself so hard that his immune system was weakened and he developed bronchitis and other infections. Several times he was diagnosed with "exhaustion" and was confined to a hospital bed. To friends, he wrote: "The doctors tell me I can't get by on two or three hours of sleep a night. I try to do it, and I learn I just can't."

For more than a decade, Martin had suffered from insomnia. He worried that he had not earned the accolades that had been thrust upon him. And, as he tired, his sensitive nature began to feel hurt by the severe criticism. That sensitivity had also periodically developed into full-scale depression. By the time 1967 rolled around—and his efforts yielded little or no results—Martin's moods tended to fluctuate.

"In the later years," recalled Andrew Young, "he was given to a kind of depression that he had not earlier [experienced]. . . . He talked about death all the time. He was spiritually exhausted." Family and friends worked constantly with him to cheer his spirits—and sometimes they were successful. But as Coretta remembered: "He just always talked about the fact that he didn't expect to have a long life. Somehow he always felt that he would die early and he saw no need always to be on guard against the inevitable."

On the day John F. Kennedy was assassinated, Martin looked up from the television and said to Mrs. King: "This is exactly what's going to happen to me. I just realized it. I don't expect to survive this revolution."

---

"Whenever men and women straighten their backs up, they are going somewhere, because a man can't ride your back unless it's bent."

Martin Luther King, Jr.,
April 3, 1968

---

"The forces that threaten to negate life must be challenged by courage. . . . This requires the exercise of a creative will that enables us to hew out a stone of hope from a mountain of despair."

Martin Luther King, Jr.,
1963

---

"I have a job to do. If I were constantly worried about death, I couldn't function. I must face the fact, as all others in positions of leadership must do, that something could well happen to me at any time. I feel, though, that my cause is so right, so moral, that if I should lose my life, in some way it would aid the cause."

Martin Luther King, Jr.,
January 1965

# MARTIN LUTHER KING, JR., ON LEADERSHIP

★ Your job is too great and the days are too bright to be bickering in the darkness of jealousy, deadening competition, and internal ego struggles.

★ There is nothing to be afraid of if you believe and know that the cause for which you stand is right.

★ Seek to transform your suffering into a creative force.

★ Courage breeds self-affirmation. It faces fear and thereby masters it.

★ A refusal to be stopped, the courage *to be,* the determination to go on *in spite of,* is the hallmark of great movements.

★ Do not be intimidated. Do not be harassed. Do not be silent. Be heard.

★ Whenever you see injustice, take a stand against it.

★ Remember that the road ahead will not always be smooth. There will be rocky places of frustration and meandering points of bewilderment. There will be inevitable setbacks here and there.

★ Whenever you set out to build a temple, you must face the fact that there is a tension at the heart of the universe between good and evil.

★ There is no painless way to have a revolution.

★ No leader can be great, or even fit for office, if he attempts to accommodate to injustice to maintain his political balance.

★ A firm sense of self-esteem is the most powerful weapon against slander and vilification.

"I have a dream that one day on the red hills of Georgia, sons of former slaves and sons of former slave-owners will be able to sit down together at the table of brotherhood. . . . I have a dream my four little children will one day live in a nation where they will not be judged by the color of their skin but by the content of their character. I have a dream today!"

Martin Luther King, Jr.,
August 28, 1963

"A movement is led as much by the idea that symbolizes it. The role of the leader is to guide and give direction and philosophical under-building to the movement and this is what I have tried to do in this struggle."

Martin Luther King, Jr.,
spring 1963

# 16 / Inspire People with Your Dream

During the week after Thanksgiving of 1967, the SCLC held a seven-day staff retreat at Frogmore, South Carolina, where they hatched an ambitious and daring master plan—with new goals and new tactics—to take the civil rights movement into the future. This session was precipitated by Martin King's opening remarks a few months earlier at the organization's annual convention in Atlanta.

Deeply concerned about widespread violence and rioting, the rise of the militant Black Power movement, and a general lack of progress, Martin addressed the need for some new thinking. "Our real problem is that there is no disposition by the Administration or Congress to seek fundamental remedies," he said. "We must devise tactics to create a situation in which they deem it wise and prudent to act with responsibility and decency."

Then, in what was a striking departure from his previous guidance, Martin suggested a serious escalation in action. "To raise protest to an appropriate level for cities," he said, "it is necessary to adopt civil disobedience. To dislocate the functioning of a city, without destroying it, can be more effective than a riot because it can be longer lasting, costly to the society, but not wantonly destructive. Moreover, it is difficult for government to quell it by superior force."

The Frogmore retreat, then, centered on creating specific plans for a massive march on Washington, D.C.—one that would disrupt the bureaucracy of the federal government. After defining the broad goals of such a campaign, the SCLC staff then broke into small groups to concentrate on the details.

Initial preparation for what was to be called a "Poor People's Campaign" would involve the recruitment and training of several hundred volunteers selected from each of fifteen different metropolitan areas around the country. At least three thousand people would then travel to Washington from their respective locations. "We ought to come in mule carts, in old trucks, any kind of transportation people can get their hands on," Martin advocated. As an example, he suggested that "People flow across the South . . . joining the Alabama group, the Georgia group, right through South and North Carolina, and Virginia. We hope that the sound and sight of a growing mass of poor people walking slowly toward Washington will have a positive, dramatic effect on Congress." Upon arrival, the people would set up a "tent city" on federal property and also camp in public parks. "People ought to come to Washington," said Martin, "sit down if necessary in the middle of the street and say, 'We are here; we are poor; we don't have any money; you have made us this way; you keep us down this way; and we've come to stay until you do something about it.'"

A mass rally, similar to the one in 1963, would then be held at the Lincoln Memorial where a list of demands would be presented to administration officials. These demands, said Martin, would cost the nation something in the form of "a massive program on the part of the federal government that will make jobs or income a reality for every American." Specific demands of the Poor People's Campaign included a $30 billion annual appropriation for a comprehensive anti-poverty effort; a full-employment commitment; a guaranteed annual income; and the annual construction of 500,000 units of low-cost housing.

After the massive rally, demonstrations and other forms of protest would then branch out. The White House switchboard would be deluged with a call-in. Local hospitals would be filled with people in need of health care. Sit-ins would be staged in government buildings—including one designed to shut down the Pentagon. Spontaneous local protests would take place all over the city. Mass arrests were expected to fill the jails. As people were carted off, hundreds of thousands of new recruits from all over the country were expected to take their places. Everything was designed to upset the smooth running of the federal government as much as possible. If that failed to result in meaningful action by Congress, additional demonstrations in other major urban areas would be instituted, followed by nationwide boycotts of specific industries. According to Martin, there was to be no time limit on the demonstrations. They were "going to stay in Washington until something is done about this extremely serious problem facing our nation. . . . We've got to go for broke this time," he said. "If necessary, I'm going to stay in jail six months."

Two days after the staff retreat ended, Martin announced the bold SCLC plan to a stunned group of reporters. He described to them how "waves of the nation's poor and disinherited" would flood the nation's capital. He stated that the campaign would be "as dramatic, as dislocative, as disruptive, as attention-getting as the [recent] riots without destroying life or property." "I would be the first one to admit to act at this time is risky," he told the press. "But not to act represents moral irresponsibility."

The SCLC staff then fanned out across the country to carry out their individual assignments. And Martin personally hit the road to raise awareness. He started on the West Coast with a series of speeches and fund-raisers in an effort to solicit as much as $400,000 that would be needed to maintain a tent city. This was going to be "a last chance project to arouse the American conscience toward constructive democratic change," he told people. Through a series of articles, he related how "my staff and I have worked three months on the planning," how they had held "workshops on nonviolence with the people who will be going to Washington." "We have an ultimate goal of freedom, independence [and] self-determination," he said. And Martin also issued a personal invitation: "Come young and old, come sick and well," he said. "Bring your whole family. . . . We are going to build a shanty town in Washington. We are going to build a town within the town. We're going to let the whole world know what it means to be poverty stricken." And, he said, they were "going to stay in Washington until we get a response from the Congress."

It was clear to everyone that the SCLC was now charting a new and different course—with new goals, new tactics, and new methods. As Martin said, they were now "escalating nonviolence to the level of civil disobedience." It was to be a new phase—a "showdown for nonviolence," as he termed it—that quite possibly could cost the federal government up to one trillion dollars (according to some government estimates).

To be sure, what Martin was proposing was a more militant form of action. But he believed a major shift had to occur because of all the riots taking place around the country. If he didn't do something on a grand scale for nonviolence, something that would serve as a channel for the people's anger, there quite possibly could be a full-scale armed revolution. And he wanted to avoid that at all costs.

But while the road map for the civil rights movement had now changed, the final destination had not. Martin's grand dream still remained the same. As a matter of fact, it would never change—just as every grand vision that guides a major movement does not change.

The first dictionary definition of a leader describes "a primary shoot of a plant, the main artery through which the organism lives and thrives." In much the same way, organizations prosper or die as a result of their leader's ability to create, embody, and communicate the company's vision. Effective visions provide context, give purpose, and establish meaning. They inspire people to mobilize, to act, to move in the same direction. And once an accepted vision is implemented, a consensus builds that often results in enhanced understanding of the organization's overall purpose.

In creating and gaining widespread acceptance of a vision, leaders provide the only effective mechanism that can truly overcome the natural human tendency to resist change. A vision is a powerful thing. Once everyone has bought in, people start to set goals to achieve the vision. They begin to lay out battle plans to reach the goals. They're mobilized, they're acting—they're changing. With an accepted vision there is no fear or resistance. Fear and resistance are replaced by purpose, by excitement, by desire, by courage—and by action.

History has demonstrated a clear difference between mediocre leaders who failed and great ones who were able to achieve success, in part, by creating a shared vision. Where Herbert Hoover failed to avert the Great Depression, Franklin Roosevelt combined vision and action to pull the nation out of it—and then led the free world to victory in World War II. Where James Buchanan gave up the notion of holding the Union together, Abraham Lincoln stepped in and provided a clear direction and vision of what needed to be done. In doing so, he united the North in a common purpose, won the Civil War, and ultimately reunited the entire nation.

Moreover, all the world's greatest leaders—George Washington, Thomas Jefferson, Mohandas K. Gandhi, Winston Churchill, Harry Truman, among many others—understood the need and possessed the skill to create a common, effective, and widely shared vision. Each understood the importance of laying out a long-term strategy in a world dominated by human nature's tendency to focus on short-term rewards. Each understood that a vision too mired in details usually fails in rapidly changing times; and that the best long-term plans are flexible when events threaten to alter the course.

Every good leader also realizes that effective visions cannot be forced upon the masses. Rather they must be set in motion by means of persuasion and inspiration. People must accept and implement new ideas wholeheartedly and without reservation. When this is achieved, people move forward with enthusiasm, commitment, and pride. Martin King harnessed his vision through the implementation of his own exceptional roving leadership style. By interacting frequently with the people—by "marching" with them—he was able to see to it personally that the word got out. He also very clearly understood that leadership is more inspiration than administration; that "people derive inspiration from their involvement," and that "you can't get persons to respond to anything if they aren't stimulated."

Furthermore, by continually advocating that the future can be better than the past, Martin was strategically tying his vision to one of the most basic tenets of humanity—the human desire for a better tomorrow. It is a doctrine that many successful leaders have embraced.

In his first inaugural address, for example, Jefferson spoke of the United States of America as "the world's best hope." During the Civil War, Lincoln constantly portrayed the conflict as a "struggle to maintain that form of government whose leading object is to elevate the condition of men . . . to afford all an unfettered start and a fair chance in the race of life." And Theodore Roosevelt, on July 4, 1886, eloquently stated his understanding of this timeless principle: "The Declaration of Independence derived its peculiar importance," he said, "not on account of what America was, but because of what she was to become; she shared with other nations the present, and she yielded to them the past, but it was felt in return that to her, and to her especially, belonged the future. . . . So it is peculiarly incumbent on us here today so to act throughout our lives as to leave our children a heritage, for which we will receive their blessing and not their curse."

Martin King's vision for the civil rights movement was specifically and skillfully tied to the American ideal—to what he called "a struggle for genuine equality." It involved a "faith in the future" with which people would be able to "work together, to pray together, to struggle together, to go to jail together, to stand up for freedom together, knowing that we will be free one day." And he pointed out constantly that "a special feature of our struggle is its universal quality [where] every social stratum is involved—lower, middle and upper class—and every age—children, teenagers, adults and senior citizens."

Nowhere did Martin more eloquently articulate his vision than in Washington, on August 28, 1963. He had prepared extensively for a brief ten-minute oration that was to be the culmination of the original March on Washington. Standing on the steps of the Lincoln Memorial, looking out on the Capitol building before a crowd of 250,000 people, Martin began reading from his handwritten draft.

"In a sense we've come to our nation's capital to cash a check," he said. "When the architects of our republic wrote the magnificent words of the Constitution and Declaration of Independence, they were signing a promissory note to which every American was to fall heir. This note was the promise that all men, yes, black men as well as white men, would be guaranteed the unalienable rights of life, liberty, and the pursuit of happiness.

"It is obvious today," he went on to say, "that America has defaulted on this promissory note in so far as her citizens of color are concerned. . . . We refuse to believe that there are insufficient funds in the great vaults of opportunity of this nation."

As Martin neared the conclusion of his prepared remarks, he became energized by the crowd's enthusiastic response and instinctively decided to continue speaking. At about that time, the famous singer Mahalia Jackson, who was sitting close by on the stage, shouted out: "Tell them about the dream!" And so Martin went on to speak for another five minutes extemporaneously—completely from his heart and soul.

"So I say to you, my friends, that even though we must face the difficulties of today and tomorrow, I still have a dream," he began. "It is a dream deeply rooted in the American dream that one day this nation will rise up and live out the true meaning of its creed—we hold these truths to be self-evident, that all men are created equal.

"I have a dream," he repeated, "that one day on the red hills of Georgia, sons of former slaves and sons of former slave-owners will be able to sit down together at the table of brotherhood. . . . I have a dream my four little children will one day live in a nation where they will not be judged by the color of their skin but by the content of their character. I have a dream today!"

Then he brought the crowd to its highest emotional peak in an eloquent alliterative peroration resplendent with repeated key phrases:

> So let freedom ring from the prodigious hilltops of New Hampshire.
>   Let freedom ring from the mighty mountains of New York.

Let freedom ring from the snow-capped Rockies of Colorado.

Let freedom ring from the curvaceous slopes of California.

But not only that.

Let freedom ring from Stone Mountain of Georgia.

Let freedom ring from Lookout Mountain of Tennessee.

Let freedom ring from every hill and molehill of Mississippi, from every mountainside, let freedom ring.

And when we allow freedom to ring, when we let it ring from every village and hamlet, from every state and city, we will be able to speed up that day when all of God's children—black men and white men, Jews and Gentiles, Catholics and Protestants—will be able to join hands and to sing in the words of the old Negro spiritual, "Free at last, free at last; thank God Almighty, we are free at last."

When he finished, the massive crowd thundered its approval with shouts and applause, with cheers and tears. Martin had spoken about his dream over the previous few years, but never before had he been quite so eloquent or quite so passionate. So profound was the impact that when he was received at the White House later that afternoon, even President Kennedy greeted him by simply saying: "I have a dream."

It is of interest to note that as Martin King articulated his vision to the masses, he did not say (as is common in many modern organizations): "I have a corporate mission statement" or "I have a statement of intent." He did not even say, "I have a vision." He simply said, "I have a dream."

That reference to a "dream" was not only unusually simplistic, it was powerfully symbolic. A dream infers hope for the future and, in and of itself, is a symbol for rudimentary change. Not only that, everyone can relate to a dream because every human being has had dreams—dreams of a better life for their children, of a better life for themselves, of economic and social equality. In addition, all Americans (not just African-Americans)—of which he was speaking to a quarter of a million in person and millions more through the medium of national television—believed in the American dream as articulated in the Declaration of Independence.

By speaking of his dream and, in particular, equating it to the American dream, Martin was strategically tapping into (as the definition of leadership states) *the values—the wants and needs, the aspirations and expectations,* of the people he represented. Nothing could have been more powerful to inspire the masses—or to unify them in a common bond.

And there is clear evidence that Martin not only *naturally* referred to his vision as a dream—but that he did so *strategically* and *purposefully.* He had earlier referred to the question posed by poet Langston Hughes, who asked: "What happens to a dream deferred?" In a rhetorical response related to the dreams of African-Americans, Martin stated that "these dreams were not deferred, they were denied and repudiated by vicious people through subtle patterns of exploitation."

Clearly, Martin King understood that he was tapping into the hopeful emotions of all the people when he referred to "a grand dream" that would result in "the creation of the beloved community—where men will live together as brothers." And he also appealed to their angry emotions by suggesting that the American dream had been "deferred" and "denied" by their own government.

"A movement is led as much by the idea that symbolizes it," Martin once wrote. "The role of the leader is to guide and give direction and philosophical and under-building to the movement and this is what I have tried to do in this struggle."

In mid-March 1968, Martin received a call from his old friend Rev. James Lawson in Memphis, Tennessee. Lawson explained how a group of sanitation workers (approximately 1,300 in number) had organized and gone on strike in order to improve their working conditions. But the all-white city leadership refused to even talk with them about their demands. The mayor of Memphis was threatening to fire everybody if they did not return to their jobs—and a local judge had issued an injunction against the daily protest marches. Things were looking bleak; people were losing hope; and Rev. Lawson asked Martin if he would come down to Memphis and help out.

Several members of the SCLC staff advised against it due to a hectic schedule related to preparations for the Poor People's Campaign. They pointed out as well that Martin himself was going to undertake an extensive People-to-People trip across Georgia, Alabama, and Mississippi. But in response to their objections, Martin reminded them: "These are poor folks. If we don't stop for them, then we don't need to go to Washington. These are part of the people we're going there for."

It was then quickly decided that he and key members of the SCLC staff would make a stop in Memphis while on the tour. And then, in a remarkable burst of energy, Martin crisscrossed the South speaking in countless counties to thousands of people. On one day in Mississippi, for instance, he addressed rallies in Batesville, Clarksdale, Greenwood, Grenada, Hattiesburg, Laurel, and Marks. A similar frenetic pace with as many stops occurred in the other states.

On March 18, Martin (who had rearranged his schedule) hopped a plane to Memphis. After first conferring with Lawson and other local leaders, he was escorted to the local Mason Temple where he thought he was to deliver a few remarks. But upon arrival, he was surprised to find more than fifteen thousand people singing freedom songs while they waited to hear him speak.

"We are tired of being at the bottom . . ." he told the crowd. "We are tired of having to live in dilapidated, substandard housing. We are tired of working our hands off and laboring every day and not even making a wage adequate with the daily basic necessities of life. . . . We are tired; we are tired; we are tired," he echoed again and again and again—just as he had done in the very first mass meeting in Montgomery in 1955. And then he vowed that "we're not gonna let any dogs or water hoses turn us around. We aren't gonna let any injunction turn us around. We've gotta march again. . . ." When he finished, the audience cheered and applauded in a ringing endorsement of his remarks. So uplifted was Martin at the enthusiastic response that he declared to his staff that he would return to Memphis to personally lead the next march.

That march was scheduled for Thursday, March 28, and, over the next few weeks, Martin shuttled in and out of Memphis to help prepare for the event. All black people were encouraged to boycott their jobs for one day and take part in the demonstration. And all black students were asked to stay out of school that day.

When the downtown march began, King and Abernathy were at the front of the line. After only a few blocks, however, the sound of smashing glass at the rear of the procession interrupted the peaceful walk. Members of several Memphis youth gangs were shouting "Black Power" and had started breaking store windows. Others began looting the stores. Local police quickly descended on everyone with riot gear, nightsticks, and guns. Martin and Ralph left immediately because, as Martin phrased it: "I will never lead a violent march." The demonstration then metamorphosed into something of a riot and, by the time it was all over, more than a hundred downtown stores had been damaged and sixty people were injured—including one black teenager shot and killed by police. To help restore order, the governor of Tennessee called out the National Guard and a town curfew was imposed.

Martin, meanwhile, was terribly distressed at what had happened. It had been thirteen years since the Montgomery bus boycott. During that time he had led countless demonstrations in the name of nonviolence. He had preached the doctrine of Christian love. Surely, the people in Memphis were familiar with his teachings. How then, he wondered, could such a disaster have occurred? He and his staff realized that this was the very first time a march he had led had erupted in violence. And Martin was inconsolable. He couldn't sleep, wouldn't eat, and began to spiral down into another state of depression.

But, then, the very next day, he appeared in front of reporters with his old characteristic resolve. He announced that he and the SCLC had been unprepared for the previous day's march. But that wouldn't happen again. He told reporters that he was unaware that gang youths had been threatening to turn the demonstration into a violent confrontation. Had he been informed of that fact, he said, he would have met with them and tried to talk them out of such a thing—just as he had done in Chicago. If they could not be dissuaded, said Martin, there would have been no march. He then vowed that he was going to return to Memphis within a week. And this time, he said, he would lead "a massive *nonviolent* demonstration"—just as he had always done before.

Martin and his associates then flew back to Atlanta to regroup. In the meantime, the national media had a field day with the unfortunate events in Memphis. Among other things, the press now said that Martin Luther King, Jr., ran out on the marchers in Memphis when the going got tough; that his "credibility" was now "shattered"; that he hid behind the "facade of nonviolence" only to "provoke violence"; that the words "King" and "violence" were one and the same; and that the entire nation now doubted his word.

At a hastily assembled staff meeting at Ebenezer Baptist Church, many members of the SCLC staff lobbied heavily against further participation in Memphis. Some even suggested that the Poor People's Campaign be called off. An argument ensued and some harsh words said. Disconcerted, angry, and depressed, Martin stormed out of the meeting and Ralph Abernathy ran after him to find out if he was okay. "I just can't take it anymore," Martin told Ralph. "But don't worry, I'll snap out of it."

On the morning of April 3, Martin, Ralph, and several staff members boarded a plane to fly to Memphis in preparation for the scheduled April 5 march. Their plane was delayed at take-off due to a bomb threat. But Martin's spirits were up, in part because Lyndon Johnson had recently announced that he would not run for reelection in the fall. Maybe now, he thought, something would be done about that terrible war in Vietnam.

Once they arrived in Memphis, the group not only met with local leaders, they made it a point to spend a great deal of time with the youth gang that had caused all the violence in the previous march. Helped out by Martin's personal presence and heartfelt appeals to the young men, they agreed to assist in the upcoming march and keep it nonviolent. And when informed by a reporter that a U.S. district court judge had issued an injunction against the proposed protest demonstration, Martin responded matter-of-factly: "We are not going to be stopped by Mace or injunctions," he said.

That night he was scheduled to give another address at the Mason Temple. But Martin was tired, complaining of a sore throat, and didn't want to go. So he asked Ralph to speak in his place. But when Abernathy got there he recognized that the audience was plainly disappointed. Martin had already changed into his pajamas when Ralph called and asked him to reconsider his decision. "I think you should come down," he said. "The people want to hear you, not me. This is your crowd." Reluctantly, Martin changed back into his suit and headed down to the temple in the midst of a violent rainstorm.

When he arrived, the crowd cheered thunderously—drowning out the noise of the storm raging outside. Martin approached the rostrum and began his extemporaneous remarks by calling Ralph Abernathy "the best friend that I have in the world." He also commended the local leadership as "noble men."

Then Martin proceeded to elevate the events in Memphis to a higher level. "The masses of people are rising up," he said. "And wherever they are assembled today, whether they are in Johannesburg, South Africa . . . or Memphis, Tennessee—the cry is always the same: 'We want to be free.'

"Now, I'm just happy that God has allowed me to live in this period, to see what is unfolding," he went on to say. "And I'm happy that he's allowed me to be in Memphis. . . . I can remember when Negroes were just going around . . . scratching where they didn't itch and laughing when they were not tickled. But that day is all over. We mean business now, and we are determined to gain our rightful place in God's world. . . . We are determined to be people. . . . The issue is injustice," he said. "This issue is the refusal of Memphis to be fair and honest in its dealings with its public servants, who happen to be sanitation workers."

Martin also put in a passionate plea for his philosophy of nonviolence. "We don't have to argue with anybody," he implored the crowd. "We don't have to curse and go around acting bad with our words. We don't need any bricks and bottles, we don't need any Molotov cocktails, we just need to go around and say, 'God sent us by here, to say to you that you're not treating his children right. And we've come by here to ask you to make the first item on your agenda—fair treatment.' "

He also said he was in Memphis because he cared about the people. "Either we go up together," he said, "or we go down together." Martin then told the biblical parable of the Good Samaritan—about how he had stopped to help a man in need after a Levite and a priest had not. "The first question the priest asked," explained Martin, "was 'If I stop to help this man, what will happen to me?' But then the Good Samaritan came by, and he reversed the question: 'If I do not stop to help this man, what will happen to him?' The question is not,

'If I stop to help this man in need, what will happen to me?' The question is, 'If I do not stop to help the sanitation workers, what will happen to them?' That's the question."

Martin further reminded the audience that they lived in America—and he called them to action. "If I lived in China or some other totalitarian state, maybe I could understand the denial of certain basic First Amendment privileges, because they hadn't committed themselves to that over there. But somewhere I read of the freedom of assembly. Somewhere I read of the freedom of speech. Somewhere I read of the freedom of the press. Somewhere I read that the greatness of America is the right to protest for right. And so just as I say, we aren't going to let any injunction turn us around. We are going on.

"Let us rise up tonight with a greater readiness," he went on. "Let us stand with a greater determination. And let us move on in these powerful days, these days of challenge to make America what it ought to be. We have an opportunity to make America a better nation. . . . We're going to march again. We've got to march again."

During this moving speech, Martin additionally became nostalgic and told stories of the past—stories that tended to inspire. He recalled the sit-ins of 1960, "when students all over the South started sitting-in at lunch counters. And I knew that as they were sitting-in, they were really standing up for the best in the American dream. And taking the whole nation back to those great wells of democracy which were dug deep by the Founding Fathers in the Declaration of Independence and the Constitution."

He recalled some of the events in Birmingham—how Bull Connor would let the dogs loose and turn on the high-pressure fire hoses—but "there was a certain kind of fire that no water could put out," he said. "We'd go on before the water hoses singing 'Over my head I see freedom in the air' . . . [and] we would just go in the paddy wagon singing, 'We Shall Overcome.'" And Martin also recalled being stabbed by a "de-

mented woman" in Harlem and later receiving a letter from a
little white girl who had read that if he had sneezed, he would
have died. "I'm simply writing to you," said the girl, "to say
that I'm so happy that you didn't sneeze."

"Well, I don't know what will happen now," he concluded.
"We've got some difficult days ahead. But it doesn't matter
with me now. Because I've been to the mountaintop. And I
don't mind. Like anybody, I would like to live a long life.
Longevity has its place. But I'm not concerned about that
now. I just want to do God's will. And He's allowed me to go
up to the mountain. And I've looked over. And I've seen the
promised land. I may not get there with you. But I want you
to know tonight, that we, as a people will get to the promised
land. And I'm happy, tonight. I'm not worried about anything. I'm not fearing any man. Mine eyes have seen the glory
of the coming of the Lord."

The next day, April 4, 1968, Martin met with his executive
staff to work out details of the upcoming Memphis march.
Ralph Abernathy, Andrew Young, Jesse Jackson, Hosea
Williams, Bernard Lee, James Bevel, James Orange, and Martin's brother, A.D., were there with him. Martin and A.D.
also took time between meetings to telephone their mother
for a quick chat. "She's always so happy when A.D. is with
me," Martin told Ralph after the call. Then the group met
again with gang members and other militant black youths in
hopes of turning them away from violence. Also that day,
good news arrived that a judge had lifted the injunction and
was going to allow the march to proceed.

At around 6:00 P.M., Martin and Ralph were preparing to
leave the room they shared together at the Lorraine Motel for
a dinner engagement. While Ralph was making some last
minute preparations, Martin stepped out onto the balcony
overlooking the interior parking lot. Leaning against the iron
railing, he began chatting amiably with his friends who had assembled below.

He was standing there alone when a single rifle shot suddenly rang out. The bullet struck Martin in the face and neck, knocked his feet out from under him, and drove him onto his back. Blood was everywhere. His anguished friends attended to him and called an ambulance, which immediately whisked him away to the nearest hospital. But there was nothing anyone could do.

An hour later, Martin Luther King, Jr., died.

---

"We are simply seeking to bring into full realization the American dream—a dream yet unfulfilled. A dream of equality of opportunity, of privilege and property widely distributed; a dream of a land where men no longer argue that the color of a man's skin determines the content of his character; the dream of a land where every man will respect the dignity and worth of human personality—this is the dream. When it is realized, the jangling discords of our nation will be transformed into a beautiful symphony of brotherhood, and men everywhere will know that America is truly the land of the free and the home of the brave."

Martin Luther King, Jr.,
July 19, 1962

---

"The end is the creation of the beloved community."

Martin Luther King, Jr.,
August 11, 1956

---

"If a man hasn't discovered something that he will die for, he isn't fit to live."

Martin Luther King, Jr.,
June 23, 1963

# MARTIN LUTHER KING, JR., ON LEADERSHIP

★ The road map for your movement may change, but your final destination should remain the same.

★ Your organization will prosper or die as a result of your ability to create, embody, and communicate a vision.

★ An effective vision may provide an effective mechanism that can truly overcome the natural human tendency to resist change.

★ Leadership is more inspiration than administration.

★ People derive inspiration from their involvement.

★ You can't get people to respond to anything if they aren't stimulated.

★ Tie your vision to the human desire for a better tomorrow.

★ Call your vision "a dream." It will be more meaningful, more simplistic, and more symbolic.

★ Make sure your dream taps into the emotions of the people.

★ Your role, in part, is to guide and give direction and philosophical underbuilding to your movement.

★ If you can't stop for an average person in your organization, then you don't need to pursue your lofty goals.

★ Tell the people that you either go up together, or you go down together.

★ The question is not "What will happen to you?" The question is "What will happen to them?"

# Epilog

"If you one day find me sprawled out dead," Dr. King had once said during a mass meeting, "I do not want you to retaliate with a single act of violence. I urge you to continue protesting with the same dignity and discipline you have shown so far."

But the feelings of anguish, anger, and rage experienced by millions of people after hearing of Martin King's murder could not be restrained. Almost immediately, major rioting spontaneously erupted in 130 cities across the United States. More than sixty thousand National Guard troops were called out—as were federal troops in Baltimore, Chicago, and Washington, where the violence was particularly severe. Before it all subsided, twenty thousand arrests were made and at least forty-five people had been killed. Why the violence took place may have been best explained by, of all people, Stokely Carmichael: "When white America killed Dr. King last night she declared war on us," he lamented. "He was the one man in our race who was trying to teach our people to have love, compassion, and mercy for white people."

President Johnson declared a national day of mourning for King's funeral, Tuesday, April 9. Schools and government agencies closed. Flags flew at half staff on all public buildings. And several hundred thousand people followed his coffin as it was pulled on an old wagon by two Georgia mules through the streets of Atlanta. Legions of people from all over the country felt impelled to be there. Many dropped everything, hopped planes, trains, or buses so they could walk in the funeral procession. Once there, thousands sang freedom songs and held hands with others whom they had never met before nor would ever see again. It was one of the greatest outpourings of grief the nation had ever experienced.

Within a week, Congress passed the Civil Rights Act of 1968 (also known as the Open Housing Act) and President Johnson immediately signed it into law. "Martin King may have paid for this piece of legislation with his life," Johnson was quoted as saying. The Poor People's Campaign went on as scheduled. A tent city was set up. Rallies and speeches were held. But the disruption of the federal government was insignificant compared to what it probably would have been had Martin been there. It was abundantly clear to everyone involved that an era was over.

But in no way did that diminish his legacy or what had been achieved. "In only 12 years of public life," wrote Harry Belafonte and Stanley Levison, "he evoked more respect for black people than a preceding century had produced." The *Saturday Review* noted: "Negroes in this past decade experienced the birth of human dignity—eating in restaurants, studying in schools, traveling in public conveyances side by side with whites for the first time in a century." But it was Dr. King himself who, in his 1967 book, *Where Do We Go from Here,* pointedly explained what had been accomplished:

> Since the beginning of the civil rights revolution, Negro registration in almost every southern state has increased by at least 100 percent, and in Virginia and Alabama, by 300 and 600 percent, respectively. . . . A decade ago, not a single Negro entered the legislative chambers of the South except as a porter or a chauffeur. Today, eleven Negroes are members of the Georgia House. . . . Ten years ago, Negroes seemed almost invisible to the

larger society, and the facts of their harsh lives were unknown to the majority of the nation. Today civil rights is a dominating issue in every state, crowding the pages of the press and the daily conversation of white Americans.

Also during the civil rights movement, a consistent and significant amount of federal action was achieved. The Civil Rights Act of 1957 established a Civil Rights Commission and a Civil Rights Division of the Justice Department. The Civil Rights Act of 1960 authorized judges to assist African-Americans with registration and voting. In 1961, the Interstate Commerce Commission banned segregation in public transportation. In 1963, the Supreme Court ruled that the segregation laws of Birmingham, Alabama, were unconstitutional. The Civil Rights Act of 1964 guaranteed African-Americans the right to vote and authorized the federal government to desegregate public facilities and schools. And in the years that followed the tragedy of 1968, the greatest social gains since the end of the Civil War took place. African-Americans were appointed to the president's cabinet, the Supreme Court, as ambassador to the United Nations—and to countless other federal, state, and local positions.

Others around the world were also affected. When the Berlin Wall was being torn down, East Germans and West Germans, united at long last, sang the freedom song "We Shall Overcome"—as did young Chinese revolutionaries at Tiananmen Square. And, after being released from a South African prison following thirty years of confinement for his beliefs, Nelson Mandela quoted Martin Luther King, Jr., and told of how his example provided hope and courage to those struggling for freedom in his country.

It was Abraham Lincoln who once said that "In granting freedom to the slave, we assure freedom to the free." The undeniable truth is that, through Martin King's leadership, millions of poor and oppressed people of all races, all over the world, were granted new respect, were provided new hope, and were given the personal courage to speak out against tyranny. He led a successful effort to extend the boundaries of freedom not just for African-Americans, but for all people everywhere.

Dr. King once said that when a crisis is placed right out in the open, "leaders will naturally emerge out of the situation." And yet it was he who naturally emerged. It was *his* leadership that made the difference. It was in his honor that a national holiday was proclaimed in 1986.

Why?

Why Martin Luther King, Jr.? Why did he rise from the great masses of people? What made him different? Why did people follow his lead?

Well, for starters, he was one of the people. He experienced what they experienced. He rode at the back of city buses, sat in separate waiting rooms, drank from separate water fountains, utilized separate rest rooms, and ate in separate eating establishments. As a result, he was able to articulate the dreams, the desires, the aspirations, and the values of millions of people.

Moreover, Martin King's leadership style was creative, imaginative, and bold. He was able to learn, think, connect, and then create something new. He took Gandhi's idea of nonviolent direct action and combined it with the Christian doctrine of love to give birth to an effective weapon that people could utilize to combat oppression. And nonviolence itself is symbolic of true leadership—aimed at winning over the oppressor through persuasion as opposed to coercion.

And Dr. King learned as he went along. He came to see that leadership is more inspiration than administration, that change is more evolution than revolution. He learned what the great leaders learned—that they must persuade their adversaries and inspire their followers. And he understood that character is the foundation upon which all other elements rest. Accordingly, he made decisions based on the dictates of his conscience—choosing good over evil, justice over injustice, and acting "because it is right to do it."

Two of the most fundamental principles resting on the foundation of character are achievement and compassion. And Dr. King strategically combined a decisive drive to achieve with personal empathy. "We must combine the toughness of the serpent and the softness of the dove, a tough mind and a tender heart," he said. "To have serpent-like qualities devoid of dove-like qualities is to be passionless, mean, and selfish. To have dove-like qualities without serpent-like qualities is to be sentimental, anemic, and aimless. . . . What is more tragic than to see a person who has risen to the disciplined heights of toughmindedness but has at the same time sunk to the passionless depths of hardheartedness?"

Dr. King not only cared about everybody and everything, he constantly urged others to care. "Make a career of humanity," he told 26,000 students in 1959. "You will make a greater person of yourself, a greater nation of your country, and a finer world to live in." When the people despair, he also said, "the leader has the responsibility of trying to find an answer."

Martin Luther King, Jr., also practiced what he preached. Like George Washington during the American Revolution, he "rode to the sound of the guns"—in Montgomery, in Albany, in Atlanta, in St. Augustine, Selma, Chicago, Harlem, Cleveland, and Memphis. He came up with new ideas and then transformed them into real action, into tangible results. He not only talked the talk, but walked the walk. He backed up his words with his deeds. He meant what he said. And he did what he said.

And Dr. King was a humble man. "A man all wrapped up in himself is a mighty small package," he once remarked. So he chose the ministry as his profession. After earning his degree, he went back to the South where he was needed, he lived in modest surroundings, drove to work in an old Rambler, worked twenty hours a day, took no salary from the SCLC, accepted very little and gave away much.

At every moment, he was "conscious of my limitations." He admitted he didn't have all the answers. "I am still searching myself," he said, "I don't know everything." He wouldn't "have any money to leave behind" but just wanted "to leave a committed life behind." "He who is the greatest among you shall be your servant," he often quoted from the scripture. "I want to be a servant."

And he didn't want "a long funeral," not even "a eulogy of more than one or two minutes," he said. On that day, he wanted no mention of his Nobel Peace Prize or the hundreds of other awards he had received. Rather, he said, "I'd like somebody to mention that Martin Luther King, Jr. tried to give his life serving others . . . tried to love somebody . . . tried to feed the hungry . . . to clothe those who were naked . . . to visit those who were in prison . . . tried to love and serve humanity." "Say that I was a drum major for justice, a drum major for peace, a drum major for righteousness." Through his words and actions, it's clear that Dr. King wanted people to remember of him that: "I did try. . . . I did try. . . . I did try. . . ."

Martin Luther King, Jr.'s, principles of leadership are appropriate for all times, for all leaders in any situation with any organization. But they are especially effective during tough times—when there is a major transition taking place, a major period of change. And that's exactly what was going on during the American civil rights movement. "We stand today between two worlds—the dying old and the emerging new," Dr. King said of the times in which he lived. "We are witnessing the birth of a new age [and] we must face the responsibilities that come along with it."

He recognized that "we will be living tomorrow with the very people against whom [we are] struggling today; that "all inhabitants of the globe are now neighbors"; and that "this world-wide neighborhood" had been created largely as a result of "modern technological revolutions." He stated that humanity had "inherited a large house, a great 'world house' in which we have to live together—black and white, Easterner and Westerner, Gentile and Jew, Catholic and Protestant, Moslem and Hindu—a family unduly separated in ideas, culture and interest, who, because we can never again live apart, must learn somehow to live with each other in peace."

As far as Martin King was concerned, the great period of transition and change that the world was experiencing was not to be looked at with despair and anxiety but, rather, with hope and opportunity—"opportunity to create a new spirit of class and racial harmony." To make it happen, he said, would take true leadership. "There is a dire need for leaders who are calm yet positive," he said, "who avoid extremes, who understand the issues, who possess opinions and a will, who will not lie, who can stand before a demagogue and damn his treacherous flatteries without winking." He called for leaders with "wise judgment and sound integrity"; leaders "not in love with money, but in love with justice; not in love with publicity, but in love with humanity; leaders who can subject their particular egos to the greatness of the cause."

"A time like this demands great souls with pure hearts and ready hands," he said. "Leaders whom the lust of office does not kill. Leaders whom the spoils of life cannot buy . . . dedicated, courageous, and intelligent leaders."

People had tried and failed before Martin King was able to make significant advances in the area of civil rights. But he was able to achieve something great, in part because he portrayed the cause as bigger than any one person. "If I had never been born this movement would have taken place," he said. "I just happened to be here. You know, there comes a time when time itself is ready for change."

He also raised the bar in terms of meaning. He placed the movement in context with an American dream that, as he said, "reminds us that every man is heir to the legacy of worthiness," that tells us "freedom is not only from something, but to something," and that cries out: "Freedom is one thing—you have it all, or you are not free."

On November 13, 1956, the United States Supreme Court rendered its historic decision that declared Alabama's laws on bus segregation unconstitutional. After more than a year of struggle, the people of Montgomery, Alabama, led by Martin Luther King, Jr., had won their victory over injustice.

The next night, however, outraged and out-of-control members of the Ku Klux Klan rode through Montgomery's African-American neighborhoods in an attempt to terrorize the residents. Earlier that day, they had threatened "to burn down fifty houses" and hang dozens of people "from the same tree."

"Ordinarily, threats of Klan action were a signal to the Negroes to go into their houses, close the doors, pull the shades, or turn off the lights," Dr. King recalled in *Stride Toward Freedom*. "Fearing death, they played dead. But this time . . . when the Klan arrived—according to newspapers 'about forty carloads of robed and hooded members'—porch lights were on and doors open. As the Klan drove by, the Negroes behaved as though they were watching a circus parade. Many walked about as usual; some simply watched from their steps; a few waved at the passing cars. After a few blocks, the Klan turned off into a side street and disappeared into the night."

No one feared the Klan that day. The people's attitude of fear and helplessness had been transformed into determination, resoluteness, and pride. Somehow, Martin King had successfully transferred his own personal courage to the people of Montgomery, Alabama.

As this story indicates, Dr. King was able to provide people with a sense of hope. Even when things look their bleakest, he would express optimism: "Somehow, I still believe we're going to get there," he'd say. And then he encouraged everyone to take control of their own destiny, to get involved, to "accept the task of helping make the world a better place to live in," to "stand up and protest against injustice wherever we find it."

"Human progress never rolls in on the wheels of inevitability," he said. "It comes through the tireless effort and the persistent work of dedicated individuals."

"Will we continue to march to the drum beat of conformity," he asked, "or will we, listening to the beat of a more distant drum, move to its echoing sounds?"

"Shall we say the odds are too great? Shall we tell them the struggle is too hard? Or will there be another message, of longing, of hope, of commitment?

*"The choice is ours,"* said the Reverend Dr. Martin Luther King, Jr.

*"I still have a dream. It is a dream deeply rooted in the American dream. I have a dream that one day this nation will rise up and live out the true meaning of its creed: 'We hold these truths to be self-evident, that all men are created equal.'"*

MARTIN LUTHER KING, JR.,
AUGUST 28,1963

# Bibliography

Ansbro, John J. *Martin Luther King, Jr.: The Making of a Mind.* Maryknoll, NY: Orbis Books, 1990.

Ayres, Alex. *The Wisdom of Martin Luther King, Jr.* New York: Meridian, 1993.

Bennett, Lerone, Jr. *Before the Mayflower: A History of Black America.* New York: Penguin Books, 1993.

———. *What Manner of Man: A Biography of Martin Luther King, Jr.* Chicago, 1964.

Bennis, Warren, and Burt Nanus. *Leaders.* New York: Harper & Row, 1985.

Burns, James MacGregor. *Leadership.* New York: Harper & Row, 1978.

Calloway-Thomas, Carolyn, and John Louis Lucaites, editors. *Martin Luther King, Jr., and the Sermonic Power of Public Discourse.* Tuscaloosa: University of Alabama Press, 1993.

Carson, Claiborne, editor. *The Papers of Martin Luther King, Jr.,* 3 vols. Berkeley: University of California Press, 1992–1997.

Covey, Stephen R. *Principle-Centered Leadership.* New York: Simon & Schuster, 1990.

———. *The Seven Habits of Highly Effective People.* New York: Simon & Schuster, 1989.

Gandhi, Mohandas K. *The Story of My Experiments with Truth: An Autobiography.* Boston: Beacon Press, 1957.

Gardner, Howard. *Creating Minds.* New York: Basic Books, 1993.

———. *Extraordinary Minds.* New York: Basic Books, 1997.

———. *Leading Minds.* New York: Basic Books, 1995.

Garrow, David J. *Bearing the Cross: Martin Luther King, Jr., and the Southern Christian Leadership Conference.* New York: William Morrow, 1986.

———. *Chicago 1966: Open Housing Marches, Summit Negotiations, and Operation Breadbasket.* Brooklyn, NY: Carlson Publishing Company, 1989.

Katzenbach, Jon R., and Douglas K. Smith. *The Wisdom of Teams.* Boston: Harvard Business School Press, 1993.

King, Coretta Scott. *My Life with Martin Luther King, Jr.* New York, 1969.

———. *The Words of Martin Luther King, Jr.* Newmarket Press, NY, 1983.

King, Martin Luther, Jr. Collected papers. Mugar Memorial Library, Boston University.

———. *The Strength to Love.* New York: Harper & Row, 1963.

———. *Stride toward Freedom: The Montgomery Story.* New York: Harper & Row, 1958.

———. *The Trumpet of Conscience.* New York: Harper & Row, 1968.

———. *Where Do We Go from Here: Chaos or Community?* New York: Harper & Row, 1967.

———. *Why We Can't Wait.* New York: Harper & Row, 1964.

King, Martin Luther, Sr. *Daddy King: An Autobiography.* New York: William Morrow, 1980.

Levine, Michael L. *African Americans and Civil Rights: From 1619 to the Present.* Phoenix: Oryx Press, 1996.

McCullough, David. *Mornings on Horseback.* New York: Simon & Schuster, 1981.

———. *Truman.* New York: Simon & Schuster, 1992.

McPhee, John. *Assembling California.* New York: Farrar, Straus & Giroux, 1993.

Man of the Year cover story, 1964. *Time*, 3 January.

Morris, Edmund. *The Rise of Theodore Roosevelt*. New York: Coward, McCann & Geoghegan, Inc., 1979.

Morrison, Ann M., *The New Leaders: Guidelines on Leadership: Diversity in America*. San Francisco: Jossey-Bass Publishers, 1992.

Moses, Greg. *Revolution of Conscience: Martin Luther King, Jr., and the Philosophy of Nonviolence*. New York: The Guilford Press, 1997.

Nanda, B. R. *Gandhi and His Critics*. Delhi, India: Oxford University Press, 1985.

Oates, Stephen B. *Let the Trumpet Sound: A Life of Martin Luther King, Jr*. New York: Harper-Collins, 1982.

Peters, Thomas J. *Thriving on Chaos*. New York: Alfred A. Knopf, 1987.

————, and Nancy K. Austin. *A Passion for Excellence*. New York: Random House, 1985.

————, and Robert H. Waterman. *In Search of Excellence*. New York: Harper & Row, 1982.

Phillips, Donald T. *The Founding Fathers on Leadership*. New York: Warner Books, 1997.

————. *Lincoln on Leadership*. New York: Warner Books, 1992.

Raines, Howell, editor. *My Soul Is Rested: Movement Days in the Deep South Remembered*. New York: Viking Penguin, 1983.

Reddick, L. D. *Crusader without Violence: A Biography of Martin Luther King, Jr*. New York, 1959.

Schulke, Flip. *He Had a Dream: Martin Luther King, Jr., and the Civil Rights Movement*. New York: W. W. Norton & Company, 1995.

————. *Martin Luther King, Jr.: A Documentary . . . Montgomery to Memphis*. New York: W. W. Norton, 1976.

————, and Penelope O. McPhee. *King Remembered*. New York: W. W. Norton & Company, 1986.

Senge, Peter. *The Fifth Discipline*. New York: Doubleday, 1990.

Tannen, Deborah. *You Just Don't Understand: Women and Men in Conversation*. New York: Ballantine Books, 1990.

Ward, Geoffrey C., *Before the Trumpet: Young Franklin Roosevelt 1882–1905*. New York: Harper & Row, 1985.

Washington, James M. *A Testament of Hope: The Essential Writings and Speeches of Martin Luther King, Jr*. New York: HarperCollins Publishers, 1986.

Watters, Pat. *Down to Now: Recollections of the Civil Rights Movement.* New York: Pantheon Books, 1971.

Williams, Juan. *Eyes on the Prize: America's Civil Rights Years, 1954–1965.* New York: Penguin Books, 1987.

Young, Andrew. *An Easy Burden: The Civil Rights Movement and the Transformation of America.* New York: HarperCollins Publishers, 1996.

# Notes

Opening epigraph: *Where Do We Go from Here,* 1967.

## Introduction

Opening epigraph: Television interview with Mike Wallace, 2-13-61; "angriest I have ever been," Interview, 1-65; "I felt just as if a curtain had come down," Bennett, p. 26; "I did not conquer it," *Time,* 1-3-64; "best mother in the world," *Autobiography of Religious Development;* Boston University paper, 1953; "Our mother was behind the scene," Letter, 10-48; "Perhaps my strong determination," *Face the Nation,* 1964; "I always had a desire to work," Reddick, p. 50; "History has thrust me into this position," Interview, 10-64; "I went back south," Television interview with Mike Wallace, 2-13-61; "when I get to be a man," Schulke and McPhee, pp. 9–10.

## PART I: Preparing to Lead

Opening epigraph: Speech, 8-11-56.

### Chapter 1: First Listen: Lead by Being Led

Opening epigraphs: *Stride Toward Freedom,* 1958; Speech, 3-3.

56; "It is a significant fact," Speech, 5-2-54; "From the beginning," *New York Post,* 5-13-56; Rosa Parks, *Time* magazine, 1-3-64; "Somebody has to do it," Coretta King, p. 116; Speech; 12-5-55; "great awakening," Oates, 1982; Hegel, Oates, 1982; "suddenly catapulted," *Letter from Birmingham Jail,* 4-16-63; "Everything happened so quickly," Speech, 11-29-59; "I neither started the protest," *Stride Toward Freedom,* 1958; "we started our struggle together," *Stride Toward Freedom,* 1958; "unprepared for the role," Speech, 11-29-59; "This is not the life I expected to lead," Unpublished notes, 1956; "a struggle for the whole of America," 4-24-56; "three sins," 3-22-56; "cradle is rocking," Speech, 3-31-56; "Many persons would have been arrested," Speech, 11-14-56; "injunction against feet," Speech, 11-14-56; "universe is on the side of justice," Newspaper article, 11-14-56; Garrow, 1986; "I would be terribly disappointed," Speech, 11-14-56; "This is the time," MIA statement, 12-20-56; "bus driver greeted me," *Stride Toward Freedom,* 1958; "more honorable to walk the streets in dignity," *Stride Toward Freedom,* 1958; "dealing with crazy people," 1-10-57; Oates, 1982; "Tell Montgomery that they can keep shooting," 1-27-57, Oates, 1982; "a conflict between justice and injustice," Speech, 2-56; "not lose faith in democracy," Speech; 3-19-56; "we must meet hate with love," Speech; 1-30-56; Closing epigraphs: Garrow, 1986; *Stride Toward Freedom,* 1958.

## Chapter 2: Persuade Through Love and Nonviolence

Opening epigraphs: *Stride Toward Freedom,* 1958; "land of my father's fathers," Reddick, p. 22; Purpose of "Pilgrimage for Freedom," *New York Times,* 4-6-57; "Give us the ballot," speech, 5-17-57; "fed to us in teaspoons," speech, 2-12-58; mission of "Crusade for Citizenship," Garrow, 1986; "To teach is to learn twice," Joseph Joubert, 1754–1824; "In the first days," *Stride Toward Freedom,* 1958; "Living through the actual experience," Article, *Pilgrimage to Nonviolence,* 4-13-60; "a half-dozen books on Gandhi's life," *Stride Toward Freedom,* 1958; "an armed revolt," Article, 1-31-58; "did not mean that the pacifist approach," Garrow, 1986, 1951; "Gandhi's goal," *Stride Toward Freedom,* 1958; "Gandhi was probably the first person in history," *Stride Toward Freedom,* 1958; "eros, philia, and agape," *The Strength to Love,*

1963; "which seeks nothing in return," Speech, 6-27-56; "love of God operating in the human heart," *The Strength to Love,* 1963; "key that unlocks the door," *The Strength to Love,* 1963; "a potent instrument," *The Strength to Love,* 1963; "discovered the method," *The Strength to Love,* 1963; "before plunging too deeply," Article, *Ebony,* 7-59; "to India I come as a pilgrim," Statement, 2-2-59; "three-headed team," Article, *Ebony,* 7-59; "nonviolent resistance to evil," *Stride Toward Freedom,* 1958; "I came to see for the first time," *Stride Toward Freedom,* 1958; "a man who never embraced Christianity," *Stride Toward Freedom,* 1958; Letter and Martin's response, 9-19-56; "One anonymous phone-caller" story, *Liberation,* 12-56; "a method of action," Interview, summer, 1963; "step forward," *Stride Toward Freedom,* 1958; "tool of achievement," Article, 10-59; "armor of truth," Speech, 6-7-64; "constantly seeking to *persuade* his opponent," Speech, 11-16-61; "our aim is to persuade," Article, 5-65; "persuade with our acts," *Stride Toward Freedom,* 1958; "all [we] seek is justice," *Stride Toward Freedom,* 1958; "does something to the hearts and souls," *Stride Toward Freedom,* 1958; "weakens his morale," Speech, 6-23-63; "the oppressor goes along unaware," *Stride Toward Freedom,* 1958; "seeks to create a crisis," *Letter from Birmingham Jail,* 4-16-63; "transformation and change of heart," *Stride Toward Freedom,* 1958; "defeat the unjust system," *Stride Toward Freedom,* 1958; "antithetical concepts," Speech, 12-10-64; "you may murder a murderer," Speech, 3-4-67; "riots are not revolutionary," Article, 9-58; "No internal revolution has ever succeeded," Speech, 3-4-67; "as old as the insights of Jesus," Speech, 12-60; "better to fight," Speech, 12-60; "Somebody has to have some sense," Speech, 5-3-63; "guiding light of our movement," *Stride Toward Freedom,* 1958; "way of life," *Stride Toward Freedom,* 1958; "ultimate weakness of violence," Speech, 11-14-66; "learn not to hit back," Speech, 2-1-65; "learn to love the white man," *The Strength to Love,* 1963; "If you had sneezed," Speech, 4-3-68; "Don't do anything to her," Oates, 1982; "The police tried to break my arm," *New York Times,* 9-4-58; "I could not in all good conscience," Statement, 9-5-58; Closing epigraphs: Address to SCLC, 3-4-67; Article, 5-56; "power without love," Speech, 11-4-56; "eye for an eye," Speech, 5-3-63.

## Chapter 3: Learn, Learn, Learn

Opening epigraphs: *Why We Can't Wait,* 1964; *Where Do We Go from Here,* 1967; "we don't have enough money to pay salaries," Garrow, 1986; "demands of the movement," Garrow, 1986; "time has long since come," Letter, 11-29-59; "I can't stop now," Speech, 1-31-60; "a broad, bold advance," Letter 11-29-59; "I can't stand idly by," Speech, 12-1-61; "Don't stop now," Speech 12-15-61; "I expect to spend Christmas in jail," *Time,* 1-3-64; "I do not appreciate," Garrow, 1986; "kicked out of jail," Speech, 7-19-62; "happy to leave," Statement, 7-27-62; "Nothing could hurt our movement more," *New York Times,* 7-27-62; Pritchett's comment, "Albany is as segregated as ever," *New York Times,* 8-9-62; "having preached the effectiveness of going to jail," Garrow, 1986; "Approximately 5 percent," *Time,* 1-3-64; "I subject myself to endless self-analysis," *Playboy,* 1-65; Coretta's and friend's comments, from *My Life with Martin Luther King, Jr.* and Garrow, 1986; 41; *Message from Jail,* 7-14-62; "Every time I go [to jail]," Interview, 6-63; "Education is more than ever the passport," *Where Do We Go from Here,* 1967; "as armed with knowledge as they," *Where Do We Go from Here,* 1967; "Help us to see the enemy's point of view," *The Trumpet of Conscience,* 1968; "priceless qualities of character," Article, 9-10-61; "You should teach your children," Column, 9-57; "Parents should be involved," *Where Do We Go from Here,* 1967; "turn the ghettos into a vast school," *Where Do We Go from Here,* 1967; "This means *continuous education,"* Article, 9-10-61; "broken our backs," Oates, 1982; "leadership did not center," Garrow, 1986; "marches in Albany," Garrow, 1986; p. 226; "weaknesses in Albany," *Why We Can't Wait,* 1964; "If I had to do it again," Interview, 1-65; "serve as a guidepost," Article, 7-14-62; "tears welled up in my heart," Interview, 1-65; Closing epigraphs: *The Trumpet of Conscience,* 1968; *Where Do We Go from Here,* 1967; Speech, 11-17-57.

## Chapter 4: Master the Art of Public Speaking

Opening epigraphs: Speech, 9-29-59; Article, 6-66; *Why We Can't Wait,* 1964; Lomax–King correspondence, 7-5-56; "like the way he sounds," Oates, 1982; "held his [audiences] spellbound," *Daddy King: An Autobiography,* 1980; "go down in our pockets and give big money," Speech, 1-1-57; "freshness and creativity," Letter, 3-

22-61; "a great frustration," Oates, 1982; "following simple terms," Speech, 7-19-62; "David of truth," Speech, 3-31-68; "Moses stood," *Where Do We Go from Here*, 1967; "There is a Red Sea in history," Speech, 5-17-56; Atlanta airport story, Speech, 12-1-56; "doing it for my children," *Why We Can't Wait*, 1964; " 'my soul is rested,' " Speech, 9-10-61; " 'F'eedom,' " from *Why We Can't Wait*, 1964; "lost in the thick fog," Speech, 12-5-55; "smothering in an airtight cage," Letter, 4-16-63; "a cancer in the body politic," Article, 5-60; "like a boil that must be opened," Letter, 4-16-63; "a certain kind of fire that no water could put out," Speech, 4-3-68; "the plant of freedom," Speech, 5-18-66; "is like life," Speech, 7-19-62; "midnight in our world," *The Strength to Love*, 1963; "rise from the dark and desolate valley," Speech, 8-28-63; "A more enduring myth," Speech, 11-7-64; "Give us the ballot," Speech, 5-17-57; "I have a dream," Speech, 8-28-63; "How long," Speech, 5-25-65; "here this evening for serious business," 12-5-56; "Our destiny is bound up with the destiny of America," Letter, 4-16-63; "We've come to cash a check," Speech, 8-28-63; *Leadership*, 1978; *Leaders*, 1985; Lincoln, *Lincoln on Leadership*, 1992; *A Passion for Excellence*, 1985; *You Just Don't Understand*, 1990; "concerned with semantics," *Where Do We Go from Here*, 1967; "songs are the soul," *Why We Can't Wait*, 1964; "You must have slogans," *Where Do We Go from Here*; "a poison be employed," Speech, 9-29-59; "I'm not interested in pressing charges," Oates, 1982; Closing epigraphs: *Why We Can't Wait*, 1964; *Where Do We Go from Here*, 1967.

## PART II: Guiding the Movement

Opening epigraph: *Stride Toward Freedom*, 1959.

### Chapter 5: Awaken Direct Action

Opening epigraphs: *Stride Toward Freedom*, 1959; *Stride Toward Freedom*, 1959; Article 12-60; "spiritual leader of the movement," *My Soul Is Rested: Movement Days in the Deep South Remembered*, 1977; "I felt a moral obligation," Garrow, 1986; "stay in jail ten years," Oates, 1982; "Jail going wasn't easy," Garrow, 1986; "We will take direct action," *Stride Toward Freedom*, 1958; "I don't want peace," Speech, 3-18-56; "Such breathtaking, fundamental changes," Article, 1-65; Gardner, *Creating Minds*, 1993; Theodore

Roosevelt, "I felt a pleasure in action," *Mornings on Horseback,* 1981; Covey, *Principle-Centered Leadership,* 1990; Bennis and Nanus, *Leaders,* 1985; "What is needed is a strategy for change," *Where Do We Go from Here,* 1967; "This is no time for romantic illusions," Speech, 3-4-67; "incomplete revolution of the Civil War," Article, 5-64; "noble journey toward the goals," *Why We Can't Wait,* 1963; "revolution occurring in both the social order," Article, 5-60; "part of a world-wide movement," Article, 12-60; "a nation in transition," Speech, 7-23-67; "one of the most significant epics of our heritage," 1962; "he slept through a revolution," Speech, 3-31-68; "all too many people fail to remain awake," *Where Do We Go from Here,* 1967; "complete the process of democratization," Article, 5-63; "one of the grandest forms of government," Reddick, p. 22; "If the American dream is to become a reality," Speech, 7-4-65; "shaping of our own destiny," Speech, 11-14-67; "the clock of destiny is ticking out," Article, 5-63; "We must remain awake through a great revolution," Speech, 3-31-68; "walk the high road," *Stride Toward Freedom,* 1958; "nonviolence was presented," Article, 9-58; "Let us be Christian," Speech, 12-5-55; "action is not in itself a virtue," Speech, 11-7-64; "because it is right to do it," Speech, 6-27-56; "Freedom is not only from something," Speech, 11-14-56; "presence of some positive force," Speech, 2-6-57; "stand up until justice comes our way," Speech, 4-26-56; "injustice anywhere is a threat to justice everywhere," Article, 12-60; "we can't afford to slow up," Speech, 6-27-56; "Perhaps it is easy," *Letter from Birmingham Jail,* 4-16-63; "justice and injustice," Article, 1-65; "quest for freedom and human dignity," Speech, 2-6-57; "Why is it so difficult to understand," Article, 1-65; "no longer will be tolerant," Article, 1-65; "Now is the time," *Why We Can't Wait,* 1963; "If America is to remain a first-class nation," Speech, 6-6-61; "perish as fools," Speech, 6-6-61; "telling plain truths," Speech, 3-30-63; "Of the good things," *Where Do We Go from Here,* 1967; "The law pronounces [the Negro] equal," Speech, 11-7-64; "government cannot make the Constitution function," Speech, 3-30-63; "highest investor in segregation," Speech, 2-4-61; "have gone to support housing programs," Speech, 2-4-61; "Voting rights bill" specifics, Speech, -14-65; "for Americans everywhere, of every age," Article, 1-1-61; "Press on and keep pressing," Speech, 3-31-56; "end up in a deep freeze," Press conference, 4-18-64; "No lie can live forever," Speech, 3-25-65; "necessary to go backward," Speech, 2-28-54; "accumulation of many short-term victories," *Where Do We Go from Here*, 1967; "We are on the move now," Speech, 3-25-65; "Affirmative action," *Why We Can't Wait*, 1964; "Thank God, we ain't what we was," *Time*, 1-3-64; Closing epigraphs: Speech, 3-31-68; Speech, 3-31-56; "Never allow the theory," *Stride Toward Freedom*, 1959; "The chance to act is today," Article, 5-65; "Nothing will be done," Speech, 3-31-68; "substitute courage for caution," Speech, 9-15-63; "Leadership never ascends from the pew to the pulpit," Letter, 9-54.

## Chapter 6: Encourage Creativity and Innovation

Opening epigraphs: Speech, 3-14-68; Speech, 2-4-61; "test the use of transportation facilities," Speech, 5-4-61; "must develop the quiet courage of dying for a cause," Speech, 5-4-61; "CORE started the Freedom Ride," Oates, 1982; "must shun the very narrow-mindedness," *Where Do We Go from Here*, 1967; "We're faced with an extreme situation," Speech, 9-27-63; "cease imitating and begin initiating," *Where Do We Go from Here*, 1967; "The necessity for a new approach," Article, 3-9-64; "creative contribution," *Where Do We Go from Here*, 1967; "bringing the issues out in the open," Speech, 8-9-66; "reliance on mass demonstrations," Article, 11-7-64; "The innovation for this year," Article, 1-64; "We are asking you to go out and tell," Speech, 4-3-68; "had to be sustained over a period of several weeks," Comment, 9-10-61; "We had to use our mass meetings to explain nonviolence," Speech, 6-4-57; "People will work together and sacrifice," Comment, 9-10-61; "We can never assume that anyone understands," Comment, 9-10-61; "so conditioned themselves to the system of segregation," Speech, 12-60; "Today the imitation has ceased," Speech, 11-14-67; "Very few adhere to the established ideology or dogma," Speech, 11-14-67; "they are in reality standing up," Speech, 9-10-61; "Any real change in the status quo," Speech, 3-14-65; "If a man can write a better book," Article, 4-57; "an idea whose time has come," Speech, 9-10-61; "We will err and falter," *Where Do We Go from Here*, 1967; "brought blacks and whites together," Article, 4-16-68; "Anytime we've had demonstrations in a community," Article, 4-16-68; "I can see no way to break loose from an old order," Speech, 6-6-61;

"Whenever anything new comes into history," Speech, 3-31-68; "In a new era there must be new thinking," Speech, 2-4-61; "Nothing could be more tragic," *Where Do We Go from Here,* 1967; "But we are not giving up," Speech; 5-20-61; "fear not, we've come too far to turn back," Speech; 5-20-61; Closing epigraphs: *Where Do We Go from Here,* 1967; Letter, 4-16-63; "Innovative actions may serve as unifying forces," Article, 4-16-68; "Creative power can pull down mountains of evil," *Stride Toward Freedom,* 1958; "use time creatively," Letter, 4-16-63.

## Chapter 7: Involve Everyone Through Alliances, Teamwork, and Diversity

Opening epigraphs: Article, 10-66; *Stride Toward Freedom,* 1958; Speech, 3-31-68; "in many different ways," Article, 6-63; "slow to organize," Article, 6-11-67; "leadership neither planned ahead," Article, 11-7-64; "lack experience," Article, 6-11-67; "shun the very narrow-mindedness," Article, 11-65; "mark of strength, not of weakness," *Where Do We Go from Here,* 1967; "Ten percent of the population cannot by tensions alone," *Where Do We Go from Here,* 1967; "We aren't going to be free anywhere," *Where Do We Go from Here,* 1967; "have people tied together in a long-term relationship," *Where Do We Go from Here,* 1967; "Through group identity," *Where Do We Go from Here,* 1967; "Negro solidarity is a powerful growing force," Article, 8-5-62; "to sail a boat without a rudder," *Where Do We Go from Here,* 1967; "The future of the deep structural changes we seek," *Where Do We Go from Here,* 1967; "cities of the North," Article, 10-66; "Many segments must band together," Article, 8-15-64; "The only truly responsible consensus," Press conference, 6-16-65; "We begin to glimpse tremendous vistas," Speech, 11-14-67; "every alliance considered on its own merits," *Where Do We Go from Here,* 1967; "the art of alliance politics," Article, 6-11-67; "A true alliance is based upon some self-interest," Article, 6-11-67; "grand alliance of Negro and White," Speech, 11-7-64; "The economically deprived condition of the Negro will remain," Speech, 5-26-63; "there exists a substantial group of white Americans," Speech; 12-10-64; "just as determined to see us free," Interview, 6-26-66; "bound together in a single garment of destiny," *Where Do We Go from Here,* 1967; "on the basis of a Negro-white de facto alliance," Speech, 3-30-63; "Labor and the Negro have identical interests," Speech, 9-8-62; "This unity of purpose," Speech, 12-11-61; "Labor needs far more political leverage," Speech, 9-8-62; "needs more ballots to have more respect," Speech, 9-8-62; "master the art of political alliances," Article, 6-11-67; "drive a wedge into the splitting south," Speech, 3-30-63; "bring pressure on the federal government," Speech, 4-3-65; "The biggest job in getting any movement off the ground," *Stride Toward Freedom,* 1959; "conducive to deep thinking and serious discussion," Letter, 10-27-59; "Now, I want this to be informal," Speech, 1-15-68; "No parliamentary rules were necessary," *Stride Toward Freedom,* 1959; "For as long as we have men, we are going to have differences," Interview; 11-64; "carried out by 25 evangelistic teams," Letter, 10-31-56; *The Wisdom of Teams,* 1993; "organizations representing a wide variety of interests," *Where Do We Go from Here,* 1967; "insist that my staff in the SCLC be interracial." Interview, 1959; "made up in versatility," *Why We Can't Wait,* 1963; "[People] are called upon [only] to examine their heart," *Where Do We Go from Here,* 1967; "The Ph.D.'s and the no 'D's,'" *Stride Toward Freedom,* 1959; "no group can make it alone," *Why We Can't Wait,* 1963; "our world is a neighborhood," Speech, 3-31-68; "all will benefit from a color-blind land of plenty," Speech, 3-14-65; "integration is an opportunity to participate in the beauty of diversity," Speech, 11-14-66; "living tomorrow with the very people," *Where Do We Go from Here,* 1967; John Donne quotation used in Speech, 3-31-68; "a real sharing of power and responsibility," Article, 1-69 (published posthumously); "Freedom is participation in power," Speech, 1-14-66; President Kennedy, *Eyes on the Prize,* 1987; Closing epigraphs: *Stride Toward Freedom,* 1958; Speech, 3-31-68; "Winning allies is more difficult in the absence of facts," Speech, 3-4-65; "A destructive minority," Speech, 9-9-67; "When one person stands up," Speech, 3-4-65; "Life at its best," *The Strength to Love,* 1963; "Laws only declare rights," *Where Do We Go from Here,* 1967.

## Chapter 8: Set Goals and Create a Detailed Plan of Action

Opening epigraphs: Letter, 4-16-63; *Why We Can't Wait,* 1963; *Where Do We Go from Here,* 1967; Shuttlesworth, *Eyes on the Prize,*

1987; "the most thoroughly segregated city in the country," Article, 1-8-60; "never heard of Abraham Lincoln," *Why We Can't Wait,* 1963; "We decided to center the Birmingham struggle," *Why We Can't Wait,* 1963; "We were seeking to bring about a great social change," *Why We Can't Wait,* 1963; "I pleaded for the projection of a strong, firm leadership," *Why We Can't Wait,* 1963; "I am in Birmingham because injustice is here," Letter, 4-16-63; "some of the people sitting here today will not come back," Oates, 1982; "as Athena sprang from the head of Zeus," *Stride Toward Freedom,* 1959; "more long range, detailed planning on the part of the staff," Letter, 9-29-59; "must commit [them]selves to a whole long-range program," Comments, 8-26-65; "put the horse before the cart," *Where Do We Go from Here,* 1967; "What is needed is a strategy for change," *Where Do We Go from Here,* 1967; "When evil men plot," *The Words of Martin Luther King, Jr.,* 1983; "We need a chart," Speech, 8-16-67; "all united around one objective," Speech, 7-19-62; "you have to have some simple demand," Speech, 1-17-68; "Progress whets the appetite," Speech, 9-9-67; "a glowing excitement to reach creative goals," Speech, 12-11-61; "Goals must be clearly stated," Article, 5-65; "the simplest approach will prove to be the most effective," *Where Do We Go from Here,* 1967; "[Don't] aim too low," Speech, 12-15-66; "Find something that is so possible, so simple," Garrow, 1986; "to end poverty, to extirpate prejudice," *Stride Toward Freedom,* 1959; "create a beloved community," Article, 10-66; "morally and legally right," *Stride Toward Freedom,* 1959; "the goal of America is freedom," Speech, Letter, 4-16-63; "We must and we will be free," Article, 3-58; "We must gain the ballot," Speech, 8-11-56; "So long as I do not firmly and irrevocably possess the right to vote," Speech 5-17-57; "voting restrictions, the poll tax," Speech, 4-3-65; "our emphasis must be two-fold," Speech, 3-4-67; "Achievement of these goals," Article, 10-66; "We must seek to develop a constructive action program," Speech, 12-60; "long years of experience," Article, 4-3-65; "Being prepared for a long struggle," *Why We Can't Wait,* 1963; "misused the judicial process," *Why We Can't Wait,* 1963; "because of its symbolic significance," *Why We Can't Wait,* 1963; "present our bodies as personal witnesses," *Why We Can't Wait,* 1963; "Injunction or no injunction," Speech, 4-10-63; "I don't know what will happen," Comments, 4-1-63, *Why We Can't Wait,* 1963; *Letter from Birm-*

*ingham Jail,* 4-16-63; "pick up the action because the press is leaving," Garrow, 1986; Walter quotation, Garrow, 1986; Abernathy quotation, Oates, 1982; "put into effect the Gandhian principle," *Why We Can't Wait,* 1963; "I saw there, for the first time," comment, 5-7-63; "men of good will," Statement, 5-10-63; "Was there any hope?" Article, 1-65; "Action itself not a virtue," Article, 11-7-64; "remove the cause," Article, 12-60; "in terms of economic and political power," Speech, 3-4-67.

## Chapter 9: Be Decisive

Opening epigraphs: Article, 3-31-68; Article, 3-31-68; "These children," Eulogy, 9-18-63; "Oh, now wait. Let's think about this," Garrow, 1986; "I'm not going to run, Hosea," Oates, 1982; "His eyes—I don't know how to describe eyes like that," Oates, 1982; "Just hearing him speak gave you the courage to go on," Garrow, 1986; "Hello, sister," Garrow, 1986; "never worked in [a city] as lawless as this," Garrow, 1986; "I live with one deep concern," Article, 1-65; "came down on the right side," Garrow, 1986; "I consulted with my lawyers and trusted advisors," Article, 4-3-65; "all minor matters of policy," Letter, 5-24-56; "had a remarkable facility," Garrow, 1986; "One of his greatnesses," Garrow, 1986; "The tendency of many readers is to accept the printed word," *The Strength to Love,* 1963; "Our minds are constantly being invaded," *The Strength to Love,* 1963; "need for a tough mind," *The Strength to Love,* 1963; "Nothing pains some people more than having to think," *The Strength to Love,* 1963; "People of good will," Article, 1-65; "I don't believe that anyone could seriously accuse me of not being totally committed," Article, 1-65; "a genuine leader is not a searcher for consensus," Article, 3-31-68; "There comes a time," Article, 3-31-68; "I decide on the basis of conscience," Statement, 8-17-67; "We are always seeking to do the right thing," Speech, 4-26-56; "A just law is a law that squares with a moral law," Speech, 11-16-61; "The individual who disobeys the law," Speech, 11-16-61; "an element of coercion is necessary," Interview, 1961; "I believe in moral nonviolent coercion," Interview, 1961; "The absence of freedom is the imposition of restraint," Speech, 7-6-65; Tannen, *You Just Don't Understand,* 1990; "Decision means cutting off alternatives," Speech, 1-7-68; "the ability to achieve purpose,"

Speech, 2-24-65; "I want out of St. Augustine," Garrow, 1986; "a significant first step," Statement, 8-30-64; "America will be faced with the ever-present threat of violence," Article, 1-65; "twenty-two million Negroes," Speech, 12-10-64; "I must go back to the valley," Speech, 12-17-64; Closing epigraphs: *The Strength to Love,* 1963; Article, 1-65; "must be militant as well as moderate," Article, 1-65; "move past indecision to action," Article, 3-4-67.

## PART III: Winning with People

Opening epigraph: Speech, 4-26-56.

### *Chapter 10: Teach and Preach*

Opening epigraphs: Speech, 1-2-65; Speech, 12-56; Speech, 2-25-67; "Today marks the beginning," Speech, 1-2-65; "We're willing to be beaten for democracy," *Eyes on the Prize,* 1987; "I must confess this is a deliberate attempt," Remarks, 2-1-65; "Letter from a Selma Jail," *New York Times,* 2-14-65; Malcolm X: "perhaps they will be more willing to hear Dr. King," 2-4-65; "He was killed by every lawless sheriff," Speech, 2-26-65; "I can't promise you that it won't get you killed," Speech, 2-26-65; "What kinds of guns do you have?" *Eyes on the Prize,* 1987; "and then they realized how suicidal and nonsensical it was," *Eyes on the Prize,* 1987; "in our minds over and over again," Speech, 5-3-63; "the harsh language and physical abuse of police," *Why We Can't Wait,* 1963; "proved very helpful in preparing those who are engaged in demonstrations," Speech, summer, 1963; "noncommissioned officers of the civil rights movement," *Where Do We Go from Here,* 1967; "We shall have to create leaders who embody virtues we can respect," Speech, 6-11-67; "Those of you who read and think," Article, 10-24-64; "to engage in any of the demonstrations," *Where Do We Go from Here,* 1967; "before going through this kind of teaching session," *Why We Can't Wait,* 1963; "Education gives us not only knowledge," Article, 5-60; "To save man from the morass of propaganda," Article, 1947; "If an individual can't think critically," Article, 5-60; "Intelligence plus character," Article, 1947; "At emancipation only five percent of the Negroes were literate," Article, 12-60; "the gradual improvement of [their] economic status," Article, 12-60; "It is a backbreaking task," Article, 10-59; "a great deal to remove the fears and the half-truths," Speech, 9-9-67; "even the law itself is a form of educa-tion," *Stride Toward Freedom,* 1959; "early demonstrations [were] more geared toward educational purposes," *Where Do We Go from Here,* 1967; "We in this generation must stimulate our children," *Where Do We Go from Here,* 1967; "to become more efficient, to achieve with increasing facility," Article, 1947; "We must make it clear to our young people," Article, 12-60; "We must constantly stimulate our youth to rise above the stagnant level of mediocrity," Article, 12-60; "If a man is called a street sweeper," Speech, 12-56; "In the final analysis," Article, 12-60; "A productive and happy life is not something that you find," Speech, 12-56; "Historical victo-ries have been won by violence," Article, 1-65; "we must demon-strate, teach and preach," Speech, 2-25-67; "If nonviolent protest fails this summer," Article, 4-16-68; "In the vicious maltreatment of defenseless citizens of Selma," Statement, 3-6-65; "He very strongly urged us not to march," Remarks, 3-8-65; "We have no alternative but to keep moving with determination," Speech, 3-9-65; "I did it to give them an outlet," Court testimony, 3-11-65; President John-son's remarks, *Eyes on the Prize,* 1987; "Judge Johnson has just ruled," *Eyes on the Prize,* 1987; "We are tired now," Speech, 3-21-65; "So we can be free," *Eyes on the Prize,* 1987; "We have walked on meandering highways," Speech, 3-25-65; Closing epigraphs: Speech, 6-11-67; Article, 1947; "Ultimately, the thing that keeps the true fires burning," Speech, 4-24-56.

## Chapter 11: March with the People

Opening epigraphs: *Where Do We Go from Here,* 1967; Interview, 1-65; Speech, 8-66; "well, when the day comes that he stops having time to talk to a porter," Article, 6-11-67; Janitor story, Garrow, 1986; "It would literally take him an hour," Garrow, 1986; "learn the plight," Coretta Scott King, 1969; "I have seen it in Latin America," Speech, 3-31-68; "I shall never forget my agony of con-science," Oates, 1982; "I hate to hold up your pool game," Re-marks, 10-62; "walked among the desperate, rejected and angry young men," Speech, 3-2-67; "I never realized how many unknown heroes there were," Article, 5-12-62; "We walked the streets, preached on front porches," Article, 8-29-64; "little black children of Grenada, Mississippi," Article, 12-66; "I was in Marks, Mississippi, the other day," Speech, 3-31-68; "We walked from Selma to Montgomery in the middle of the road," Garrow, 1986; "We want black power," Speech, 6-16-66; "I believe in my heart that the murderers are somewhere around me," Garrow, 1986; "There's no point in fighting back," Garrow, 1986; Peters and Austin, 1985; "part of a program to dramatize an evil," Article, 10-66; "the tramp, tramp of marching feet," Speech, 8-9-66; "a ring of isolation and alienation," Speech, 11-11-67; "buoyed with the inspiration of another moment," Article, 1-65; "the beauty and dignity and the courage," Speech, 5-29-64; "The path is clear to me," Remarks, 4-13-63; "We are on the move now," Speech, 3-25-65; "Gandhi's oft-quoted statement," Article, 1963; "We came South to help you in Selma," Oates, 1982; "we've got to begin dealing with the North sometime," Andrew Young, 1996; "The purpose of the slum," Speech, 3-12-66; "You can't really get close to the poor without living and being here with them," Remarks, 1-26-66; "I understood anew the emotional pressures," Speech 12-15-66; "The moral question is far more important than the legal one," Garrow, 1986; "I met those boys and heard their stories," Speech, 3-25-65; "You mean to tell me I'm sitting here," Oates, 1982; "Freedom is never voluntarily granted by the oppressor," Speech, 7-10-66; "We aren't gonna march with any Molotov cocktails," Speech, 8-5-66; "I've been hit so many times I'm immune to it," Remarks, 8-5-66; "I march because I must, and because I'm a man," Speech, 8-66; Closing epigraphs: Speech, 9-26-66; Speech 8-9-66; Article, 1-65.

## Chapter 12: Negotiate and Compromise

Opening epigraphs: *Time*, 1-3-64; Speech, 8-26-66; Speech, 8-26-66; "Our primary objective," Remarks, 1-6-66; "We will fill up the jails here in order to end the slums," Speech, 7-10-66; "I don't think Dr. Jackson speaks for one percent of the Negroes in this country," Garrow, 1986; "we are not the creators, we are the mirror," Garrow, 1986; "All over the South, I heard the same thing," Remarks, 8-17-66; "If I come before the Mayor of Chicago some day," Garrow, 1986; "This has been a constructive and creative beginning," Remarks, 8-17-66; "I deem it a very bad act of faith," Statement; 8-19-66; "that a march in Cicero was more effective as a threat," Young, 1996; "First, we are much concerned about the injunction we face," Remarks, 8-26-66; "I want to express my appreciation," Remarks, 8-26-66; "But if these agreements aren't carried out," Remarks, 8-26-66; Covey, 1989; Tannen, 1990; "We began with a compromise when we didn't ask for complete integration," Remarks, 1-18-56; "We will always be willing to talk and seek fair compromise," Speech, 7-19-62; "The key word is respect," Speech, 8-9-66; "We must have patience," *Where Do We Go from Here,* 1967; "They seek to arouse an awareness," *Where Do We Go from Here,* 1967; "It is absolutely essential to establish a documented moral record," Article, 5-9-64; "We've got to have a crisis to bargain with," Article, 1-3-64; "We set out to precipitate a crisis," Article, 1-65; "Throughout the campaign, we had been seeking to establish some dialogue," *Why We Can't Wait,* 1963; "We will have to learn to refuse crumbs," Speech, 6-11-67; "You can't just communicate with the ghetto dweller," Article, 11-66; "We must press the city council and mayor," Garrow, 1986; "to help open channels of communication," *Why We Can't Wait,* 1963; "These businessmen suddenly realized," *Why We Can't Wait,* 1963; "Don't be too soft. We have the offensive," Note, 2-65; "We must now measure our words by our deeds," Remarks, 8-26-66; "Because we are engaged in negotiations," Speech, 8-9-66; "Humanity is waiting," Speech, 11-14-67; "men of good will," Statement, 5-10-63; "as grateful to Mayor Daley as to anyone else," Remarks, 8-26-66; "If this contract is broken," Oates, 1982; "Some people tried to frighten me," Speech, 8-26-66; Closing epigraphs: Speech, 8-9-66; *Where Do We Go from Here,* 1967; Speech, 7-19-62; "There must be more than a statement," Speech, 11-14-67.

## Chapter 13: Understand Human Nature

Opening epigraphs: *The Strength to Love,* 1963; Speech, 12-16-61; *Where Do We Go from Here,* 1967; "the emerging new order," *Stride Toward Freedom,* 1959; "perpetuate a system of human values," *Stride Toward Freedom,* 1959; "Let nobody fool you," Speech, 8-11-56; "we must be willing to confront the onslaught and the recalcitrance of the old order," Speech, 12-3-56; Speech, 4-26-56; "the inevitable counterrevolution that succeeds every period of progress," *Where Do We Go from Here,* 1967; "The guardians of the status quo lash out," *Stride Toward Freedom,* 1959; "old guards who would rather die than surrender," Speech, 8-5-62; five specific methods, Speech, 6-27-56; "When there is rocklike intransigence," *Where Do We Go from Here*, 1967; "Disappointment produces despair and despair produces bitterness," *Where Do We Go from Here*, 1967; Stokely Carmichael, "kill the Honkies," Oates, 1982; H. Rap Brown, "get their guns," Oates, 1982; "appreciate our great heritage," *Where Do We Go from Here*, 1967; "pleaded with the group to abandon the Black Power slogan," *Where Do We Go from Here*, 1967; "hostile connotations," *Where Do We Go from Here*, 1967; "we are not interested in furthering any divisions," Statement, 10-14-66; "Whenever Pharaoh wanted to keep the slaves in slavery," Speech, 8-31-66; "Men are not easily moved from their mental ruts," *Stride Toward Freedom*, 1959; "The softminded man always fears change," *The Strength to Love*, 1963; Jesse Jackson, "Dr. King said it would take from three to five years," Garrow, 1989; Andrew Young, "Martin used to say that America was a ten-day nation," Young, 1996; "absolutely convinced of the natural goodness of man," Speech, 3-4-64; "the complexity of human motives," *Stride Toward Freedom*, 1959; "The more I thought about human nature," *Stride Toward Freedom*, 1959; "I came to feel that liberalism had been all too sentimental," *Stride Toward Freedom*, 1959; "sacrifice truth on the altars of self-interest," Speech, 5-17-56; "more prone to follow the expedient [rather] than the ethical path," *The Strength to Love*, 1963; "morality cannot be legislated, but behavior can be regulated," *Stride Toward Freedom*, 1959; "Plato, centuries ago," Speech, 11-16-61; "Each of us has two selves," Article, 4-66; "a fear of what life may bring," Speech, 9-10-67; "deep down within all of us," Speech, 2-4-68; "a need that some people have to feel superior," Speech, 2-4-68; "Indeed, we are engaged in a social revolution," *Why We Can't Wait*, 1963; "For many years, the Negro tacitly accepted segregation," *Where Do We Go from Here*, 1967; "But there comes a time when people get tired of being trampled over," Speech, 12-56; "This determination springs from the same longing for freedom," *Where Do We Go from Here*, 1967; "an individual expression of a timeless longing," *Where Do We Go from Here*, 1967; "Eventually the cup of endurance runs over," *Where Do We Go from Here*, 1967; "Oppressed people cannot remain oppressed forever," Speech, 12-11-64; *Where Do We Go from Here*, 1967; "Freedom is the act of deliberating," *The Strength to Love*, 1963;

"Freedom is necessary for one's selfhood," Speech, 2-16-59; "The essence of man is found in freedom," *Where Do We Go from Here,* 1967; "discontent so deep," Article, 4-16-68 (published posthumously); "to serve as a channel," Article, 4-16-68 (published posthumously); "is not the moral way," *Stride Toward Freedom,* 1959; "acquiescence is proof of inferiority," *Stride Toward Freedom,* 1959; "to strike out against oppression," Article, 12-66; "can reap nothing but grief," Article, 1-65; "immoral because it seeks to humiliate the opponent," *Stride Toward Freedom,* 1959; "seeks to reconcile the truths of two opposites," *Stride Toward Freedom,* 1959; "I think it arouses a sense of shame," Article, summer, 1963; "It does something to touch the conscience," Article, summer, 1963; McPhee, *Assembling California,* 1993; "There is something within human nature that can be changed," Speech, 12-16-61; "There is within human nature an amazing potential for goodness," Speech, 11-16-61; "I have seen them change in the past," Speech, 3-25-68; Closing epigraphs: Speech, 2-4-68; *Stride Toward Freedom,* 1959; "non cooperation with evil is as much a moral obligation as is cooperation with good," *Stride Toward Freedom,* 1959; "Victor Hugo once said," Speech, 9-29-63; "Within the best of people there is some evil," Speech, 11-20-57; "People fail to get along with each other because they fear each other," Article, *Ebony,* 12-57; "A movement that changes both people and institutions is a revolution," *Why We Can't Wait,* 1963.

## PART IV: Ensuring the Future

Opening epigraph: Speech, 4-18-59.

### Chapter 14: Preach Hope and Compassion

Opening epigraphs: *The Strength to Love,* 1963; Speech, 12-15-66; Article, 2-16-60; "expressed in the rising expectations for freedom," Speech, 11-14-66; "We must accept finite disappointment," *The Strength to Love,* 1963; "Because when you lose hope you die," Speech, 2-68; "is a deep faith in the future," Speech, 6-27-56; "Ours is a moment based on hope," Speech, 11-16-61; "I do not come here with a message of bitterness," Speech, 4-26-56; "In spite of my shattered dreams," *Where Do We Go from Here,* 1967; "We must keep alive the great hope," Garrow, 1986; "We as leaders lifted

hope," Speech, 12-15-66; "Shall we say the odds are too great,"
Speech, 4-4-67; "to transform the fatigue of despair into the buoy-
ancy of hope," Article, 12-60; "add hope to our determination,"
*Why We Can't Wait,* 1963; "The students have developed a theme
song," Speech, 11-16-61; "Like the ever-flowing waters of a river,"
Speech, 6-27-56; "Although we stand now in the midst of the midnight of injustice," Speech, 6-10-56; "no midnight long remains,"
*The Strength to Love,* 1963; "Something beautiful will happen in this
universe," Speech, 5-13-56; "The sins of a dark yesterday," *Why We
Can't Wait,* 1963; "dark yesterdays of hatred," *Why We Can't Wait,*
1963; "radiant stars of hope," Speech, 1959; "All the darkness in
the world," Article, 2-16-60; "amid today's mortar bursts and whining bullets," Speech, 12-10-64; "Darkness cannot drive out darkness," Speech, Fall 1966; "There is a basis of hope in the democratic
creed," Speech, 3-19-56; "The American people are infected with
racism," Article, 4-16-68; "call our nation to a higher destiny,"
*Where Do We Go from Here,* 1967; "to make the American dream a
reality," Speech, 9-9-67; "I do not think the tiny nation," Speech,
1-27-66; "provide the poor with new hope and opportunity," Letter, 8-10-66; "bridge the gulf between the haves and the have-
nots," Speech, 3-31-68; "If America is to remain a first-class
nation," Speech, 9-6-60; "We must rapidly begin the shift," Article,
3-4-67; "When machines and computers," Speech, 3-4-67; "We
spend far too much of our national budget," Speech, 3-31-68; "Ultimately, society must condemn the robber," Speech 8-9-66; "true
compassion is more than flinging a coin to a beggar," Speech, 3-4-
67; "effective new nondiscriminatory training programs," Letter, 8-
10-66; "deeply interested in political matters and social ills," Oates,
1982; "in breaking down legal barriers to Negroes," Oates, 1982;
"he who is greatest among you shall be your servant," Speech, 2-4-
68; "Do something for others," Speech, 9-29-66; "My call to the
ministry," Oates, 1982; "I am here because I love America,"
Speech, 12-61; "I choose to identify with the underprivileged,"
Speech, 8-28-66; "Some people are suffering," Speech, 6-5-66; "I
am deeply grateful to both of you," Letter, 6-19-56; "Look at that
devil," Garrow, 1986; "I had a double task ahead," *Stride Toward
Freedom,* 1959; "commission to work harder," *Where Do We Go
from Here,* 1967; "Let us remember that as we struggle," Speech, 5-
17-56; "the passionless depths of hardheartedness," *The Strength to*

*Love,* 1963; "We need leadership that is calm and yet positive," Speech, 5-17-57; "We must never struggle with falsehood," Speech, 5-17-57; "[We] don't need to hate," Speech, 1-64; "the chain of hatred must be cut," Oates, 1982; "hate is too great a burden to bear," *Where Do We Go from Here,* 1967; "There is no easy way to create a world," Article, 10-66; "I believe that unarmed truth," Speech, 12-11-64; "an indescribable capacity for empathy," *Time,* 1-64; "the victim of deferred dreams," Speech, 12-67; Covey, 1990; "toughness of the serpent," *The Strength to Love,* 1963; "During days of human travail," Speech, 8-31-67; "a chronic disease that dries up the red corpuscles," Speech, 1959; "People are often surprised," Article, 1-69 (written 3-68, published posthumously); "We've got to learn to live together as brothers," Garrow, 1986; "I am optimistic," Remarks, Spring 1961; "There is nothing to keep us from molding," Speech, 3-4-67; "I think we can do it," *Meet the Press,* 8-67; Closing epigraphs: Speech, 12-61; Speech, 3-4-67; Article, 1-69 (written 3-68, published posthumously); "The one thing that keeps the fire of revolution burning," *Where Do We Go from Here,* 1967; "Remember that hope finally means," Speech, 1-17-68; "Every crisis has not only its danger points," Speech, 9-9-67.

## Chapter 15: Have the Courage to Lead

Opening epigraphs: Speech 1-27-56; *Stride Toward Freedom,* 1956; Article, 3-14-66; Speech, 3-25-68; "inextricably bound together," Speech, 7-2-65; "Violence is as wrong in Hanoi," Article, 1966; "Nothing will ever taste any good for me," Garrow, 1986; Riverside Church remarks, Speech, 4-4-67; "Martin was on fire with determination," Young, 1996; "had to stand so often amid the chilly winds of adversity," Speech, 1-65; "transferred to three different jails," Article, Summer 1963; "drains a man's energy and depletes his resources," *The Strength to Love,* 1963; "I don't think you can be in public life without being called bad names," Article, 1-65; "I have been so concerned about unity," Letter, 6-19-60; "The job ahead is too great," Letter, 6-19-60; "he who lives by the sword," Article, 5-56; "to manifest love," Article, 5-56; "Don't do anything to her," Oates, 1982; "I'm not interested in pressing charges," Remarks, 9-61; "I've been used before," Garrow, 1986; "I've been hit so many times I'm immune to it," Remarks, 8-5-66; "I was enjoined January

15, 1929," Oates, 1982; "the price one has to pay in public life," Article, 1-61; "seen youngsters refuse to turn around," *Why We Can't Wait,* 1963; "attacked by tear gas," Article, 12-66; "leap into the air to catch with their bare hands," Article, 12-66; "This is Selma, Alabama," "Letter From a Selma Jail," *New York Times,* 2-14-65; "I feel that the confidence that the people have in me," Speech, 8-1-56; "There is nothing to be afraid of if you believe," Speech, 1-1-61; "Democracy demands responsibility," Article, 3-59; "The fear of physical death and being run out of town," Article, 12-57; "I'm going to jail," Remarks, 4-1-63; "No lie can live forever," Speech, 12-11-61; "Truth crushed to earth will rise again," Speech, 12-11-61; "Man's history is a path upward," Article, 1-69 (published posthumously); "Faith can give us courage to meet the uncertainties of the future," Speech, 12-10-64; "possible for me to falter," Article, 1-69 (published posthumously); "Oh, Lord, I'm down here trying to do what is right," *Stride Toward Freedom,* 1958; "When I was growing up, I was dog bitten—for nothing," Speech, Summer 1963; "Martin was so much fun when he relaxed," Garrow, 1986; "The jetliner left Atlanta," *Time,* 1-3-64; "never had the time to be the fun-loving man that he really was," Garrow, 1986; " 'I wouldn't want my daughter to marry George Wallace,' " Speech, 9-10-67; "As my sufferings mounted," Article, 4-27-60; *Extraordinary Minds,* Gardner, 1997; "transform the suffering into a creative force," Speech, 4-27-60; "do a little converting when I'm in jail," Speech, 2-4-68; "No one can know the true taste of victory," *Where Do We Go from Here,* 1967; "You don't get to the promised land," Speech, 3-22-56; "There are as many Communists in this freedom movement," Article, 1-65; "Don't forget it," Garrow, 1986; "Though I am not perfect," Speech, 1960; "I have nothing to hide," Remarks, 2-19-60; "The pioneers in any movement," Phillips, 1992; "the agonizing loneliness that characterizes the life of the pioneer," Speech, 3-14-66; "Those who pioneer in the struggle for peace and freedom," Speech, 3-25-65; "difficult days ahead," Speech, Summer 1963; "we are still in for a season of suffering," Speech, 3-25-65; "Freedom is never free," Speech, 1-60; "the power of the mind to overcome fear," *The Strength to Love,* 1963; "the determination not to be overwhelmed by any object," *The Strength to Love,* 1963; "an inner resolution to go forward," *The Strength to Love,* 1963; "courage breeds creative self-affirmation,"

*The Strength to Love,* 1963; "courage faces fear," *The Strength to Love,* 1963; "the forces that threaten to negate life," *The Strength to Love,* 1963; "We must not permit adverse winds to overwhelm us," Speech, 11-14-67; "No, I'm going to walk," Schulte, 1976; Hosea Williams remarks, Schulte, 1976; "I've decided that I'm going to do battle for my philosophy," Speech, 8-67; "Somebody is saying stand," Speech, 3-25-68; "When a person lives with the fear of the consequences for his personal life," Article, 3-23-57; "It is better to shed a little blood," Article, 10-66; "I do plan to intensify my personal activities," Remarks, 3-28-67; "I will not be intimidated," Speech, 5-67; Article, 1967; "not going to segregate my conscience," Remarks, 2-67; "Whenever I see injustice," Speech, 9-9-67; "presently moving down a dead-end road," Speech, 4-17-67; "a radical reordering of our national priorities," Remarks, 3-28-67; "go all out," Oates, 1982; "was not the buoyant, energetic King one had known," Calloway, 1993; "almost breaking down under the continual battering," *Stride Toward Freedom,* 1958; "The doctors tell me I can't get by," Remarks, 1966; "he was given to a kind of depression," Garrow, 1986; "He just always talked about the fact," Coretta King, 1969; "I'll never see my fortieth birthday," Coretta King, 1969; Closing epigraphs: Speech, 4-9-68; Article, 1969; Article, 1-65; "the road ahead will not always be smooth," Speech, 3-4-67; "Whenever you set out to build a temple," Speech, 3-3-68; "There is no painless way to have a revolution," Article, 1966; "No leader can be great," Speech, 9-12-62; "A firm sense of self-esteem," *Where Do We Go from Here,* 1967.

## Chapter 16: Inspire People with Your Dream

Opening epigraphs: Speech, 8-28-63; Interview, Spring 1963; "Our real problem is that there is no disposition," Speech, 8-15-67; "We ought to come in mule carts," Remarks, 10-66; Garrow, 1986; "People flow across the South," Article, 4-16-68 (published posthumously); "People ought to come to Washington, sit down if necessary," Article, 4-16-68 (published posthumously); "a massive program on the part of the federal government," Interview, 10-67; "going to stay in Washington until something is done," Remarks, 11-67; Garrow, 1986; "waves of the nation's poor and disinherited," Interview, 12-4-67; "as dramatic, as dislocative, as disruptive," Remarks, 11-67; Garrow, 1986; "I would be the first one to admit at this time is risky," Interview, 12-4-67; "a last chance project to arouse the American conscience," Remarks, 8-68; Oates, 1982; "my staff and I have worked three months on the planning," Article, 4-16-68 (published posthumously); "workshops on nonviolence," Article, 4-16-68 (published posthumously); "We have an ultimate goal of freedom," Speech, 1-16-68; "Come young and old," Speech, 3-22-68; "going to stay in Washington until we get a response," Speech, 3-22-68; "escalating nonviolence to the level of civil disobedience," Interview, 10-67; "showdown for nonviolence," Article, 4-16-68 (published posthumously); "people derive inspiration from their involvement," Article, 12-56; "you can't get persons to respond to anything if they aren't stimulated," Remarks, 12-67; Garrow, 1986; "a struggle for genuine equality," Interview, 4-1-67; "faith in the future," Speech, 6-27-56; "work together, to pray together, to struggle together," Speech, 8-28-63; "a special feature of our struggle," Speech, 8-5-62; "I have a dream," Speech, 8-28-63; "these dreams were not deferred, they were denied," Article, 1-69 (published posthumously); "the creation of the beloved community," Speech, 8-11-56; "A movement is led as much by the idea that symbolizes it," Interview, Spring 1963; "These are poor folks. If we don't stop for them," Oates, 1982; "We are tired of being at the bottom," Speech, 3-18-63; "I will never lead a violent march," Oates, 1982; "a massive *nonviolent* demonstration," Interview, 3-30-68; "I just can't take it anymore," Oates, 1982; "We are not going to be stopped by Mace or injunctions," Speech, 3-18-68; "I think you should come down," Oates, 1982; "I've been to the mountaintop," Speech, 4-3-68; "She's always so happy when A.D. is with me," Oates, 1982; Closing epigraphs: Speech, 7-19-62; Speech, 8-11-56; Speech, 6-23-63.

## Epilog

"If you one day find me sprawled out," Oates, 1982; Stokely Carmichael, Oates, 1982; Belafonte and Levison, Garrow, 1986; *Saturday Review,* 11-13-65; "Since the beginning of the civil rights revolution," *Where Do We Go from Here,* 1967; "leaders will naturally emerge," Interview, 8-20-65; "because it is right to do it," Speech, 6-27-56; "We must combine the toughness of the serpent and the softness of the dove," *The Strength to Love,* 1963; "Make a career of humanity," Speech, 4-18-59; "the leader has the responsibility of trying to find an answer," Speech, 3-25-68; "A man all wrapped up in himself," Article, 9-29-62; "conscious of my limitations," Speech, 5-2-54; "I am still searching myself," Speech, 11-14-66; "have any money to leave behind," Speech, 2-4-68; "He who is the greatest among you shall be your servant," Speech, 4-9-67; "a eulogy of more than one or two minutes," Speech, 4-9-67; "I'd like somebody to mention," Speech, 2-4-68; "Say that I was a drum major for justice," Speech, 2-4-68; "I did try," Speech, 4-9-67; "We stand today between two worlds," Speech, 12-3-56; "We must face the responsibilities that come along with it," Article, 4-57; "we will be living tomorrow with the very people," *Where Do We Go from Here,* 1967; "all inhabitants of the globe are now neighbors," *Where Do We Go from Here,* 1967; "inherited a large house," *Where Do We Go from Here,* 1967; "opportunity to create a new spirit of class and racial harmony," Article, 4-16-68; "There is a dire need for leaders," Speech, 6-27-56; Speech, 8-11-56; Speech, 12-15-56; Article, 4-57; "A time like this demands great souls," Speech, 8-11-56; "If I had never been born this movement would have taken place," Garrow, 1986; "reminds us that every man is heir to the legacy of worthiness," Speech, 7-19-62; "freedom is not only from something," Speech, 11-14-56; "Freedom is one thing," Article, 6-20-64; "Ordinarily, threats of Klan action," *Stride Toward Freedom,* 1958; "Somehow, I still believe," Article, 8-67; "accept the task of helping make the world a better place," Article, 1-65; "stand up and protest against injustice," Speech, 4-66; "Human progress never rolls in on the wheels of inevitability," Article, 3-68; "Will we continue to march to the drum beat of conformity," Speech, 9-25-66; "Shall we say the odds are too great," Speech, 4-4-67; Final epigraph: Speech, 8-28-63.

# Acknowledgments

I'd like to thank Dexter King of the Martin Luther King, Jr., Center for Nonviolent Social Change and Phillip Jones and Tricia Harris of IPM in Atlanta, Georgia, for granting permission to utilize the words of Dr. Martin Luther King, Jr., and for their support and encouragement of this project.

I also acknowledge and appreciate very much the courtesy and assistance provided by Dr. Clayborne Carson, Director of the Martin Luther King, Jr., Papers Project at Stanford University, and staff members Susan Carson, Randy Mont-Reynaud, and Kerry Taylor. Access to Dr. King's unpublished speeches, sermons, and letters was invaluable during the research for this book.

Larry Kirshbaum, Maureen Egen, and Rick Wolff at Warner Books deserve tremendous credit for turning my idea into reality—as does Bob Barnett, my friend and the best literary agent in the business. I can't imagine working with better people.

A very special thanks to my good friend Jim Goodwin, of the Oklahoma Eagle Publishing Company in Tulsa, Oklahoma, for reading the manuscript, for his insightful comments, and for his uplifting encouragement.

As always, my wife, Susan, my sons, Steven and David, and my daughter, Kate, couldn't have provided more love and support during research and writing. I am very fortunate to have them in my life.

DTP
Fairview, Texas

# Index